Economic Management Of Resources
A Critique of Classical Economics

ECONOMIC MANAGEMENT OF RESOURCES

A CRITIQUE OF CLASSICAL ECONOMICS

DAVID HETHERINGTON

PUBLISHED FOR THE
CENTRE OF MIGRATION & DEVELOPMENT STUDIES
UNIVERSITY OF WESTERN AUSTRALIA

First published February 1996.

Printed in Singapore by Fabulous Printers Pte. Ltd.
Distributed by: API-Toppan Company(S) Pte. Ltd.
38 Liu Fang Road, Jurong Town, Singapore 2262

National Library of Australia
Cataloguing-in-publication entry

Hetherington, David, 1939-
Economic Management of Resources

Bibliography
Includes index.
ISBN 0 86422 438 9   100132274X

1. Natural resources - Management. I. University of Western Australia. Centre for
   Migration and Development Studies. II. Title.

333.7

Jacket design by Ms Judy Shilkin.

To Rosemary and Mark

Preface

Every author owes a great debt of gratitude to a multitude of people, both the living and the dead. As one whose great interest is in "the grand themes", as they have been described, the intellectual debts are probably greater than ever. Of those among the living who have acted as my mentors, Professor Appleyard deserves my greatest thanks for reading through the first draft of this book several years ago and for encouraging me to continue with the project. The essay which I am now offering to the general public is very different in concept though not in content from my original draft.

I am also very grateful to Dr Ruth Barton for so painstakingly reading through the manuscript of the second draft and making recommendations from her perspective as an historian on how to improve the essay. Her very perceptive criticisms enabled me to remove many of the obscurities which so easily creep into one's writing. I would also like to express my gratitude to Dr Joan Wardrop who, likewise, read through the manuscript and kindly offered constructive criticism.

My thanks must also go to Dr John Prestage for taking the time from his point of view as an economist to read the manuscript and give me his views on it. I am also very grateful to Mr Alf Holmen who very diligently read through the manuscript and pointed out my stylistic errors.

I am deeply grateful to Dr Rony Gabbay and Dr Robin Ghosh for reading the manuscript and for recommending that it be published under the auspices of the Centre for Migration and Development Studies at the University of Western Australia.

My thanks must also be given to my colleagues at Curtin and Murdoch Universities for their support and encouragement over the years which I have been working on the book. A special note of thanks in this respect must go to Associate Professor Geoffrey Crockett for allowing me to use the facilities of the Economics Department.

My very real thanks go to Mrs Glenys Walter for typing and preparing the final manuscript in "camera-ready" format for presentation to the printer.

While my debt of gratitude to those who have offered their criticisms of this essay is very great, the views expressed herein are my own and I gladly accept this responsibility.

Economists today enjoy a very mixed reception amongst society at large. The reason for this is that they have considerable influence over the direction of government policy, an influence which has at times been beneficial, and at other times baneful. The effect which policy directives have will depend on the extent to which they are ideologically motivated as opposed to being empirically based. This book goes into publication in the hope that economic theory will become less ideological and more empirical.

David Hetherington
January 1996

Contents

Introduction

"Religion is ultimately more important than politics, and politics is ultimately more important than economics or technology. " Harris Harbisson.[1]

Four developments took place in the religious, political, economic and technological life of Europe in the fifteenth and sixteenth centuries which have done more to shape the history of our modern world than almost any other series of events in human history. The first of these was the invention in the fourth decade of the fifteenth century of the three masted sailing ship, a development which when combined with other technical inventions, such as the compass, the gun, and the stern-post rudder, gave the European maritime powers their technological and commercial advantage over the rest of the world. The second were the transoceanic voyages of discovery which, beginning in the middle of the fifteenth century with the Portuguese expeditions to West Africa, culminated at the end of the century in the discovery of the sea routes to South Africa, the West Indies and India, and resulted in the establishment of a single world market, an event whose economic importance has not been sufficiently appreciated. The third was the development in Western Europe in the course of the fifteenth century of that uniquely European political phenomenon, namely the nation state. The fourth was the Protestant Reformation, a religious event in essence, but one which was destined to have liberating effects not only on the nations of Northern Europe where its initial impact was first felt, but on the rest of the world.

It was these developments, the first in the technological field, the second in the commercial and economic, the third in the political and the fourth in the religious field, that transformed the mediaeval world

---

[1]   Harbisson, E Harris, *Christianity and History*, Princeton University Press (1964). p.132.

into the modern and shaped the course of economic development in succeeding centuries. It is these events which, perhaps more than any other in history, give credence to the fundamental thesis of this book, namely that, insofar as the economic growth and development process is concerned, technology is the *limiting* factor, the market is the *essential* factor, the state is the *critical* factor, and culture and religion are the *determining or governing* factors.

The claim that technology is the limiting factor will occasion little if any opposition from economists. The role of technology in the economic development of the world is well understood. The Classical Economists saw economic growth as a competition between population growth on the one hand and technological innovation on the other. Their pessimistic view of the world caused them to see the former outstripping the latter with dire results for human kind. Events, not for the last time in history, proved them wrong. Technology has well and truly outstripped population growth in many countries of the world with the result that standards of living have risen consistently this century.

Nevertheless, technology still remains the limiting factor insofar as economic growth and development is concerned. The level of skill achieved by the nation's populace determines what can and cannot be done at any point in time. Skill potential can, of course, be increased, as the history of technology demonstrates only too well. Whether that happens largely depends, as we shall see, on social and cultural attitudes towards growth and development on the one hand and on the attitude of the political leadership on the other. The will to expand must be present if expansion is to take place. If the will is not present, technological innovation will not take place.

While technology is the limiting factor, the market has undeniably been an essential factor in the development of the modern world. The attempt of the command economies of Eastern Europe to function without the market system has demonstrated the futility of that experiment. For while the Russian economy has performed very well insofar as the production of producer goods is concerned its performance in the field of consumer goods leaves much to be desired. Whenever and wherever the market is able to perform effectively, it should be allowed to do so. The limits to its effectiveness are considerably greater than market economists are often prepared to allow, as the existence of imperfect competition so clearly demonstrates. Entrepreneurial activity, the protégé of the market system, has undoubtedly added significantly to the wealth of society;

without it, the world would be a very much poorer place. The measure of success which entrepreneurs enjoy, however, is determined by the political and cultural conditions of the era. When the state provides the necessary protection and support which entrepreneurs require as happened in Britain during the Mercantilist era, in America and Germany in the latter part of the nineteenth century, and in Japan during the twentieth century, progress may be swift.

Economists, however, are apt to treat the market as given, and to ignore the very important role played by the state in the economic development process, as chapter one seeks to demonstrate. History, on the other hand, shows that the state has played a major role in the formation of the market. Indeed, an important theme of this book, as stated in chapter two, is that economic growth and development are the result of the pursuit by national governments of policies designed to further the economic well-being of the nation and its people. Successful nations, as we shall see, are those which have managed their resources effectively usually by pursuing expansionist economic policies. Fifteenth century Portugal - the subject of chapter three - is a case in point, for by undertaking the voyages of discovery, Portugal created a world market, stretching from Brazil in the west to China and Japan in the east. The success of the British - the subject of chapter four - was due to their ability not only to create the largest captive overseas market, but, by building a network of canals across the kingdom, to integrate the overseas market into the national market. The process of market integration at the national level went one stage further in the nineteenth century with the construction of the railways. The steady urbanisation of national societies in the twentieth century, another example of market widening, has been effected by a further development in the transport system, namely the petroleum based engine. Throughout history, the state has played a critical role in the economic development process by *facilitating* the development of transport systems, and *ipso facto* of markets at both the national and the international level. Our failure to recognise this all important fact lies at the root of much of our current inability to manage our economies effectively.

The state, therefore, is the critical factor in the economic development and growth process, as the history of Western Europe shows conclusively. The economists of the German Historical School understood that only too clearly. It is the fundamental shortcoming of the Classical Economists, and therefore of modern economic thought in general, that it has failed to appreciate that point. In consequence, macro- economics has ceased to be empirical, as chapter one of this book endeavours to make clear. The notion that politics -national security and self-esteem - is ultimately more important than economics - our freedom to trade - receives a very stony reception from economists, particularly those of the classical school. Perhaps the supreme irony of the situation is that the father of the school, Adam Smith, was a political realist; he understood the importance of the Navigation Acts. Nevertheless the notion that the market will provide the optimum result for society at large without any direction or intervention by government dies very hard. The importance of balanced development is forgotten with the result that countries like Australia become exporters of raw materials and importers of finished goods, and consequently losers in the international economic stakes.

The claim that religion and culture are the fundamental determinants of economic progress has substantial support from history, as this book shows. There has been strong opposition to technological innovation throughout much of human history with the result that many societies which should have progressed economically have failed to do so. Societies in which slavery or serfdom predominate are generally inimical to technological innovation. The key to successful economic development is the existence of the right environment. If the environment is not right, technological progress will be inhibited and economic development will not occur. The Puritan Revolution had to occur before England was ready for continuous technical innovation. Cultural attitudes have great influence on the way in which a country progresses or fails to progress economically, as chapter five of this book demonstrates.

For this reason the role of the Jews in the economic growth and development process has received considerable attention. The presence of Jews in any community has a stabilising effect which in itself facilitates the economic growth and development process, as European history unreservedly testifies. Chapter five elucidates the reasons why economic advancement was more rapid in those countries in which the Jewish and Protestant faiths prevailed.

Given the applicability of this thesis to Europe, the question arose whether it could be used to explain the economic development process in other parts of the world. China was chosen because in the period of history which Europeans refer to as the mediaeval era, she was more technologically sophisticated and therefore more economically developed than her western counterpart. Moreover, the comparative economic development of the two continents provided ample evidence of the truth of the thesis of this book, namely that religion and culture were the *governing* factors in the economic development process and politics the *critical* factor, the market the *essential* factor and technology the *limiting* factor. The question that then arose in China's case was which religion was the dominant influence, Confucianism, Legalism, Taoism, Buddhism, Nestorian Christianity, Islam or Judaism, all of which had representation in China at some time during either the T'ang or the Sung dynasties. The current state of knowledge does not unfortunately permit an authoritative answer to that question. Historians know that there was a community of Jews in Kaifung, the commercial centre of China in the ninth century; their influence on the cultural and economic life of the country, however, awaits the efforts of the researcher. What is certain, however, as chapter six of this book shows, is that China's failure to modernise her economy in the nineteenth century was due to the superior cultural attitudes which prevailed among the leadership at that time. By contrast, economic development in Japan from 1870 onwards reflected a totally different cultural ethos.

One problem, however, remained. Why was it that those very people, the Jews, who have given so much to the economic advancement of the modern world, are very largely responsible for the present state of economic theory and consequently the current bankruptcy of economic policy? Chapter eight is an attempt to answer that question.

Any new approach to economic theory inevitably necessitates some re-thinking of policy. That has been done in this book in the light of the Australian situation, and with good reason for the contemporary Australian scene depicts both the tragedy of the current approach to economic problems on the one hand and the very great possibilities for economic development that that Continent continues to offer on the other. Much of what has been said in the Australian context, however, has applicability to other countries.

1 Economic Management of Resources

THE FAILURE OF CLASSICAL ECONOMICS

"He who considers things in their first growth and origin, whether a state or anything else, will obtain the clearest view of them." Aristotle.

"Economic theories must be capable of testing if they are to add to human understanding; the refinement of abstract models is insufficient." Eamonn Butler.

Eamonn Butler's words[2] in his guide to the economic thought of Milton Friedman emphasise the fundamental importance of the empirical approach in economics, an approach which has acquired almost universal acceptance among modern economists. Yet as the author of one of these textbooks states: *"Economics appears currently to be in a state of crisis. After a long period of the development of theories of macroeconomics, evidence has accrued that is not easily explained within the existing framework of theories."[3]* Richard Lipsey offers no explanation why economic theory has failed so miserably; to find one, however, would not be difficult. For economics to be genuinely empirical in character, it must take account of economic realities, of economic conditions in the real world; it must therefore consider history. History is the touchstone of economics. If economics cannot be validated at the bar of history, then economists of whatever persuasion should consider whether the theories by which they set so much store can be regarded as truly empirical. Indeed any claim which economists

---

2   Butler, Eamonn. Milton Friedman, *A Guide to his Economic Thought*. Gower, Aldershot, England (1985).

3   Lipsey, R.G., Langley, P.C., & Mahoney D.M., *Positive Economics for Australian Students*, 2nd.ed., Weidenfeld & Nicholson, London (1985), p.13.

make regarding the empirical character of their discipline can only be justified if the theories which they propose explain the central feature of modern economies, namely the economic growth and development process. Such a view would not enjoy the support of the majority of contemporary economists, who believe that the principal function of economics is to create models of the economy designed to provide them with a deeper understanding of the actual mechanics of its operation. Their activities would be highly commendable if the models which they devised were of the linear variety, and could be used to explain the dynamics of the growth and development process. Most economic models, as Eli Hecksher[4], the Swedish economist of Mercantilism, observed seventy years ago, are principally concerned with static situations. Their primary concern is with the attainment and retention of equilibrium conditions.

Economic development is a dynamic process, and one which will therefore bring disequilibrium into the economic situation. Economic historians are concerned to explain, not when and why economies come to rest in equilibrium (if indeed they do), but when and why they change. They want to know why it was that for approximately two millennia of human history, comparatively little economic progress was made. They want to know why it was that economic progress was faster in China than in Europe between the eighth and the thirteenth centuries. They want to know why, in the words of R.M. Hartwell, the Australian born economic historian, *"it was European civilisation long in the making that provides the matrix of modern economic growth."*[5] For this reason equilibrium models are of little value in the real world as an explanation of the economic growth and development process, as first year students of economics sometimes appreciate.

No theory of economics, moreover, will suffice that does not explain why economic development took place more rapidly in Europe than in China from the fifteenth century onwards, why it was the Iberian kingdoms and not the Italian city states that engaged in transoceanic voyages of discovery, how Holland became the leading commercial nation in the world in the seventeenth century, why Great Britain and not France, her much more populous neighbour, became the leader of the world economy in the nineteenth century, how America and Russia

[4] Hecksher, Eli, *Mercantilism*, Garland , New York & London (1983).
[5] Hartwell, R.M., *The Industrial Revolution and Economic Growth*, Methuen & Co. (1971), p.11. (All quotations in this chapter are taken from Ch.1 of Hartwell's book, entitled, *Lessons of History.*)

emerged as the two super-powers of the twentieth century, and why Japan succeeded so well in the modernisation of her economy in the latter part of the nineteenth century whereas China failed so miserably. Perhaps no economist understood the importance of the empirical approach better than Adam Smith. Smith's objective in writing his inquiry into the causes of the increase in the Wealth of Nations was to state the case for the untrammelled operation of the market system, the only economic system which he believed to be compatible with the concept of 'natural liberty'. Smith's argument was that economic growth and development had been more rapid in those countries in which the market system had been given greatest vent.[6] Smith breathed the air of eighteenth century rationalism. His nineteenth century successors were less sanguine. As Benjamin Higgins in his book entitled "Economic Development of a Small Planet" says: *"The classical economy posited a closed system within which the race for economic development was seen as a battle between population increase and technological progress. The classicists saw technological progress as the source of higher profits, which, in turn, were seen as the means whereby investment could be raised, thus increasing the wages fund. A larger wages fund was seen as the source of increased employment opportunities, and therefore, so it was thought, of further increases in population. A higher population, however, was seen as the harbinger of diminishing returns, on account of higher food costs, which in turn would reduce profits, lower investment and retard economic progress."[7]*

Population growth is certainly no guarantee of economic growth, as Hartwell has observed. *"History can only show that although economic growth has always been accompanied by population growth; population growth has not always been accompanied by economic growth."[8]* The Malthusian situation which confronted China and Ireland in the nineteenth century, and India, Sudan and Ethiopia at different times during the twentieth century, bears a tragic testimony to that grim fact. If population growth is to result in economic growth, as happened

---

[6]   Smith, Adam, *The Wealth of Nations*, edited by Edwin Cannan, Norman Berg, Georgia (1976). Refer Book *III Of the different progress of opulence in different nations*, p.356 ff.

[7]   Higgins, Benjamin & J.H., *Economic Development of a Small Planet*, W.W. Norton & Co., New York. p.34. The Classical Model.

[8]   Hartwell, R.M., *The Industrial Revolution and Economic Growth*, Methuen & Co. (1971), p.15.

in Germany, Britain and America in the nineteenth century, it must be accompanied by technological innovation.

Nor will geography explain why some nations are more successful than others at the economic development game. Europe's long coastline may have been a contributing factor in her maritime expansion. Likewise, China's long coastline may have been a contributing factor in her maritime expansion, but it cannot explain why the Chinese, in the early fifteenth century, sent much larger maritime expeditions to India and East Africa than any European power ever dispatched to the east before the nineteenth century. Nor will it explain why the Chinese failed to follow up their advantage.

Neither terrain nor climate adequately explain the economic development process. That the seven most highly developed countries in the world all lie in or near the temperate zones is not evidence that tropical countries cannot develop advanced economies. The ancient civilisations of the world were not restricted to the temperate zones. Many of them flourished in the tropics, namely Ceylon, Java, and the empires of West Africa.

Natural resources are likewise no guarantee of economic advancement, as the comparison between Peru, one of the wealthiest countries in the world from the point of view of natural resources, and Japan, one of the poorest, shows. *"The possession of natural resources represents only the potential for growth,"* as Hartwell has reminded us.[9]

Nor will the presence of finance capital necessarily suffice to ensure the successful outcome of the economic development process. Europe recovered rapidly after World War II because it had the technological know-how and organisational expertise - the human capital - to utilise the financial resources made available under the Marshall Plan. The developing countries can only benefit in proportion to their capacity to utilise effectively the capital stock thus provided. Again, Hartwell's thesis is valid. *"There is general agreement among economists that a flow of capital to an undeveloped country will not alone produce growth."*[10]

Nor is the money supply a determinant of economic achievement. However important sound effective monetary management may be for the efficient operation of a modern economy. For, as Milton Friedman has said: *"Money is a veil. The real forces are the capacities of the*

---

[9]   Ibid.
[10]   Ibid.

people, their industry, and ingenuity, the resources they command, their mode of economic and political organisation."[11]

Population growth, technological innovation, natural resources, capital accumulation, markets, and the money supply have all played their part in the economic growth and development process. So too has human industry and ingenuity. But none of these factors alone will adequately explain why certain nations at different times in their history have performed better than others economically. It is only as we examine that most controversial element of all, namely the role of government, that we shall get an insight into the operation of the economic development process.

Economic liberals have always had the greatest difficulty reconciling their doctrine of 'laissez-faire' with economic realities. In a remarkable passage on the progress of commerce in England since the reign of Elizabeth, Smith states that *"there is no country in Europe, Holland not excepted, of which the law is, upon the whole, more favourable to this sort of industry. Commerce and manufactures have accordingly been continually advancing during all this period."*[12] A little further on, he compares the progress of agriculture in France with that of England, and observes: *"The cultivation and improvement of France is, upon the whole, inferior to that of England. The law of the country has never given the same direct encouragement to agriculture."*[13] Such sentiments are curiously at variance with Smith's comments on the corn law bounty which he claims had nothing to do with England's agricultural performance in the eighteenth century.

It was Smith's attitude towards the Navigation Acts which reveals the dichotomy which lies at the heart of economic liberalism, for, while on the one hand, the legislation was a patent contradiction of the whole philosophy of economic liberalism, he nevertheless praised it as *"wise as if they had all been dictated by the most deliberate wisdom."*[14] The defence argument is one which has always created the utmost difficulty for economic liberals on account of its manifest irreconcilability with their dogma. Being a realist at heart, Smith accepted that national security overrode all other considerations,

---

[11]   Friedman, Milton & Schwarz, Anna J., *A Monetary History of the United States of America (1867-1960).* Princeton University Press (1963), p.696.

[12]   Smith, Adam, *The Wealth of Nations*, edited by Edwin Cannan, Norman Berg, Georgia (1976), p.393.

[13]   Ibid. - p.394-5.

[14]   Ibid. - p.431.

including that of the growth of national income. The Navigation Acts highlight a problem which lies at the heart of economics, namely that in the real world it is impossible to separate economic considerations from political and strategic factors.

The prime mover in Europe's remarkable expansion was the nation state; without it, the other three engines of growth, the global commercial empires of the European Powers, the national economies and space exploration, would not have occurred. It was the maritime states of Western Europe, led by Portugal and Spain, that created the global commercial empires, thereby bringing into existence for the first time in human history, a genuinely world economy. The era which followed has been described by the Indian historian, K.M. Pannikar as *"an age of maritime power, of authority based on control of the seas by the European nations alone."*[15] It was the nation states of Europe, led by Britain, that in the eighteenth century created the national economies which facilitated the industrialisation of the modern world, thus effecting the greatest change in economic conditions that mankind has ever witnessed in its history. It was the nation state that pioneered space exploration in the twentieth century, thus opening up one of the most promising avenues of economic expansion ever available to man.

Traditionally, Anglo-Saxon economists and historians have tended to take the role of the state for granted. A long line of English historians including Toynbee Senior,[16] Unwin,[17] Ashton,[18] Clapham,[19] Lipson,[20] Deane[21] and Hartwell[22] have taken the view that the role played by the state in Britain's rise to economic hegemony in the nineteenth century was minimal. For them the observation of Phyllis Deane holds good; *"the first industrial revolution occurred in Great*

---

[15] Pannikar, K.M., Quotation taken from Boxer, C.R., *The Portuguese Seaborne Empire 1415-1825*. Hutchinson,London (1969).

[16] Toynbee, Arnold, *Lectures on the Industrial Revolution in England*, Augustus M. Kelly (1962), p.72.

[17] Unwin, George, *Studies in Economic History. The Collected Papers of George Unwin*, ed. by R.H.Tawney., Frank Cass, London (1958). See Introd. Memoire section ix.

[18] Ashton, T.S., *The Industrial Revolution 1760-1830*. Oxford University Press (1968).

[19] Clapham, J.H., *An Economic History of Modern Britain*, C.U.P. (1930).

[20] Lipson, E., *The Growth of English Society. A short Economic History*. Adam & Chas. Black, London (1959). 4th ed. Chs. 6 & 10.

[21] Deane, Phyllis, *The First Industrial Revolution*, C.U.P. (1979).

[22] Hartwell, R.M., *The Industrial Revolution and Economic Growth*, Methuen & Co. (1971).

Britain and is of particular interest in that it occurred spontaneously, without the government assistance which has been characteristic of most succeeding industrial revolutions."[23] "Laissez-faire" was their watchword. Such a view is perhaps all the more comprehensible in view of the distinct political advantages which England had scored over her continental competitors. For England had been politically united since Norman times; since the reign of Henry II (1154-89), she had enjoyed a uniform legal system; by the middle of the fourteenth century, internal tolls had been abolished and the country thereafter enjoyed the unique advantage in Europe of possessing a national customs network; standardisation of weights and measures was slower to eventuate, but even in that field, as Eli Hecksher has told us, England was ahead of Continental Europe.

Few nations were more aware of the advantages which Britain had acquired than the Germans. Writing from the viewpoint of a nation which had suffered acutely as a result of a lack of political unity, of the absence of a central government able to exercise its authority effectively throughout the nation, from the viewpoint of a country which had been forced to protect such industry as it had managed to develop through the creation of a customs union, Frederick List had this to say: *"The assertion that the English have attained their present commercial eminence and power, not by means of commercial policy, but in spite of it, appears to be one of the greatest falsehoods promulgated in this century."[24]*

The Germans reserved their strongest diatribes for the Smithian notion that: *"the improvement and prosperity of Great Britain is due to the natural effort of every individual to better his own condition, an effort which when suffered to exert itself with freedom and security, is so powerful a principle that it is alone, and without any assistance, not only capable of carrying on the society to wealth and prosperity, but of surmounting a hundred impertinent obstructions with which the folly of human laws too often encumbers its operations."[25]*

"History teaches," List replied, *"that individuals derive the greater part of their productive powers from the social institutions and*

---

[23]   Deane, Phyllis, *The First Industrial Revolution,* C.U.P. (1979).

[24]   List, Friedrich *The National System of Political Economy,* Longmans Green & Co., London (1885).,Ch. 4 - The English. p.35ff.

[25]   Smith, Adam *The Wealth of Nations,* Edited by Edwin Cannan, Norman Berg, Georgia (1976). p.508.

conditions under which they are placed."[26] Another German, Gustav Schmoller, put his finger on the heart of the matter when he wrote; *"In every phase of economic development, a guiding and controlling part belongs to someone or other political organ of the life of the race or nation.*"[27] Schmoller's corollary that *"the idea that economic life has ever been a process mainly dependent on individual action.... is mistaken with regard to all stages of civilisation"* [28] deserves far more attention from Anglo-Saxon historians and economists than it has been given.

The Germans have not been alone in their criticism of Smith and those economists and historians who subscribed to his belief in competitive enterprise, free trade and *"laissez-faire"* as a sufficient explanation of Britain's rise to economic hegemony of the world in the nineteenth century. Fernand Braudel has added the weight of his erudition in favour of the view that England's rise to economic leadership was from the beginning the result of a carefully conceived and consistently pursued policy originating in the sixteenth century. Writing with rare perspicacity of England's reaction to the domination of her trade by the Italian, Hanseatic and Flemish merchants, Braudel has this to say: *"England's reaction was vigorous, the Hanseatic merchants were stripped of their privileges in 1556, and deprived of the Stahlof in 1595; it was against Antwerp that Gresham founded in 1556-8 what would later become the Royal Exchange; it was against Spain and Portugal that the Stock Companies were in fact launched; against Holland that the Navigation Act of 1651 was directed and against France that the aggressive colonial policy of the eighteenth century was aimed. England as a country was tense, watchful and aggressive.*"[29]

There are increasing signs today that Anglo-Saxon historians are coming to realise that Britain's Industrial Revolution was neither spontaneous nor sudden, but that its origins lie far back in the past, and that the mercantile period in English History is indeed of vital importance for the understanding of what happened in the last quarter

---

[26]   List, Friedrich, *The National System of Political Economy*. Publ. in Eng. by Longmans Green & Co., .London (1885). Ch.10. p.507.

[27]   Schmoller, Gustav, *The Mercantile System and its Historical Significance*, Augustus M. Kelly, New York (1967), p.2.

[28]   Ibid. p.3,4.

[29]   Braudel, Fernand, *Civilization and Capitalism: The Fifteenth to the Eighteenth Centuries*, Vol.3. The Perspective of the World. Fontana Press, London (1985). p.355.

of the eighteenth century. Charles Wilson describes the 1660-1760 era as *"a time when commercial enterprise, often closely allied with state power and aided by legislation and military or naval force, was changing the face of an agrarian economy. The dynamic of the time was commercial."*[30] A re-appraisal of the mercantile period in English History is long overdue. The time has come when British and American historians should recognise that the first industrial revolution, whilst it can in no sense be regarded as a *'planned'* event, was nevertheless the result of the persistent and relatively consistent pursuit of economic policies designed to ensure British economic hegemony of the world. As Cunningham observed over a century ago, *"the politicians of the sixteenth, seventeenth and the greater part of the eighteenth centuries were agreed in trying to regulate all commerce and industry, so that the power of England relative to other nations might be promoted."*[31]

Just a century later, C.H. Lee, whose work broke new ground inasmuch as it is one of the first to apply the new quantitative methods to the writing of economic history, has affirmed that both in the eighteenth and the nineteenth centuries, *"government did exert a considerable influence on economic development."*[32] Peter Matthias has this to say: *"Government in terms of aggressive economic nationalism, actively underwrote the development of trade, bound up with imperial expansion and naval potential. Politics,"* he continues, *"can no more be ignored when looking at any wider issues in economic history; indirectly the state and the legal framework were of great importance in shaping the context within which the process of growth occurred and in influencing the process itself."*[33] Perhaps the last word rests with Britain's chauvinistic Foreign Secretary, Lord Palmerston, who declared that it was the business of government *"to open and secure roads for the merchant."*[34]

The American economy has long been portrayed as the apotheosis of competitive enterprise, free trade and *laissez-faire*, a description which even the most ardent economic liberals know to be

---

[30] Wilson, Charles, Quoted in *The Growth of English Overseas Trade* by W.E. Minchinton,. Methuen, London (1969), p.37

[31] Cunningham, W., *The Growth of English Industry and Commerce*, Kelley, New York (1968).

[32] Lee, C.H., *The British Economy since 1700, A Macroeconomic Perspective*, C.U.P. (1986).

[33] Mathias, Peter, *The First Industrial Nation: An Economic History of Britain. (1700-1914)*, Methuen & Co., London (1968).

[34] Morris, James, *Pax Britannica*, Penguin Books, p.109

inaccurate. Barry Poulson[35], a committed liberal, allows that governments did in the pre-Civil War period stimulate some activities through tariff protection and legal monopolies such as charters for roads, bridges and canals. Simon Kuznets tells a different story, however, when he says: *"Even in the USA every decade marked some decision by the state on currency, on tariffs, on internal improvements , on land, on labour, on immigration, and each one was reached after explicit discussion in which its importance for the country's economic growth was recognised."*[36] Goodrich declares that America's *"economic development was conditioned from the beginning and in very substantial degree by government subsidy and participation of public agencies of every sort."*[37] Heilbroner is more emphatic. America's *"economic growth and development gives the lie to the liberal thesis. The government acted as the promoter of business, the regulator of the economy, and guarantor of the economy."*[38] Harold Vatter, who along with Faulkner *et al* considers the period between 1860 and 1913 to be a kind of *laissez-faire* era in American history, nevertheless concedes that *"the Federal Government took limited interventionist action in favour of such measures as the protectionist tariff, the Homestead Act, an income tax law that the Supreme Court invalidated, some conservation of natural resources under Theodore Roosevelt, some anti-trust and railroad rate legislation."*[39],[40] The impartial observer could be excused for questioning Vatter's use of the word '*limited*' in view of the very considerable overall direction of the economy that is represented by the interventionist measures which Vatter cites. Perhaps, however, once again, the final word rests with the politicians. *"We must,"* says Warren Harding, *"give government co-operation to business; we must protect American business at home,*

---

[35] Poulson, Barry W., *The Economic History of the United States of America*, MacMillan, New York (1981).

[36] Kuznets, Simon, *Towards a Theory of Economic Growth*, W.W. Norton & Co, New York (1968).

[37] Goodrich, B., *Government Promotion of American Canals and Railways 1800-90*, Greenwood Press.

[38] Heilbronner, *The Economic Transformation of America. A Short Introduction in collaboration with Aaron Singer*, OUP.

[39] Vatter, H.G., *The Drive to Industrial Maturity. The U.S. Economy (1860-1914)*, Greenwood (1975), p.77.

[40] Faulkner, H.U., *American Economic History*, 7th.ed. ch.21. p.420. Harper (1954).

and we must protect it abroad. "[41] Harding's sentiments were uttered in the mid-1920s, an era when the European nations were re-building their war torn economies in the wake of the Great War. They admirably reflect the thinking of American Presidents from the time of Lincoln onwards. The role of the state in the economic development of the modern American economy was critical.

While historians, Anglo-Saxon in particular, have generally been very reticent to admit the significant role which the state has played in the economic growth and development of the Anglo-Saxon countries, the role of the state in the development of the nations of Continental Europe has been far more readily recognised. Schmoller's perceptive comments on the mercantilist era in the history of the maritime states of Western Europe deserves citation. *"Everywhere,"* he writes, *"new state systems of economy and finance were arising, able to meet the needs of the time."*[42] Commenting on the policies of the Dutch Government, Schmoller says: *"Colonial policy, naval policy, the regulation of the Levant trade, of the herring and whale fisheries, were all centralised."*[43] Writing of Colbert's administration (1662-83), Schmoller had this to say: *"The submission of the towns to a uniform ordinance, the partial abolition of the provincial Estates, the diminution of the power of the provincial governor, and his replacement by the intendant; these were measures which, like his great road and canal works, his interest in post and insurance, in technical and artistic education, in exhibitions and model buildings created by the state, in private and public model industrial establishments, his reform of river tolls, his union of the inner provinces in a uniform customs system - all aimed at the one thing, to make of the French people under its brilliant monarchy a noble and united body, united in civilisation as well as in government, and worthy of the name of nation."*[44]

Schmoller was no less emphatic about the role of the state in the economic development of his own country. *"The whole character of Prussian administration from 1680 to 1786,"* he wrote, *"was determined by the way in which this state, with its small and broken*

---

[41]   Harding, Quoted in Knowles, L.C.A., *Economic Development in Nineteenth Century France, Germany, Russia and the United States*, Augustus M. Kelly, New York (1968).

[42]   Schmoller, Gustav. *The Mercantile System and its Historical Significance*, by Augustus M. Kelly New York, London (1967).

[43]   Ibid. p.53.

[44]   Ibid. p.55.

geographical basis, set about combining a national policy in pursuit of German-Protestant and mercantilist objects. "[45]

Writing almost a half a century after Schmoller, Eli Hecksher, the Swedish historian had this to say of the mercantilist era: *"The statesmen of that period had a clearer understanding of essentials than the school of 'laissez-faire', and their view has been amply confirmed in modern times."*[46] With regard to the Dutch, the strength of whose central government has been called in question by a number of historians, including Peter Geyl and P. Jeannine who remarked that the Republic was *"a state with little capacity for intervention"*,[47] Hecksher tells us that *"the Dutch trading companies were among the most famous undertakings of the mercantilist period. It is curious that the influence of the state on their formation was more pronounced than was the case with the English companies."*[48] With regard to France, Hecksher, who is always more considerate in his judgements than many Anglo-Saxon historians when discussing the work of the great French minister, Jean-Baptiste Colbert, says: *"Colbert's regiments are an inspiring proof of the effectiveness of French mercantilism when it was upheld by its stringent protagonist. They prove that, in these cases, central authority was not lacking in consciousness of purpose or vigorous energy."*[49]

While the Dutch were the most successful mercantilists in the seventeenth century, and the English in the eighteenth century, it was the Germans who showed what could be done in the nineteenth century when the power and authority of the state was harnessed in the cause of industrial expansion. W.O. Henderson tells us that GDP per capita rose by 21.6% per decade between 1870 and 1914 against Britain's paltry 12.5%. *"Germany's industrial expansion,"* he says," *had been achieved partly by private enterprise and partly by vigorous state intervention."*[50] Lillian Knowles concurs. *"German industrial expansion was a conscious development. It was carried out by an autocrat in each state, and was systematic, designed to a definite*

---

[45]   Ibid. p.57.
[46]   Hecksher, Eli, *Mercantilism.*, Garland, New York & London (1983).
[47]   Geyl, Pieter, *The Revolt of the Netherlands*, Vol.1., (1555-1609), Vol.2., (1609-48), Benn, London.
[48]   Hecksher, Eli, *Mercantilism*, Garland, New York & London (1983), p.356.
[49]   Ibid. Vol.1. p.159.
[50]   Henderson, W.O., *The Rise of German Industrial Power (1834-1934)*, Temple Smith, London (1975), Ch.5.

end. "[51] The real motives of the Germans are well summarised by W.H. Dawson who wrote: *"The struggle was not now for intellectual and political ideals, but for sheer mastery in the realm of matter, and for political ascendancy among nations."*[52]

The role played by the state in the economic development of Russia has not been seriously questioned by any economists or historians. Alexander Gerschenkron summarises the whole process of development in that country when he says, in connection with Russia's victory over the Turks in the war of 1877 and their failure to secure their gains at the Congress of Berlin one year later: *"There is little doubt that military considerations had a good deal to do with the Russian government's conversion to a policy of rapid industrialisation."*[53] Similar observations could be made of Peter the Great's decision to drag his country out of its mediaeval past following its defeat at the Battle of Narva in 1704 by Charles XII of Sweden, or of Stalin's far more effective plan to industrialise the country when he assumed full control in 1927. Russian history has, as Gerschenkron says, been characterised by drives towards modernisation, towards industrialisation, and, it may now be added, towards space exploration, interspersed by periods of recuperation.[54] The role of the state in this process requires little amplification.

The role played by the state in the economic development of modern Japan has long been recognised both by the Japanese themselves as well as by economists and historians outside Japan. *"There can be little doubt,"* writes G.C. Allen, *"that state influence on development has been profound,"* for *"the government undertook the task of providing a modern infrastructure for Japan and its colonies."*[55] Yoshihara Kunio affirms that *"the Japanese Government was much more extensively involved in economic development than were the governments of western countries. In the early Meiji era, governments pioneered industry by setting up modern factories and*

---

51   Knowles, L.C.A., *Economic Development in Nineteenth Century France, Germany, Russia and the United States*, Augustus M. Kelly, New York (1968).

52   Dawson, W.H., *The Evolution of Modern Germany*, Quoted in L.C.A. Knowes, p.11. (see above in 50).

53   Gerschenkron, Alexander, *Economic Backwardness in Historical Perspective*, The Belknap Press, Harvard University Press (1966).

54   Ibid. Ch.6 "Russia: Patterns and Problems of Economic Development (1861-1958)".

55   Allen, G.C., *A Short Economic History of Modern Japan (1867-1937)*, MacMillan (1981).

introducing machine technology from the West. State enterprise remained important throughout the pre-war period in the production of iron and steel, machinery and armaments. Government took responsibility for railroads, communications and other types of overhead capital. Governments also gave subsidies and incentives to promote the development of certain industries, provided heavy industry with protection from foreign competition in the 1920s and 30s, and aided the zaibatsus in establishing a dominant position in the economy.[56] Kunio's view is firmly endorsed by T.C. Smith who describes that era, 1868-1880, as a period *"when Government enterprise was dominant. Government ownership and management of industry were a salient feature of the early Meiji period and were partly the result of the new government's inheriting the enterprises developed by its predecessors; in extending the principle to new fields of industry, the Meiji Government was following Tokugawa example. Centralised power and ruthless utilitarianism go far toward explaining Japan's rapid industrialisation.*[57]

The extent of the dilemma which economic liberals are faced with when reconciling economic history with economic theory may be seen from Milton Friedman's observations on the Meiji Revolution in Japan in a book entitled "Free to Choose", which he co-authored with his wife, Rose D. Friedman. *"The Meiji Government did intervene in many ways and played a key role in the process of development. It sent many Japanese abroad for technical training. It imported foreign experts. It established pilot plants in many industries and gave numerous subsidies to others. But at no time did it try to control the amount or direction of investment or the structure of output. The state maintained a large interest only in shipbuilding and the iron and steel industries because they were not attractive to private industry and required heavy government subsidies. These subsidies were a drain on Japanese resources.*[58]

The nation state is the distinguishing feature of European civilisation. No other civilisation in history has developed a similar political structure. The existence of a heterogeneous group of

---

[56]   Yoshihara, Kunio, *Japanese Economic Development. A Short Introduction*, Oxford University Press, London (1979).

[57]   Smith, Thomas C., *Political Change and Industrial Development in Japan: Government Enterprise (1868-80)*, Stanford University Press (1955).

[58]   Friedman, Milton & Rose, *Free to Choose*, Harcourt, Brace & Jovanovich (1980).

contiguous territorial units, each having its own political and economic life, with its own distinct language, literature and history, yet all sharing in a common cultural and religious background, and all participating in common artistic, intellectual and philosophical movements is one of the unique features of European civilisation. Most civilisations have based their political organisation on the imperial principle, e.g. Rome, Babylon and China, in which one single political authority controls the whole of the territory which it has conquered, differences of language, literature, history and religion notwithstanding. Europe, since Roman times, has only ever paid lip service to the imperial principle. The title, Holy Roman Emperor, which was first used at Charlemagne's coronation on Christmas Day AD 800 and finally abandoned by the Habsburgs at Napoleon's behest in 1806, reflected an ideal, not a reality. The parallel existence of city states and feudal states in the Middle Ages and of nation states in modern history has effectively prevented every effort at continental domination due to the mutual jealousy of the rival powers.

The nation state today enjoys a very considerably tarnished image, largely on account of the conflicts for which it is unfairly blamed. Europe has certainly paid a high price in terms of blood and treasure for the luxury of the nation state. It is important to remember, however, that it was not the nation state that was the original perpetrator of war. If the scale of conflict and destruction has been far greater under the nation state than under its predecessors, that is due to the double-edged impact of technical advance.

To see the nation state, therefore, in a negative light is to miss the real significance of this unique institution. For no other civilisation in history has spawned such a rich diversity of literature, art, painting, music, scholarship and science. No other civilisation has produced painters of the quality of Rembrandt, Rubens, Turner, Gainsborough, and Constable. No other civilisation has produced composers of the calibre of Bach, Mozart, Beethoven, Schubert, Brahms, Chopin or Tchaikovsky. No other civilisation has produced such giants of the pen as Shakespeare, Milton, Goethe, Schiller, Victor Hugo, or Dickens. No other civilisation has produced scientists of the calibre of Copernicus, Galileo, Newton, Faraday or Einstein. No civilisation in the whole of human history has produced such a wealth , such a diversity of talent and ingenuity as Europe.

The significance of the nation state from an economic viewpoint, however, lies in the stimulus which it has provided to the economic growth and development process. Familiarity with the economic literature, whether academic or pamphleteering, of Europe over the last few centuries should suffice to confirm the role played by the competitive factor in the economic development of Europe. Christopher Dawson's statement that: *"From the fifteenth century onwards, the history of Europe has been increasingly the history of the development of a limited number of sovereign states as independent power centres and of the ceaseless rivalry and conflict between them,"*[59] has been abundantly justified by events. It was under the stimulus of competition that the Portuguese first engaged in transoceanic voyages of discovery in the fifteenth century with a view to finding the sea route to India, thereby capturing the spice trade from the Arabs and the Venetians. It was under the stimulus of competition that the Dutch Republic created the Dutch East India Company and took control of both the production and distribution of spices. It was under the stimulus of competition that Englishmen and Frenchmen alike looked, not without envy, at the wealth of the Dutch - Richelieu described it as *"irrefutable proof of the value of trade"* - and concluded that if maritime commerce could enrich a small nation such as Holland on such a scale, then they too should apply themselves with due propriety to the establishment of their own merchant marine and commercial empire. In the eighteenth century, when Englishmen were bewailing the state of commerce, the Frenchman, Dutôt, was writing with admiration of the enormous advantages which Britain had already secured from her commercial empire. France, he concluded, should equip herself with a powerful navy and with more colonies.[60]

In the nineteenth century, it was the Germans' turn to express their profound admiration at the immense lead which Britain had established. List, however, was convinced that Germany had the capacity to compete with England. *"The advantages which England has in manufacturing, navigation and commerce need not therefore discourage any other nation which is fitted for manufacturing production by the possession of suitable territory, national power and intelligence, from entering into the lists with English manufacturing*

---

[59]   Dawson, Christopher, *The Dynamics of World History*, The New American Library of World Literature (1962), p.243

[60]   Dutôt, Political *Reflections on the Finances and Commerce of France*, Augustus M. Kelly (1974).

supremacy.[61] Similarly it was under the stimulus of economic competition that the Meiji rulers of Japan set about the modernisation of their backward country in the 1870s. It was under the stimulus of competition that Russia embarked on an economic development program in the 1930s which was designed to make *"socialism safe in one country"*. It was likewise under the stimulus of competition that the European nations established, in the aftermath of World War II, the European Common Market, or Economic Community, as it has subsequently been renamed. Economic development, whether we like it or not, is in no small way due to the competitive instinct which the existence of an array of separate political entities each jealously guarding its own sovereign territory has engendered. Economists who ardently defend competition as the mainstay of the market system, as the liberals do, should always remember that it had its origin in the competitive trading conditions which were fostered by the existence of the world-wide commercial monopolies of the Western European maritime nations. Its adoption by Smith was motivated by the desire to see Great Britain acquire an even greater economic advantage than she already enjoyed over her competitors.

Hartwell's view that *"history gives little comfort to the advocates of government action for growth"*[62] must therefore be repudiated. The free enterprise, free trade, *"laissez-faire"* economy belongs very largely to the myths of history rather than to its realities. Only Britain ever came remotely near the liberal ideal during the second half of the nineteenth century, and even then British governments, as the English social historian, G.M. Trevelyan tells us, were reform minded rather than *"laissez-faire"* orientated.[63] The paradox of which Hartwell writes when he says: *"past growth was achieved in the context of what can broadly be described as free enterprise or market economies: it is now argued that growth in underdeveloped countries' economies is not possible without vigorous government leadership, and also that continued growth in developed countries is not possible without some overall direction of the economy,"*[64] is no paradox at all, for economic

[61] List, Friedrich, *The National System of Political Economy*, Longmans Green & Co., London (1885).
[62] Hartwell, R.M., *The Industrial Revolution and Economic Growth*, Methuen & Co. (1971), p.19.
[63] Trevelyan, G.M., *English Social History*, Longman, Green & Co., London (1942).
[64] Hartwell, R.M., *The Industrial Revolution and Economic Growth*, Methuen & Co. (1971), p.19.

development, both before, during and since the mercantilist era of European history (1650-1850), has been the result of the pursuit by governments of sound, effective macro-economic management policies. Economic growth - the expansion of total output, of gross national income, and economic development - the improvement of productivity - are the result of the purposeful, rational decision-making by governments. Those who argue that economic growth and development is contingent upon state action have history on their side.

"The appeal to history," on the other hand, as Hartwell warns us in his essay entitled "Lessons of History", *"can be the most dangerous as it is probably the most common of all the bases of decision-making."*[65] There can be no doubt whatsoever of the truth of Hartwell's statement as a century which has witnessed two of the most detestable dictatorships of all time, both of which have used history as a justification for their theories and their inhuman behaviour, can demonstrate. The abuse of history, however, is no argument for its rejection. European civilisation is rooted in history, probably more so than any other world culture, and understandably so, in view of the fact that Europe's two principal religions, Judaism and Christianity, are themselves rooted in history.

---

[65]   Ibid.

2 MANAGEMENT

"The role of the state is of strategic importance." Simon Kuznets.[66]

Adam Smith once defined Political Economy as *"the art of managing the resources of a people, and of its government"*.[67] To Smith, management was to be equated with "laissez-faire". Free the people from the archaic restrictions on the movement of goods. Permit people to move freely in search of work, to pursue their own economic interests, for in so doing they will automatically benefit the community at large. Allow the market to be the unfettered arbiter of resource allocation, the determinant of the effective utilisation of the factors of production. Permit competitive business enterprise and free trade between nations, and industry and commerce will flourish and national income increase. Restrict government to its traditional functions of the maintenance of law and order, the defence of the realm, the education of the young and the construction of those facilities, such as ports, harbours, roads and highways which are essential to trade, but which no individual or private corporation has the resources to provide. Such in a nutshell was the Smithian philosophy.

It is to Smith's credit that he saw the impracticability of some of his ideas. He recognised that there were many situations in which men were not free to enter into voluntary contracts with their fellowmen, that the economic, social and political power of eighteenth century landlords was such that tenants who farmed their lands were obliged to pay the rents demanded.[68] He was aware of the economic power that the large

[66] Kuznets, Simon, *Towards a Theory of Economic* Growth, W.W. Norton, New York (1968).

[67] Oxford *English Dictionary*, 2 Vol. ed.

[68] Smith, Adam, *The Wealth of Nations*, Eds. Edwin Cannan, Norman Berg, Georgia (1976), p.49.

corporations, which in his time were only in their infancy, were able to exercise in the market-place, thus dictating prices, and holding down wages.[69] He was only too well aware of the power, social, economic and political, which employers could wield against their workers.[70] Significantly enough he was far more concerned about the dangers of employers' confederations than he was of trades unions, a concern which was more than justified in the light of the Combination Acts which the British Parliament legislated in 1799. He remained sceptical of Britain's ability ever to become a free trading nation, because he realised how powerful the merchant and manufacturing classes were and how strongly supportive of mercantilist policies they were.[71] He did not foresee the time when Britain's technological lead would result in those very same people demanding the abolition of tariff barriers on a wide range of goods. Least of all can he be blamed for failing to perceive the remarkable transformation that the Industrial Revolution, then only in its infancy, would have on the world in which he lived. The astonishingly rapid increase in the rate of technological innovation, the growth of factories, the emergence of the large technologically based corporation with its need for efficient and effective management - all these developments lay in the future when Smith was writing. Yet it is these developments in the microeconomic sphere that have provided us with a totally new appreciation of what management is all about.

The emergence and growth of the business enterprise as a factor in our social and economic life is very much a phenomenon of the Industrial era. Other societies have had their managers, just as they have had their governments, their doctors, their lawyers and their priests. In Roman times, it was by no means unusual for the wealthy owners of land to go off and leave their estates in the hands of a steward. Soldiers of patrician families, who were away on active service, would entrust their farms and their households to the care of their most intelligent and energetic slaves. Wealthy merchants anxious to increase their overseas business, would embark on foreign trips leaving their affairs in the hands of their most trusted servants. Whatever the legal and economic status of the individuals in whom responsibility was entrusted, their function was to care for the property of their master. Business management as we know it today, however, is very much a phenomenon of the industrial era. Never before in human

---

69   Ibid. p.577.
70   Ibid. p.67.
71   Ibid. p.437-8.

history have so many people committed their lives and their careers to it.

The decisive factor in the emergence and growth of management is the development of technology. The invention of the steam engine revolutionised not only the method by which textiles could be manufactured, but the whole financial and economic system of the day. The emergence of the factory with its two or three, in some cases, five hundred employees, established the need for management. Initially, this was provided by the owner or owners themselves. As the size of the enterprises to be managed increased, the demand for non-familial managers grew. The real impetus, however, to the growth of a professionalised cadre of managers in the nineteenth century was provided by the development of another technology, namely the railways.

Whereas the textile mill, and even the ironworks, could be run by the owner and his partner with very little help from outside their respective families, the railway could not. To begin with the railway was not a family business, but a joint stock company. Railway investors were people who had made their money elsewhere and were looking for an attractive investment with a good return. They were a class of stockholders who had no real, immediate interest or concern with the efficient management of the operation, provided that their investment gave them a dividend at the end of each year. The Directors of such companies, while they had a financial stake in the operation, were not generally men with the knowledge or experience to manage the railway. Accordingly, men from other walks of life, such as canal companies, or even the armed services, were selected for the job. The expansion of the railway network throughout the length and breadth of the country coupled with the development and expansion of both existing and new technologies combined to provide more and more opportunities for those bright young men who considered management as a career. The boom in the electrical industry in the 1870s and 80s, the emergence of the chemical industry, and the succession of discoveries and innovations which have accompanied its growth, all provided an enormous impetus to the opportunities for professional management.

With the arrival of the twentieth century, and the long steady succession of technological improvements that have changed every aspect of our lives, the stage was set for an unprecedented growth in the demand for professional management. There was the same tendency in many of these new technology areas for the owners to manage the business themselves initially. But the growth in scale of many private enterprises, coupled with the growth in the size and scope of public utilities, such as electricity generating stations, gas works, postal services, telecommunications and broadcasting, provided even more opportunity for men and talent and managerial skill. With the passage of time, there emerged on the industrial scene a new phenomenon, the giant corporation, employing over 100,000 people, with assets running into millions of dollars, and sales, in many cases, of commensurate value, too large, too complex, and too sophisticated to be managed along traditional functional lines, and therefore requiring a cadre of highly trained professionals whose job it was to ensure the smooth efficient functioning of the business. It was the United States of America, with its mass market of 100 million people, that first saw the emergence of these giants of the industrial scene. For the Industrial Revolution in America was the age of Rockefeller, Vanderbilt, Carnegie, the Du Pont family, Thomas Edison and Henry Ford, men who made their fortunes out of the newly developed technologies of the day, and, while, where possible, these men kept the business as much under their own personal control as possible, the enterprises which they built up became so large that they required professional managers to run them.

The emergence of the giant corporation on the European scene was only a matter of time. I.G. Farben was established in Germany in 1925. The British government countered by creating Imperial Chemical Industries in 1926. Amalgamations, mergers and take-overs in other industries have resulted in the post-war period in the emergence of a number of giant corporations on the European scene comparable in size to those of North America. Today these corporations control a sizeable portion of the commercial market, both in their home countries and abroad.

The management of such vast enterprises necessarily demanded the development of a set of ideas according to which they could be controlled. The philosophy of Management by Objectives provided the corpus of theory that was needed. Beginning with the notion that business undertakings, whatever their size, must be managed effectively if they are to survive, let alone succeed in the competitive world of modern industrial and commercial capitalism, the pundits of MBO developed their ideas. Managements, they claimed, could only be effective when they knew and understood the business for which they were responsible.

To understand the business, its strengths and weaknesses, the reasons for its successes as well as its failures, was the key to effective management. It was not enough to identify the business by its principal product or products, by the nature of the technology in which it was engaged, or even by the market segment which it served. These attributes of the enterprise could certainly help in determining the nature of the business, but none of them individually could identify the real nature of the business. To understand the business properly, managements have to take all these factors into account, specifically, however, they have to look at the world outside the business enterprise and try to identify the services and the value their particular company provided to the community at large. To understand why the customer was willing to part with his money to purchase the goods and services which the company produced was considered vitally important in determining the unique contribution which the firm could make to the community at large. The result areas as they became known, were the key areas, and a proper understanding of what the customer wanted and was prepared to pay for, was the key to business success. To put it another way, business success depended on a thorough knowledge of the market together with a careful and intelligent assessment of the contribution which the individual business enterprise could, with the resources at its disposal, make in the market.

The process of understanding the business was not complete until the corporate audit had been undertaken. For whereas analysis of the market and the opportunities which it offered, provided the understanding of where the business could be won, only a knowledge of one's own enterprise, its strengths, capabilities, and potential, could provide the all-important information regarding the ability of the business to meet the demands of the market. The corporate audit entailed a complete review of the technological and material resources available to the company, with a view to ascertaining whether they would suffice to achieve the results which the business wanted to obtain in the market place. Typically, the audit would encompass the material assets of the enterprise and the natural resources which it could access. Of much greater importance than this, however, was the managerial and technological competence of the enterprise. The recruitment, training, and development of technical expertise and managerial ability were the twin pillars on which the success of the technologically based companies was built, and it was excellence in these fields that determined the success of the business and the advantage which it might acquire over others in the same field. Ultimate success in the market place, leadership in the technological area in which the business specialised, and economic performance were all independent of the human factor, and it was to the corporate audit that management looked to identify whether it has the resources which it considered it needed to achieve the results required. The corporate audit, with its precise detailing of managerial needs and technical expertise in all aspects of the enterprise's operations, be they production, marketing, selling or finance, was seen as the cue to the establishment of business competence.

Whilst the market analysis and the corporate audit provided the understanding of the business which was so important to success, it was the definition of the enterprise's objectives that determined the direction in which the company should be going. The greatest confusion still pervades the sphere of objectives and objective setting, largely due to the fact that the indices of profit and profitability obtrude on the scene. But this is to confuse objectives and economic performance. Performance is the economic reward earned through effort. The financial results of the company - its economic performance indices - indicate how successfully the enterprise has performed its task of supplying the goods and services which the public needs. Objectives are the hard, measurable, precise, quantitative, statistically stated facts about the business which have to be achieved if the firm is to continue to grow or survive. They relate in the first place to the result areas, such as market share, market standing, customer service, product sales, and technological innovation. They are also seen as applicable to such resource areas as manpower planning, labour relations, and management performance, since the latter are as significant for industrial and financial success as the former. The exercise of setting objectives is hard work, because it necessitates thinking through the requirements of the business in the light of its priorities. Managerial fads, products which executives are proud of but which customers only buy when they would rather have something else, procedures which were established to meet conditions which existed years ago, and are no longer relevant to the needs of the market, all these and similar managerial irrelevancies have to go. Goals have to be set, which given the managerial muscle have to be achieved if the business is to grow and flourish, for every division of the firm, every department and every section within that department. They have to be established for overseas subsidiaries and similar undertakings. The main purpose of all such effort is to ensure that every manager is aware of the common goals and every manager and his staff knows what is expected of him during the forthcoming year.

Once the goals have been established, corporate strategies aimed at achieving those ends have to be developed and resources allocated to the ends agreed. The process of strategy development may well involve some modification of the original objectives; the nature of the business, its sheer size, and complexity often require that some of the objectives be thought through in the light of what later examination reveals was entailed in putting them into operation. Strategy development will often require the sloughing off of unprofitable operations, the expansion of certain key product lines where marketability has shown them to be good, the development of new markets hitherto untouched, the elimination of an overseas operation or the closure of certain production facilities. It may reveal fundamental shortcomings in the research and development area which would have to be made good if the company is to achieve its objectives; it may reveal weaknesses in other areas, inadequacy or unreliability of plant and equipment, or even uncertainty regarding the availability of raw materials and other purchased parts. Strategy formulation of this type often leads to the development of sub-objectives which are every bit as important as the attainment of the original objectives.

The process of resource allocation which provides the means by which the agreed objectives are turned into labour and material requirements follows that of strategy formulation and goal setting, and provides for every managerial unit within the enterprise, the financial resources and goals that are expected of that unit for a future period. The process is, like the goal setting and strategy formulation activities that precede it, a lengthy one involving the drawing up, discussion and revision, where necessary, of plans at every level in the organisation in the context of the goals which have been set. The magnitude of the task in a multi-national corporation can well be imagined; small wonder that executives complain that so much of their time is taken up with the production of next year's budget.

Goal setting, strategy formulation, resource allocation and budgeting are only the prelude to the execution of the practical tasks of implementation. Within a division of a large multi-national corporation, implementation requires a high degree of effective communication, co-ordination and managerial teamwork amongst the staff of the division. The secret to effective implementation is the identification and concentration on key tasks. The process of achieving goals is dependent on the performance of certain essential functions. The key tasks may well be the improvement of morale, efficiency or effectiveness of the sales force through the execution of a carefully devised and thought out training program. It may be the elimination of several major bottlenecks in the production or distributive processes, the presence of which is inhibiting sales, or it may be the completion of a Research and Development project the results of which materially effect sales performance. Whatever it is, the performance of a job is dependent on the completion of the key tasks.

Corporate control of the market, despite the immense power available to the modern technological enterprise, is never so complete that management's plans are implemented without default. Industrial unrest delaying the completion of a capital construction project, the discovery by a rival enterprise of an alternative and seemingly superior process or product, the failure of the sales staff to match the expectation of the market's research and intelligence unit, the loss of an export market, an adverse movement in currency values - all these eventualities are part and parcel of the real world in which modern management has to perform its task.

The process of monitoring achievement in the modern business enterprise has been immensely facilitated in recent years by the development of the electronic computer. Information in the pre-computer era necessitated the expenditure of many hours of clerical labour, and even then what was available to management only provided a very limited appreciation of the state of the business. The computer not only revolutionised the speed and accuracy with which management received information, but it rendered possible the production of a much wider range of data and thus provided better informed executives. Concurrent with the development of the computer, there has been a vast increase in the size and the scope of the managerial function, an increase which has necessitated the availability of much more information than was previously demanded. Economic performance indices for all aspects of the production, marketing, financing, distribution and technical sides of the business are now available to management. So great indeed is the volume of information available to management that the problem of deciding what is relevant and significant on the one hand, and irrelevant and insignificant on the other is critical for modern management.

The corpus of theory which the management theoreticians have developed is not complete without the process of review. Review forces the corporation as a whole to undertake a very serious examination of itself. Review obliges the Boards of Directors of large concerns to look critically at the goals they have set their enterprises to see whether they were the result of plain, hard, judicious thinking, or whether they were the result of shallow optimism, faulty strategies and misdirection of resources. Review compels the company to look very carefully at the goals which it has set itself, to see whether they were realistic or even appropriate to its resources and the opportunities which are available to it in the market place. Review compels a company to look carefully at its human resources and the potential of its management cadres to see just how capable are its assets in that area. In short, the review process forces a company to ask itself some very searching questions, and not until these are answered satisfactorily will the company be in a position to know where it went wrong and more fundamentally why it went wrong.

The thesis of this work is that the economic development and growth process is the result of the successful application of these management principles by governments. Successful states have been those whose leaders understood the contemporary world situation, analysed the opportunities for economic development which presented themselves, recognised the relative strengths and weaknesses, capabilities and deficiencies of their own and other states, and had the courage not only to perceive but to exploit the opportunities available to them. It is this process of evaluation which has heralded the ascent to economic power and prosperity of the various nation states which have dominated the world political and economic scene over the last five hundred years. The competence and integrity of the national leadership is the decisive factor, the dynamic element in the economic development of the modern nation state. The evidence of history is undeniable on that issue! It is successful men who produce successful nations, and the successful nations are those which have the good fortune to produce a succession of very capable leaders. As Braudel, the great French economic historian, has remarked, *"success depends on sensing the opportunities of a given period, on doing so time and time again, and piling advantage on advantage."*[72]

---

[72]   Braudel, Fernand, *Civilization and Capitalism: the Fifteenth to the Eighteenth centuries.*, Vol.3. "The Perspective of the World". Fontana Press, London (1985), p.50.

The essence of the economic development task is leadership, and the essence of effective leadership is the capacity to get the right things done. Leadership requires both character and performance, as Drucker tells us in his epoch-making work on management,[73] but it also needs vision and courage. Vision is important because it enables the leadership to see the world not as it is, but as it could be after it has been transformed by the collective efforts of the leaders and the people. Vision is thus required if the leadership is to inspire in the people the desire and willingness to undertake the risks entailed. Courage is indispensable, for without the courage to undertake the tasks involved, to bear the risks and burdens associated with the re-direction of effort and enterprise which economic growth entails, naught will be achieved. All the great leaders of history have been men of vision and courage. The courage to focus the nation's efforts on the exploitation of those alternatives which appear to offer the greatest rewards is the supreme test of leadership. Effective leadership is dynamically motivated, teleologically orientated, economically expansionist, technologically innovative, and strategically minded. Effective leaders know how to determine their objectives, and also how to achieve them. They have a deep appreciation of the value of resource management, whether at the human, the material or the financial level. They recognise that the determinants of national economic achievement are the nation's people, their character, enterprise, energies, their willingness to work and their skills, and they treat all other factors, material and financial as subordinate to those factors.

The essence of the approach is a correct understanding of the contemporary world situation. Appreciating where one's own country stands in relation to others in terms of comparative levels of economic development and in terms of the opportunity for development is the first step towards a correct assessment of the situation. It is task which is not easily done, for it requires an understanding of the opportunities available to one's own nation as well as some perception of the way in which other nations will respond to one's own initiatives. Analysing where the opportunities for economic development lie is essential if the task is to be undertaken effectively, for it is only as we elucidate the alternatives that the national leadership will know in which direction to point the nation. The task is not an easy one. The information available to the leadership is always deficient, and hindsight always provides a

---

[73]   Druker, Peter, *The Practice of Management*, Pan Books.

more accurate perception of events than the present can ever do. The task requires commitment, dedication, tenacity, courage and the resolve to see the project through to the end. Mistakes will be made, human fallibility being what it is; they can readily be excused, however, if they are due to lack of knowledge rather than lack of foresight. Appreciating the relative strengths and weaknesses of other states is a fundamental part of the exercise, but under no circumstances should this be used as a pretext for procrastination or even project repudiation. Many an individual, many a country, has taken calculated risks which, at the time, appeared foolhardy, but which in the light of later events, proved highly successful. Such undertakings have often had unperceived consequences. Finally, no amount of appraisal, analysis or appreciation of the risks involved will have any significance if the willingness to exploit the opportunities available is not present. Understanding the contemporary world situation is where the management process begins. Nations that succeed at this point are very likely to succeed along the line. Those that fail here will almost certainly be stragglers.

"No man builds a tower without first calculating what it is going to cost him."[74] As it is with business houses, so it is with nations. The national audit - the term here is used here in its broader sense - is as essential to the state as the corporate audit is to the business enterprise. The task of determining what resources the nation has and what those resources are capable of achieving, is a pre-requisite to success. Determining a nation's own strengths and weaknesses, its assets and deficiencies, is essential. Every nation's principal resource is its people. Their character and skill and the quality of the national leadership are the fundamental determinants of achievement. Character is of prime importance both among the people at large and among its leadership. Level of technique is a limiting factor, which given time, can always be improved. A lack of capital or the absence of natural resources should never deter any nation from proceeding with a development project for the simple reason that such facilities can always be obtained through trade. A nation's greatest asset is its people, and its greatest strength is its unity, its awareness of its homogeneity.

National homogeneity requires time to develop, for it is the product of the nation's shared experiences, of its history, and it is not infrequently enshrined in its literature. Homogeneity - that awareness of being part of the nation, of belonging - is much easier to attain in

---

[74] Mark 14:28.

nations whose people have enjoyed a long history of shared experiences and who speak one language, as the history of Western Europe demonstrates. A common language, however, is not essential as the experience of Switzerland shows, provided that the nation has other features which enable it to achieve a sense of identity.

Leadership requires vision and understanding to perceive the direction in which the nation should go, particularly at critical junctures in its history. Setting it on the correct path is a major task of no small importance, particularly when such a course of action necessitates a complete revolution in thinking and direction. The determination of objectives is therefore of paramount importance if the leadership is to know where it is to go. As with the business enterprise, so with the nation, objectives to be of any value, must be time-related tasks, achievement of which are measurable. Normally, no one single objective will suffice, though exceptions can always be gleaned from history which prove the rule. Generally life is too complex for that. Conversely, there is a very real danger that if too many goals are established, conflict will arise in the attainment of them.

The determination of the objectives to which the state is working is one of the most fundamental tasks of leadership. The goals which are established will reflect the determination of the leadership to steer the ship of state on a new course, a course for which its previous history and experience has suited it, but which nevertheless requires a re-orientation of the energies of the nation. It was on just such a course that the leaders of Portugal launched their small nation at the end of the fifteenth century when they set their captains the task of finding the sea route from Europe to India. Peter the Great launched his state on an entirely new course two centuries later when he attempted to bring his protesting countrymen into the modern world. A radically different course was adopted by the Meiji leaders of Japan when they attempted to bring their nation into the modern world in the latter part of the nineteenth century. The nations of Africa and Asia are engaged in a struggle to re-orientate the direction of their countries in an attempt to industrialise, for industrialisation is for them an entirely new path, and therefore one strewn with obstacles and difficulties. It is as important psychologically for a nation to have goals as it is for an individual. For goals centre a nation's energies on what has to be achieved in just the same way in which they centre an individual's resources on what he has to achieve. Goals enable the aspirations of the nation to be given direction and purpose. Goals make the task of achievement specific and tangible.

With the goals defined, the task of determining the most appropriate measures to be used to achieve them, of delineating strategy, arises. Strategic thinking is essentially long-term, and it involves a commitment to policy decisions which have long-term implications. There are essentially three areas in which strategic decisions have to be made. The first relates to the degree of involvement by the state in the economic development process. The second concerns the nature and extent of the assistance which the nation may require from other nations. The third raises the issue of the commercial relationship of the state to other states.

The strategic area has always been and still is the most contentious field in economics, theory in many cases giving entirely different answers from historical experience. Economic liberalism teaches the doctrine of *"laissez-faire"*. Historians know only too well that *"laissez-faire"* is a doctrine which has been observed only in the breach by governments, and never in reality. Economic liberalism teaches the doctrine of free trade. Historians know that free trade has enjoyed very little currency on the international scene. Indeed, only one nation has practised free trade for any length of time and that was Great Britain in the second half of the nineteenth century. The reason for that was that Britain had secured such an overwhelming technological advantage over the rest of the world that she could afford to trade on the terms which she laid down.

Economic liberalism, likewise, teaches us that international trade balances will always equilibrate given that governments do not interfere with the market forces of supply and demand both for goods and currencies. Historians know that international trade balances rarely ever do equilibrate regardless of the degree of interference in the process by governments. Economic liberals show little appreciation of the significance of cultural and religious considerations. Historians, as Braudel et al have observed, have stopped thinking of *"economic history as a neatly defined territory which one could study in isolation from the outside world"*.[75] All human actions, according to Raymond Forth *"have an economic aspect, a social aspect and a cultural aspect"*.[76] It is the cultural factor which, as historians are now

---

[75]   Braudel, *Civilization and Capitalism: the Fifteenth to the Eighteenth centuries*, Vol.3. "The Perspective of the World". Fontana Press, London (1985), p.19.

[76]   Ibid.

recognising, has had a far greater impact on economic strategy than has been hitherto realised. Cultural considerations have had far more to do with the choice between planning and the market economy in many countries than is commonly realised.

Strategy determination will to a large extent determine the mode of resource allocation. The role of the market, with its obvious imperfections, on the one hand, and of centralised planning, with its equally obvious imperfections, on the other, need to be viewed in the light of history. Market failure, long ignored by economists in the capitalist world, is now being given proper attention, just as the manifest weaknesses of the 'planned' economy are now being observed in those countries which have adopted imperative planning techniques as part of their economic development strategy.

The key resource is labour, its capabilities being the prime determinant of achievement. Yet the under utilisation of labour both in the developed as well as the developing world, remains what, throughout history, it has traditionally been, namely one of the greatest evils of all time. The effective utilisation of the nation's manpower is, as history shows, a major determinant of achievement. No nation can operate to full capacity, or for that matter, with maximum efficiency with a substantial part of its workforce out of commission, just as no businessman would think or operating with idle manpower on his books. Manpower wasted is talent destroyed and opportunity foregone.

The task of economic development is a complex one, ranging as it does across a whole spectrum of issues from the management of human resources to the management of the financial and material resources of the nation. To select any one of these and identify it as a key task is to give it a priority which it would not otherwise have. Just as there are key tasks in industry, jobs which if not attended to will result in the goals of the firm not being obtained, so it is with nations. If there are tasks which are not done, the state will fail in its obligations to its people and fail to achieve its objectives.

There are four areas, which traditionally have been vital for the success of the economic development process - agriculture, manufacturing, transport and education. To these must be added a fifth, namely environmental preservation.

The fundamental importance of agriculture has been well understood by rulers since the days of the ancient Egyptians. Governments, ancient mediaeval and modern, have always been acutely aware of the dangers in which they place themselves if their people do not have enough to eat. The French and Russian Revolutions both provided examples of what can happen to governments if the food supply in the capital city is insufficient to meet requirements. Peasant rebellions have been a recurrent feature of China's past. They have frequently been occasioned by the failure of the government to ensure an adequate supply of food. Empires which have been dependent on foreign supplies of food have always placed a high priority on control of shipping lanes. It was as important for the Roman Empire, dependent as the city of Rome was on Egypt for its supply of corn, to control the shipping lanes of the Mediterranean, as it was for Britain in the nineteenth and early twentieth centuries, dependent as she was on North America for her food supply, to control the shipping lanes of the world. Governments, ancient, mediaeval and modern, have accordingly placed a high priority on the production of sufficient food to satisfy the needs of their peoples. City states have, on account of their inability to satisfy their citizens' requirements from their own resources, been more vulnerable to disruptions in the food supply than nation states. The attention, however, which the latter have given to agriculture in modern times reflects the deeply ingrained belief that governments that fail to ensure an adequate food supply for their people have no right to govern. The Physiocrats were not mistaken in giving pride of place to agriculture; they were mistaken in assuming that manufacturing was economically superfluous.

The Mercantilists, on the other hand, understood the importance of manufacturing for the economic well-being of the state. They realised, what modern governments have increasingly come to recognise, that the production of manufactured goods not only provides employment but raises the level of skill among the workforce and therefore adds to the nation's wealth. Manufacturing, as the Mercantilists appreciated, was the basis of commerce and trade, and a favourable balance of trade was an essential ingredient in the nation's economic prosperity. Nations that neglect manufacturing, as we shall see, are doomed to economic demise. The almost universal propensity of governments to protect their industries is comprehensible in view of the political uncertainties that threaten our world. The modern state cannot survive either economically or militarily without a strong manufacturing industry. Moreover, economic development must be balanced if it is to meet national requirements effectively. A nation which is dependent on others for its high technology goods will be at the mercy of its more powerful suppliers in times of political emergency. Political economists who espouse the cause of liberalism should remember that competition works on the winner takes all principle. They are in danger of forgetting that inefficient industries may be preferable to no industry at all.

Technical innovation has been the source of mankind's extraordinary economic expansion over the last two hundred years. Yet there remains one area in particular in which innovation has been more critical than any other, namely transport. For it is transport revolutions that have converted our world of nucleated villages into one large global village, and in so doing has brought the wealth of the world to our front doors. Throughout history it is improvements in transport technology that have revolutionised man's capacity to improve his lot. It is to advances in transport that we owe the development of the market. Indeed, the market is a creation of the transport system. At every stage in the development of the market there has taken place an improvement in transport. Trade depended on the adequacy of the transport system. The developments of the last five hundred years have resulted in the creation of much larger markets than were even conceivable in times past.

Economic development is contingent on what is now described as human capital investment, and the extent to which a country can commit resources to it determines the level of skills which its people possess. The skills acquisition process is the most important investment which any nation can make, for it is on the quality of that input that the nation's output is to a large extent contingent. The correlation between the education level of a country and its level of national wealth is one which cannot be ignored. The richest countries today around the world are those which have the highest levels of academic attainment. The poorest are those which have little educational input.

Care of the material environment is a key task to which more attention has been given in recent years than was hitherto the case. The problems associated with ecology and the preservation of the environment continue to plague our societies just as much as man's rape of the earth in ancient times destroyed so much of the earth's fragile biosphere. Agrarian societies have always been faced with the very real problems associated with over-cropping, deforestation, salinity and soil erosion. These persist in our time only they are exacerbated by the folly of the destruction of the equatorial rain forests around the world. The wholesale destruction of fishing grounds is but a further reflection on the inadequacy of the market system to provide adequate protection for common property resources. Simultaneously, industrialism has contributed to the problem through environmental pollution due to ineffective or insufficient methods of waste disposal. The failure to manage the physical environment effectively is due to that indubitably human propensity to consider only the short-term results of our actions, and ignore the wider long-term considerations. Mankind's future on planet earth is contingent on his ability to manage the environment effectively. It is a problem which was until recently completely ignored by market economists. Indeed, the problem has only received proper attention since governments, mainly at the behest of their people, have been prevailed upon to take appropriate action.

The management process is not complete until the question how well have we done is both asked and answered. The Chinese in the thirteenth century had little difficulty not only in asking the question, but in answering it. They saw themselves for what they undoubtedly were, the leaders of the world, culturally, politically and economically. The Venetians in the fifteenth century had little doubt about the position of economic hegemony which they enjoyed in the Mediterranean and in Europe. The Iberian powers had every reason to be proud of their achievements in the sixteenth century, likewise the Dutch in the seventeenth and the British in the nineteenth centuries. The twentieth century has witnessed first the dominance of the United States of America, and is now witnessing a bid for supremacy by Japan.

Success, however, breeds pride, as the attitude of late fifteenth century Venice demonstrates. The Venetians, sadly, were not alone. Their failure to understand the signs of the times is redolent of the attitudes of other nations at similar periods in their history, the Dutch in the mid-seventeenth century and the British in the mid-nineteenth century, to name but two examples. It is this failure, as much as a failure of leadership as anything else, which accounts for the inability of nations to maintain the lead which they have established. It is a sad, but undeniable fact that nations only really arrive at a true assessment of their situation when they have experienced military defeat. Russia's history exemplifies this point better than that of any other nation. Japan's response to the decimation of her land in 1945 provides a further example. The process of review forces a nation to ask itself not so much how it succeeded in getting where it did, but where it should go next.

The role of the nation state in the process of European economic development has been seriously underestimated by the economic liberals in their anxiety to defend the market economy. For the nation state played a very vital part in the creation of the global commercial empires of the European maritime states from the fifteenth century onwards, in the promotion of scientific research and technological innovation in the seventeenth and eighteenth centuries, in the creation of those conditions in the eighteenth and nineteenth centuries not the least of which is the national market, without which industrialisation could not have taken effect as it did, in the promotion of those projects, e.g. the development of the three-masted sailing ship, canalisation, railway and highway construction, and space research without which our modern world would not be what it is today. Demographic growth, geographical expansion and technological innovation have been the hallmarks of European history for the past six centuries, centuries which have witnessed the most rapid economic development in the entire history of man. The direction and rate of material progress has been contingent on the capacities of the leadership, political, commercial, industrial, technological, and financial to achieve their national objectives. Their ability to utilise the resources available to the nation, to grasp the opportunities which present themselves, to focus the energies of the people on those objectives which the nation considers desirable, to select the strategies most appropriate for the development of the nation's resources through the most appropriate channels, and to ensure that the task or tasks are completed - these are the hallmarks of effective leadership.

3 The Portuguese Experience

Contemporary economic thought considers that economic management began with Keynes and the Great Depression. J.F. Wright's book, *"Britain in the age of Economic Management"*[77] reflects this viewpoint well. Certainly the 1930s witnessed a significant increase in the degree of involvement by the state in the economic development process as leaders of the various national economies struggled to revive their battered economies. Even Milton Friedman has conceded that *"the Rooseveltian administration achieved a considerable measure of success in relieving immediate distress and restoring confidence"* in the economy.[78]

Economic management, however, enjoys a much more distinguished history than most economists realise. The word 'management' was first used in the English language in the Elizabethan era, at a time when the country was beginning to feel its sea-legs, to develop those commercial maritime activities for which it subsequently became famous.

Economic management, however, has an even older pedigree than that, dating back as it does in Europe to the fifteenth century when the Iberian nations first undertook the voyages of discovery which have transformed our world. *"The discovery of America, and that of a passage to the East Indies by the Cape of Good Hope, are the two greatest and most important events in the history of mankind. Their consequences have already been very great; but, in the short period of between two and three centuries which have elapsed since these discoveries were made, it is impossible that the whole extent of their consequences can have been seen....By uniting, in some measure, the*

---

[77]   Wright, J.F., *Britain in the Age of Economic Management. An Economic History since 1939*, Oxford University Press (1979).

[78]   Friedman, Milton & Rose, *Free to Choose*, Harcourt, Brace and Jovanovich. p.94.

most distant parts of the world, by enabling them to relieve one another's wants, to increase one another's enjoyments, and to encourage one another's industry, their general tendency would seem to be beneficial."[79]

Contemporary economic historians are less inclined to eulogise about the voyages of discovery than was Smith, if only because they are well aware of the disadvantages as well as the advantages which the native peoples suffered under European domination. Nevertheless, their significance has not been lost on Milton Friedman who has nothing but high praise for the intrepid sea-captains who pioneered these early exploratory journeys into the unknown. Certainly men such as Diaz, Da Gama, Cabral, Columbus and Cabot deserve the highest commendation for their remarkable achievements. Their vigour, courage, tenacity and perseverance in the face of extreme difficulties merit the adulation which generations of historians have given them. It was through their efforts that the modern world economy was born; without them the global commercial empires of the European nation states would not have come into existence, the world economy would not have been controlled from Europe and industrialisation, which has done so much to raise the standards of living for so many people around the globe, would not have taken place.

Portugal was the first of the Western European maritime nations to break out of geographical isolation to establish a commercial empire beyond her shores, a commercial empire that stretched across four continents, a truly international and intercontinental trading emporium, the first of its kind in the world. Portugal's unique achievement lay in the ability of her leaders to create the first genuinely world economy, to bring together the commerce of the Far East, the East Indies, India, Persia, the Arab World, the sub-Saharan kingdoms of Africa and Brazil. In so doing, she destroyed the Arab-Venetian monopoly of the spice trade, and established the first of the European based global commercial empires. The Portuguese voyages of discovery opened up a new era in the history, not only of the European nations, but of the world.

Trade between sub-Saharan Africa and Europe, between the Orient and the Occident had carried on since Roman times, but it had only been a mere trickle compared to what it was to become later, on account of the inadequacies of the transport modes, the camel and the

---

[79] Smith, Adam, *The Wealth of Nations*, Eds. Edwin Cannan, Norman Berg, Georgia (1976), p.590.

caravan, on which it depended. Even when, as happened with the spice trade, goods were shipped from the Indies to mainland India, thence to Aden and Suez, to be carted across the isthmus to Alexandria before being shipped to Venice, the handling costs involved were considerable, the profits which each merchant took were exorbitant in relation to the risks entailed and the end product was priced at a level which only the wealthy could afford. Inter-regional trade did take place, but it was trade between regions which were virtually self-sufficient, and which accordingly only traded a few luxury goods. The voyages of discovery accomplished a sea change in the scale and hence the character of international commerce. In the language of economics, they pushed the aggregate supply curve firmly to the right, bringing more food, more goods, and more services within the range of more people, thus raising European living standards, qualitatively as well as quantitatively. The consequences for Europe were significant; a better diet led to larger populations. Increased demand for timber for shipbuilding and grain for feeding Europe's burgeoning population resulted in the expansion of trade particularly in the Baltic. In the course of time, the demand for more ships boosted expansion of the minerals industries, coal, tin, lead, copper and iron. As populations expanded, demand for textiles, silks, laces, and building materials, e.g. brick, stone and glass, all received an impetus. The process was slow and gradual, but happen it did, albeit interruptedly.

Portugal's remarkable achievement has been attributed to several factors. The organic evolutionist school of thought, of which Malyn Newitt is a representative, has emphasised population expansion as the principal driving force behind the attack on Morocco and the settlement of the Atlantic islands in the early part of the fifteenth century.[80] The gist of Newitt's argument is that the northern valleys, whence most of Portugal's emigration has come, were over-populated in relation to existing technology, that movement to the south was impossible on account of the feudal conditions which existed on the large estates, and therefore that migration was the only acceptable alternative. As an explanation of the first stages in Portugal's maritime expansion, Newitt's argument has some merit, although demand for sugar had much to do with the settlement of the North East Atlantic islands. It does not, however, explain why the Portuguese established one of the largest maritime empires in history. That cannot be explained in terms

---

[80] Newitt, Malynn, *The First Portuguese Empire*, University of Exeter (1986).

of population pressures, as Cipolla has observed: *"European expansion after 1400...cannot be described as the result of Malthusian pressures."*[81]

Portugal's geographical position at the western end of the European littoral has been adduced as a major factor explaining her achievement. Certainly, geography conferred a natural advantage on the country, but it cannot explain why Portugal behaved as she did at that particular time in her history, nor why the Basques, the Bretons, the English or the Flemings did not engage in voyages of discovery. Nor will it explain why the French, the Catalans or the Castilians, all of whom made voyages into the north-east Atlantic in the fifteenth century did not also embark on voyages of exploration. Least of all will it explain why the Genoese, who provided the sea-captains for the earliest Spanish and English Atlantic voyages, did not themselves undertake exploration in their own right. Genoa certainly did not lack the financial resources; it was they who provided some of the funds for the Spanish and Portuguese voyages.

The explanation for Portugal's remarkable achievement in the fifteenth and early sixteenth centuries is to be found in the writings of Olivera de Marques, the Portuguese historian: *"The essence of the Portuguese expansion, was a state enterprise to which private interests and initiatives were applied. The presence of a strong royal authority permitted effective direction and efficient organisation, the consequent disengagement for internal political problems and the national cohesion necessary for common efforts."*[82] Portugal's accomplishments cannot be understood apart from the capabilities of her leaders, political as well as commercial and maritime. The achievements of Portugal's merchants, sea-captains and viceroys could not have come to fruition, but for the financial support and encouragement of the monarchs who backed them.

From the twelfth century onwards, Portuguese monarchs played a very positive part in the commercial, maritime and economic development of their countries. King Dinis (1279-1325), whom Baillie Diffie regards as *"king of a sea-minded people, and the most apt of a*

---

[81]   Cipolla, Carlo, M., *Guns, Sails and Empires. Technological Innovation and the early phase of European Expansion, 1400-1700*, Sunflower University Press, Kansas (1965).

[82]   Oliveira de Marques, A.H., *History of Portugal*, Vol. 1 "From Lusitania to Empire", Columbia University Press (1972), p.263,4.

long line of commerce-minded monarchs ",[83] sponsored a project for
the afforestation of the dunes north of Lisbon in order to ensure a ready
supply of timber for shipbuilding. The forest was to serve the double
purpose of providing a windbreak for inland agriculture; it was
therefore one of the earliest examples in European history of the
enactment of a policy of environmental preservation. A century later,
King Fernando (1367-83) enacted legislation designed to increase
shipbuilding. Lisbon merchants who were willing to build ships of more
than one hundred tons were exempted from the tithe on wood, iron and
sailcloth, as well as various other duties and taxes levied on shipping.
Portuguese commercial activity, however, had one distinguishing
feature, namely the degree of involvement by the monarchs themselves
in commerce. Portuguese kings owned their own ships and traded as
principals both in Lisbon and in foreign ports. It was this direct
involvement of the monarchy in the commercial life of the nation that
forged the all-important alliance between politics and commerce
without which Portugal's maritime expansion would have been
impossible. The politico-commercial alliance, therefore, was a key
factor in Portugal's economic development just as it had been in the
development of Venice, and as it was to become in the life of the Dutch
Republic, the British Empire, the United States of America and
Imperial Japan.

The view that mediaeval Portugal was a commercially minded
society has been challenged in recent years by Professor Boxer who
argues that *"it is an exaggeration to write of Portugal as possessing a
powerful commercial class largely emancipated from feudal
control. "*[84] Boxer observes that commerce was and remained very
much looked down upon in Portugal, an activity largely for foreigners
and Jews. Even Portugal's involvement in fisheries has been over-
emphasised, he argues, there being more people engaged in that
industry in modern times than in the mediaeval period.

No historian of the mediaeval Portuguese scene, however, can
fail to be impressed by Portugal's commercial activity. Ever since the
twelfth century, the Portuguese had been engaged in trade with
Northern European countries, with England, France, Flanders and
Acquitaine. Exploiting what little resources nature had given them, they

---

[83]   Diffie, Bailey W., *Prelude to Empire. Portugal Oversea before Henry the
         Navigator*, University of Nebraska Press (1980), p.39.
[84]   Boxer, C R *Portuguese Seaborne Empire, 1415-1824*. Hutchinson, London
         (1969).

had succeeded in extracting from their relatively poor soil such products as olive oil, wines, wax, cork, honey and dried fruits. These they had used to trade for cloth and other luxury goods of Northern Europe. Also, they had cashed in on the very rich fishing fields which nature had given them, with the result that fish and salt were two of their major export revenue earners. Mercantile interests had come to the fore very early in Portuguese history, as may be seen from the very real part played by all groups in society, not only the merchants themselves, but the clergy, nobles, princes and monarchs, not to mention the ordinary people, in the commercial life of the nation. Commerce had become the life-blood of the nation and the development of shipbuilding as a major industry in thirteenth century Portugal owes much to the country's need not only for a fishing fleet but for a mercantile marine. Contemporary chroniclers vouch for the presence of merchants from Genoa, Florence, Venice, England, Flanders, and Acquitaine in the streets of Lisbon in the fourteenth century. The city was, in Oliveira de Marques' words, cosmopolitan. Likewise, Portuguese merchants were to be found in such far distant places as Constantinople and Alexandria.[85]

C.R. Boxer, in his study of Portugal's sea-borne empire, has drawn attention to the fact that political factors in Europe strongly favoured Portugal's efforts at maritime expansion.[86] Most of the states of Western Europe were engaged, during the fifteenth century, in prolonged conflict of one kind or another either with one another or with the Turks. England and France were both embroiled in the One Hundred Years War until 1453. Thereafter, England was torn asunder by the Wars of the Roses until Edward IV assumed control in 1471. The reign of Louis XI (1461-83) was likewise one of dissension and strife in France. Louis, however, did have the good fortune to see three of the largest fiefs in his kingdom fall into his hands by virtue of their being no male inheritor. No king of England or France, however, showed any interest in exploration until the very end of the fifteenth century, after the Iberian monarchs had led the way. English and French kings, when they were relieved of the pressures of having to deal with their recalcitrant barons, were much too intent on acquiring wealth through campaigns in France or Italy to concern themselves with such

---

[85]   Oliveira de Marques, A.H., *History of Portugal*, Vol. 1 "From Lusitania to Empire", Columbia University Press (1972), p.263,4.

[86]   Boxer, C.R., *Portuguese Seaborne Empire 1415-1825*, Hutchinson, London (1969).

highly risky projects as John II (1481-95) of Portugal engaged in. Both Edward IV (1471-83) and Henry VII (1485-1509) of England conducted successful expeditions against France for the sole object of acquiring money. Charles VIII of France invaded Italy in order to secure his claim to the Neapolitan throne; there is little doubt, however, that he intended it to be a financial success. While there was wealth to be obtained in Europe, mediaeval kings were unlikely to turn their attentions outwards. Moreover, it was only when the Moors had been finally driven from the soil of Spain that Ferdinand and Isabella were willing to consider Colombus's outlandish proposal to find the westerly route to China.

Understanding the contemporary world situation and taking advantage of the opportunities available is a prerequisite for success in the task of economic management. The Portuguese leadership, when it was not embroiled in war with Castile or Morocco, took advantage of its opportunities to further the cause of exploration. Given their vision, what were the objectives of the Portuguese leadership?

C.R. Boxer has identified four objectives which the Papal Bulls authorising the voyages of exploration mention - the spread of Christianity, the discovery of a new route to the sources of gold in West Africa, the discovery of the legendary kingdom of Prester John, and the discovery of a new sea-route to the spice islands of the East.[87] There is no doubt that evangelisation played a very important part in Portugal's imperial expansion. Wherever the Portuguese went, so too did the monks and nuns of the Catholic church, with the result that communities of the faithful were established in countries as widely separated as Brazil, West Africa, East Africa, India (Goa), China and Japan. Our highly materialistic age is apt to regard the juxtaposition of two such objectives as the spread of Christianity and the encouragement of commerce with undue cynicism. The Portuguese, however, were by no means alone in their regard for the spiritual welfare of the peoples with whom they came into contact. Similar motivations influenced the settlement of North America by the Puritans in the seventeenth century. David Livingston's journeys into the heart of the African Continent in the nineteenth century were likewise motivated by a desire to bring the blessings of both Christianity and commerce to the inhabitants of that continent.[88]

---

[87] Ibid, p.22,23.
[88] Seager, George, *David Livingstone, His Life and Letters*, Lutterworth Press, London (1957).

Time was, however, when explanations of Portugal's world-wide expansion were laid almost exclusively at the feet of one man, Prince Henry the Navigator, as he has erroneously been described. To Henry was ascribed the initiative for, in the words of Baillie Diffie, *"establishing a school of cosmography, astronomy and navigation, for the design of new types of ships and navigational instruments, and for founding the first astronomical observatory in Europe, all with a view ultimately to finding the sea route to India."*[89]

The researches of a stream of historians, both within and without Portugal, have concluded that there is insufficient evidence to prove this contention. Prince Henry now appears in an altogether different light, as a feudal prince typical of the renaissance era, with a mild interest in science, but pre-eminently concerned with his princely way of life, his feudal retinue and an income substantial enough to support him and his dependants. According to this view, Henry's real interest in the discoveries, which was by no means negligible - Oliveira de Marques credits him with the initiation of one-third of all voyages made to West Africa between 1415 and 1460[90] - stemmed from the wealth which they conferred upon him. Henry's reputation as a disinterested man of science whose objective was to break through the barriers of obscurantism and technical ignorance and set his country on the road to India has been shattered.

While recent historical research has substantially tarnished the lustre of the Prince Henry's reputation, however, that of his royal successor, the Perfect Prince, as John II has been described, has certainly been magnified. Oliviera de Marques claims that it is to Prince John, who in 1474 was put in charge of overseas expansion, and who, three years later, voyaged out to the Congo to see the situation for himself that *"the creation of a comprehensive plan of discovery with its means and goals, should be credited."*[91]

The arrival of John II on the throne of Portugal eight years later provided a new dynamic to the whole enterprise of transoceanic navigation, for it was he who finally made the Portuguese accept as a first priority the search for the sea-route to India. Until John's reign, all

---

[89] Diffie, Bailey W. & Winius, George, D., *Foundations of the Portuguese Empire 1415-1580*, University of Minnesota Press (1977), Ch.7. "Henry the Navigator who followed his stars".

[90] Oliveira de Marques, A.H., *History of Portugal*, Vol.1 "From Lusitania to Empire". Columbia University Press (1972), p.144.

[91] Ibid, p.218.

talk, if any there had been, of Portugal finding a sea-route to India, was nothing but talk. Once John came to the throne, the case for circumnavigating the expanding Turkish Empire in the Middle East took on a new importance. John gave his countrymen three tasks to accomplish. The first was a journey into the heart of Africa in search of the legendary kingdom of Prester John. The second was the dispatch of a mission through the Mediterranean to the Levant and Arabia. The third was the discovery of the sea-route to India. These three objectives appeared to fifteenth century Portuguese to be much more compatible than they do to us. Contemporary knowledge of the world's geography was derived from the ancients. Ptolemy's map of the world, published in the fifteenth century, showed Africa joined to India and the Indian Ocean as a lake. The final delineation of the African Continent awaited Diaz's successful circumnavigation of the Cape of Good Hope in 1488. Even then, the voyage to India lay ten years in the future for reasons which historians are still debating, but which may well be connected with the re-design of the Portuguese man-of-war. By then John II had died and been succeeded by Manuel II (1495-1521) in whose reign the Portuguese commercial maritime empire was very largely established. While Manuel lacked the drive and tenacity of purpose of his predecessor, it is to him very largely that credit must go for completing the task of finding the sea route to India; and in 1497 that was no easy undertaking. The majority of the royal council were opposed to the project on the ground that a small nation such as Portugal did not have the resources to engage in so great an enterprise. Fortunately for mankind, Manuel had the courage to over-ride his faint-hearted advisers. His decision was more than justified by events. In 1504, when the Venetians reached Alexandria to collect their annual consignment of spices, there was none to be had. *"Le roi epicier"* as the French king derogatively referred to his Portuguese counterpart, had secured a decisive advantage, albeit temporary as subsequent events were to prove. It was very largely thanks to John's pertinacity, his vigilance and his courage that Portugal, a small, comparatively poor country on the western end of the European littoral, should have become for the better part of a century, one of the leading commercial maritime nations of Europe. It was a remarkable achievement and one which does credit to the handful of energetic, capable men who undertook it.

It is easy to criticise John II, as Portuguese in succeeding centuries have done, sometimes mercilessly, for his obvious failure to listen to the admonitions of the Genoese sea-captain, Christopher

Columbus. It is not so easy for us to remember how mistaken Columbus was, nor for that matter how ignorant men of that period were of the world's geography. Columbus believed that Cathay was only three thousand miles from the shores of Portugal. He had no premonition when he planted the Spanish flag in the West Indian islands in 1492 that he had discovered another Continent. Nor could anyone in 1494 have seen the outcome of the signing of the Treaty of Tordesillas between Spain and Portugal, according to the terms of which, Brazil, accidentally discovered in 1500 by Cabral, became Portuguese. John acted on the best advice, advice which, insofar as the distance between Europe and Cathay was concerned, was correct. The Greek astronomer, Epaphroditus, had already calculated the circumference of the world as 25,000 miles and not as Columbus believed 18,000, or as Ptolemy had stated 22,500.

Given the Portuguese objectives, what strategies did they use to achieve those ends? Carlo Cipolla, in his study of the means by which the Portuguese established their dominion over world commerce entitled *"Guns, Sails and Empire"*[92], has highlighted the significance of the technological developments which Europe had made in the fourteenth and fifteenth centuries which facilitated their achievement. The sailing ship, the principal mode by which Portugal achieved her ends, was a development from the early fishing boats and single-masted vessels which the Portuguese used in the twelfth, thirteenth and fourteenth centuries. To appreciate the problems which the Portuguese had in adapting these early models to the requirements of transoceanic navigation, we need to remember how little advanced techniques of ship design and construction really were in the late Middle Ages. It would not be true to assert that nothing had changed since Roman times, for the Vikings had developed the long ship and had voyaged to Greenland and North America. Nevertheless, much European navigation in the fourteenth century was still undertaken in galleys, the speed of the ship being determined by the capacity of the rowers when conditions were not suitable for the use of the single sail which was all most ships were equipped with. Moreover, the hazards of life in the open seas were such that, as in Roman times, ships rarely departed from the coastline when voyaging either in the Mediterranean or the North Atlantic for fear of being lost at sea. The use of the compass on

[92] Cipolla, Carlo, M., Guns, *Sails and Empires. Technological Innovation and the early phase of European Expansion, 1400-1700*, Sunflower University Press, Kansas (1965).

board European ships did not become commonplace until the fifteenth century. Even then, sailors could not be persuaded to sail far out of sight of land unless they were satisfied that the ship could return to shore without difficulty again. Both currents and wind conditions had to be taken into account; the fourteenth century sailing ship could not on any account defy them. By modern standards, navigational techniques were crude, ship design basic, and knowledge of oceanography in its infancy. The problems which the Portuguese had to face in the fifteenth century when they set out to explore the Eastern Atlantic were immense, and should not be underestimated.

The greatest difficulty facing Portuguese seamen as they fought their way south along the western shores of Africa in the first half of the fifteenth century were the prevailing currents . This is the reason why the rounding of Cape Badajoz presented such a major problem. It rapidly became clear to the Portuguese that, if success was to crown their endeavours, they would have to develop a different type of sailing ship. The invention of the three masted caravel appears to have been made in the 1430s, and no alternative explanation has been proffered concerning its origins. It marked a radical departure in ship design, but one which was necessitated by the conditions of sailing in the Atlantic. Its greatest attribute was its efficiency. The use of sails in large numbers enabled the designers to reduce manning requirements. Contemporary ships carried large numbers of rowers, for whom provisioning was quite a problem. The new ships replaced manpower with natural forces, their great advantage being their capacity to tack into the wind.

The caravel was a major step forward. Without it, the exploration of the coastline of West Africa could not have been accomplished. The caravel's inadequacies, however, came to light once the Portuguese began their exploration of the South Atlantic, where the combined forces of wind and current made the task of southbound sailing even more difficult than it had been in the North Atlantic. It was, as Diaz, discovered on his first trip to the Cape, an unsuitable ship for the India run. It was too light a vessel to handle the tough conditions of the southern archipelago. Moreover, it was too small to carry the men, materials and provisions which were necessary for the long haul to India. Inadequacy of evidence prevents conclusive statements concerning the reasons for the ten year delay between Diaz's voyage and Da Gama's, but it may well be that Portugal had once again to re-design their sailing ship before it could weather the 12,000 mile trip to

India. The ships that Da Gama took to India were larger, sturdier, more powerful vessels, capable of handling the tougher conditions of the Indian route. Moreover, the route that Da Gama took did not follow the African coastline. Diaz had realised the folly of attempting to sail into the southerly winds and currents of the South Atlantic, and hence recommended that on future voyages to the Cape, ships sail in a south-westerly direction after reaching the West African coast, towards South America, thus using the prevailing winds and currents. While adding thousands of miles to the journey, this route was a much easier one to navigate.[93]

While it was the ship that facilitated the voyages of discovery, it was the gun that enabled the Portuguese to assert their sovereignty over the Indian Ocean, to defeat the Arab and Indian navies and thereby establish a licensing system for the control of trade. The gun was a fourteenth century invention, its use in European warfare from c.1330 onwards, and its effectiveness in siege situations whether against castles or walled cities making it a highly desirable weapon to possess. Its use on battlefields, however, in those early days was not, as the Portuguese quickly learned in their wars with Castile, necessarily determinative. Perhaps for this reason its incorporation on sailing ships was long delayed. It was John II of Portugal who saw the necessity for ships travelling to the Cape and India to be equipped with heavy guns. Not only was pirate infestation of the sea lanes of the world a factor that had to be reckoned with, so also was the attitude of the Arabs and the Indians who between them controlled the maritime commerce of the Indian Ocean. Lisbon, in John's reign, became an excellent market for the cannon merchants of Europe, most of whom hailed from Flanders where the art of gun manufacture was first developed. Indeed, most of the gunners on board Portuguese men-of-war were either Flemish or German in origin. It was King John who patronised the gun-foundries of Europe and allocated the resources for the establishment of arsenals and artillery trains in Portugal itself. Under his successor, some 5,200 tons of copper was imported for the manufacture of guns. A marked improvement in ship design, generally attributed to a Breton, enabled the guns to be placed on the lower decks of sailing ships and fired through port holes.

---

[93]   Daumus, Maurice, Ed., *History of Technology and Invention - Progress through the Ages*, Vol.II "The First States of Mechanization", John Murray, London (1969).

Portugal's strategy for obtaining and maintaining monopolistic commercial power in the Orient was based ultimately on superior technology. No study of Europe's methods of enforcing her will on the rest of the world can afford to ignore the significance of the naked force factor. The gun provided Europeans with a superiority of strike power which the native peoples of the lands to which they went were unable to match. Whatever part may have been played by the horse, by disease or by simple human ingenuity, the role of the gun in the subjugation process cannot be underestimated. It was the gun that made the Portuguese carrack the formidable vessel that it became. It was the gun that enabled the Portuguese to inflict heavy defeats on the navies of the Muslim and Hindu powers. It was the gun that facilitated the establishment by Portugal of the ring of forts that surrounded the Indian Ocean, thus ensuring that mastery of the oceans which was so essential a part of her commercial strategy. The details of the stages by which the Portuguese acquired the techniques of cannon manufacture do not concern us here. Suffice it to say that it was largely due to Portuguese initiative that an invention which had originally been made in China somewhere between the tenth and the thirteenth centuries, and had subsequently been introduced into Europe where it was developed and used in land warfare, was used by Europeans for gaining control over the rest of the world.

While it was the armed merchantmen that enabled Portugal to assert control over the Indian Ocean, it was the capture of strategic trading posts and their subsequent fortification by the Portuguese that enabled them to retain that control. The man responsible for the determination and implementation of Portugal's Indian Ocean strategy was the great viceroy, Albuquerque. It was he who realised that if his country was to control the trade of the orient, the strategic trading centres of the Indian Ocean would have to come under Portuguese control, and enemy fleets would have to be destroyed. The events which constitute this story - the subjugation of the East African kingdom of Quila in 1505, the defeat of the combined fleets of Egypt and India at the Battle of Diu in 1509, the establishment of forts at Diu, Hormuz, Goa and later Malacca and the subsequent capture of Ceylon - are well known. Only in one respect was the strategy flawed, namely Albuquerque's failure to capture Aden.[94] It was to prove to be the

---

[94]   Diffie, Bailey W., & Winius, George D., *Foundations of the Portuguese Empire 1415-1580*. University of Minessota Press (1977), Ch.7. "Henry the Navigator who followed his stars".

source of Portugal's downfall, for without Aden, the Red Sea, the one remaining sea route not controlled by Portugal, could be used for commerce. The Arab-Venetian monopoly of Oriental trade, however, had been broken. Twenty years were to elapse before the volume of spices reaching Venice through Alexandria equalled what it had been before the Portuguese opened up the sea route to India. Never again was Venice to enjoy the luxury of the spice monopoly. The Low Countries, Antwerp specifically, was to become the new mart for spices in Europe. Henceforth, Northern Europe was to be of far greater importance in the economic development of the Continent than the south. The decline of Venice was assured.[95]

The maintenance of the Portuguese empire was dependent on the supply of the right quantity and quality of materials and finished goods, and on the availability of a skilled labour force. In spite of the very far-sighted policy of Dinis in the thirteenth century - an example of highly intelligent planning, not to mention conservationism, Portugal, nevertheless, suffered from a dearth of good timber, a fact which explains the relaxation of the duties on all imported wood. The realisation of this deficiency, however, made the Portuguese use Oriental sources of supply, chief of which was Goa itself. Many of the ships which Portugal used on its eastern run to China and Japan were built in Goa by craftsmen sent from Europe. Likewise, the ready supply of copper from Japanese mines provided Portugal with the opportunity to set up a cannon-foundry at Macau, thus reducing her dependence on European supplies.

Finance was Portugal's other problem, and to a large extent, she overcame it by trading textiles for African gold. The supply of gold was not sufficient, however, to meet all Portugal's needs, particularly once she entered the era of large ship construction. The enormous capital resources which such undertakings required were beyond the means of the country, even given its strong commercial propensity. Accordingly, both John II and Manuel II had recourse to the bankers of Genoa and Florence to finance the very heavy outlays which shipbuilding necessitated. Their action was more than justified in terms of the very high return which the spice trade provided once it was in Portuguese hands. In the world of the fifteenth century, a world in which trade and

---

[95]   Braudel, Fernand, *Civilization and Capitalism: The Fifteenth to the Eighteenth Centuries*, Vol. 3. "The Perspective of the World", Fontana Press, London (1985).

treasure were indissolubly linked, and capital flows were uninhibited by national frontiers, the Portuguese kings' methods were well justified.

A nation's achievement is the product of its leadership and the skills and character of its people. It is these three factors that determine what a nation accomplishes; all else, natural resources, finance capital and technology are subordinate. Portugal's remarkable rise to eminence as the first commercial maritime power to establish a truly global empire, thus creating the first genuinely world economy, substantiates this thesis unreservedly. Nature's bequest to Portugal left much to be desired; yet, what she had, her people made good use of. Their willingness to engage in commerce, essential in a country whose resource base was so limited , demonstrated the capacity both of the people and of the leadership to grasp where the future of the country lay. The freedom with which the nation's leadership supported commercial activity, and engaged in it themselves, is a further demonstration of the nation's readiness to come to terms with the realities of their world. The role played by successive Portuguese monarchs in maritime exploration cannot be ignored. *"Laissez-faire"* was a dogma wholly alien to the Portuguese way of thinking. All the key decisions in Portugal's history, the capture of Ceuta, in 1415, the discovery of the maritime route to West Africa in the 1440s, the voyages around the Cape of Good Hope and to India in 1488 and 1498 respectively, the settlement of Brazil in 1500, were monarchical in origin, and had sometimes to be made in the face of strong opposition from the Royal Council. Their execution was dependent on the skill, courage and determination of Portuguese of all walks of life - the royal prince, the nobleman, the merchant, the banker, the ship designers and builders, and last, but by no means least, the sea-captains and sailors who risked their lives on the long, arduous risky transoceanic voyages.

The role of the government in the economic development of the modern world has been very much underestimated by economic liberals. Due deference is paid to such 'real factors' as population growth and technological innovation, but insufficient attention is paid to the role of the state; for it is the political leadership alone which can canalise national energies into constructive channels, thereby producing positive results for the whole nation. It is not true to assert, therefore, that *"the great advances of civilisation have never come from centralised government".*[96] Indeed, Friedman's remark cannot easily

---

[96]   Friedman, Milton, *Capitalism and Freedom*, University of Chicago Press (1963), p.3.

be reconciled with his admission that Columbus's voyage on behalf of the King of Spain was facilitated in part by royal funds.

4 The British Achievement

Great Britain emerged at the end of the eighteenth century the most powerful and commercially advanced nation not only in Europe but in the whole world. *"A nation of shopkeepers"* was the disparaging comment of her sworn enemy, Napoleon Bonaparte, Emperor of France. Yet nothing could deny the fact that this small island of only ten million people, with its limited resources of land and raw materials, had far outstripped her larger and more populous rival, France. Her colonial empire was larger, comprising as it did strategic trading posts not only in the West Indies and West Africa, but also large areas of India and Eastern Canada. The loss of the American colonies had been a political, but not an economic, setback as the country's remarkable trade recovery after 1783 indicated. Moreover, the Eden Treaty of 1786, coming in the wake of the early economic liberal sentiments of Turgot and Adam Smith, had benefited British exports at the expense of French manufacturers. The loss of this trade with the outbreak of war in 1793 had very little adverse effect on British economic performance. By the turn of the century, one-third of all world exports emanated from the British Isles. Britain's trade, the source of her wealth, and the means by which she was able throughout the long quarter century struggle with France, not only to keep her own army and navy in the field, but to finance the efforts of her coalition partners, Austria, Prussia and Russia, exceeded by far the commerce of any other nation. It was a stupendous achievement, and one which has attracted the attention of historians and economists alike, each generation making its own contribution to our understanding both of what happened and how it happened.

Britain emerged as the leading industrial nation in the nineteenth century because it was she, rather than the Dutch or the French, who succeeded in creating not only a global commercial empire but a national economy as well; indeed Britain's greatest achievement was to integrate the national market with the global commercial empire. The timing of the emergence of the national market is generally taken to be the eighteenth century, significantly during the reign of George III. *"By 1815,"* as J.H. Plumb tells us, *"2,600 miles of canal had been built in England and Wales. They cheapened production and lowered prices."*[97] Other historians havè put the date earlier. Braudel has argued that England had a national market at the beginning of George III's reign when the total mileage of navigable waterway was 1,160 miles.[98] John Morrill, on the other hand, argues in favour of a much earlier date, contrasting the situation in 1600 when *"England still consisted of a series of regional economies striving after, if not always achieving, self-sufficiency,"* with the position in 1690 when there were *"few places"* which *"were more than twenty miles from water navigable to the sea. Gradually,"* he argues, *"a single, integrated state was emerging."*[99] Historians will debate for years to come whether England had become a national market by 1700 or whether a later date such as 1750 or even 1780 is to be preferred. Suffice it to say that it was during this period that English provincial towns first began to develop to any size; indeed while only London had a population in excess of 100,000 in 1700, by 1750 there were fourteen cities in the British Isles whose total population exceeded that figure. Urbanisation on such a scale would have been impossible but for the development of trade, and trade is impossible without an adequate transport system.

It is my purpose here to show that Britain's economic lead in the nineteenth century was in no uncertain way due to the policies, political and religious, as well as economic, which governments from the time of the Puritan and English Revolutions, followed. But for these policies, the conditions appropriate to Britain's rise to world leadership would not have been created, and Britain would not have witnessed that transformation of her social and economic life which historians have identified with the phenomenon known as the industrial revolution. The role of leadership, therefore, in all walks of life, political, industrial, commercial, and technological was critical for the future development of the country's economy. Britain's possession of such natural advantages as a fertile soil, a temperate climate, easily navigable rivers,

---

[97]   Plumb, J.H., *England in the Eighteenth Century*, Penguin Books, (1950), p.147.

[98]   Braudel, Fernand, *Civilization and Capitalism: the Fifteenth to the Eighteenth Centuries*, Vol.3. "The Perspective of the World", Fontana Press, London (1985).

[99]   Morrill, James, *The Oxford Illustrated History of Britain*, Oxford University Press, p.292.

and an abundance of good quality coal, is not denied. Her island position, moreover, meant that she did not have to shoulder the heavy burden of land fortification, which was such a drain on French resources from the time of Louis XIV onwards. The navy was her defence against all potential aggressors from the time of Elizabeth I onwards, and governments were acutely aware of it. Nor can it be denied that geography favoured the country in yet another respect, for no part of the island is more than 75 miles from the sea, a fact which, coupled with the marvellous opportunities for the development of riverine traffic and canalisation, undoubtedly facilitated the transport revolution which the country experienced in the eighteenth century. But advantages are only advantages if the nation has the wit to use them. Hence the supreme importance of leadership and its corollary, sound management.

The impressive feature of British history in the two centuries which followed the Puritan Revolution is the number of outstanding people in all walks of life that the nation produced. Few countries have enjoyed such an abundance of talent in so short a space of time. Without the initiative, courage, enthusiasm, enterprise and willingness to take risks which was the hall-mark of Englishmen in all walks of life during this era, Britain would not have become the world leader. Their contribution, however, would not have been effective if the nation's political leadership had not created the framework, social, economic and cultural within which they could operate.

Mercantilism has come in for heavy criticism at the hands of economists since the triumph of classical economic theories in the nineteenth century. We do rather less than justice to the men who not only accepted Mercantilist ideas, but made them the basis of their economic policies for the better part of two centuries, if we fail to realise that it was against the background of those very ideas that Europe, Britain in particular, engaged in an unprecedented period of economic expansion. The vital role played by the state in Mercantilist thought and practice cannot be denied. For Britain's rise to economic supremacy was achieved through a variety of means. Chief among these were the regulation of industry and agriculture - particular attention being paid to shipping and fishing - the forcible acquisition of colonial territory both from other European Powers as well as native peoples, strict control of both the domestic and colonial economies, the provision of apprenticeship schemes for young craftsmen, the fullest possible utilisation of the labour resources of the nation, the encouragement of science and technology, the encouragement of immigrants especially those who, like the Huguenots, had special skills which the country lacked, the creation of sound fiscal and debt management policies by successive governments and the development of an effective banking system in which businessmen had confidence. Finally, Parliament's role in the eighteenth century in facilitating the enclosure of land and the formation of larger farms, the construction of canals, the building of the national highway network and the provision of ports and harbours cannot be ignored. This is not to deny the very real role played by Englishmen in all walks of life, be they soldiers, sailors, merchants, industrial entrepreneurs, financiers or farmers. Their discipline, initiative, enterprise and determination contributed in no small measure to the British achievement. A nation, however, is the product of its leadership. The example of Great Britain during the Mercantilist era proves this point.

The foundation of Britain's greatness, as Braudel has argued, was laid in the reign of Elizabeth I. It was then that the country, for the first time, really began to take seriously the possibility of world exploration and world trade. The loss of Calais in 1558, followed by the closure of the port of Bruges and, then, ten years later, of Hamburg, inspired English merchants with the urge to seek new outlets for their expanding industries. The vehicle which was to be the means by which foreign trade was conducted in the next two centuries was the Trading Company. Trading companies, whether they were of the type in which individuals traded using their own capital, whilst adhering to the rules of the corporation, or of the joint stock variety in which case the profits and losses were divided amongst the investors, required a royal charter to define the geographical limits within which the company could conduct trade. They were avowedly monopolistic, understandably so in an age when the expenses not only of ship construction and voyaging, but of establishing trading posts, forts and at a later period, colonies, had to be met by the company. In Elizabeth's reign alone, companies were formed to trade with Russia, Northern Germany, the Baltic States, Turkey, the Levant and India. Thus was laid, with state initiative, the basis of English commercial power for centuries to come.

The trading company was only the first of four planks in the Elizabethan economic strategy. The second was the navy. Henry VIII had been the founder of the English navy, but it had been so neglected by his successors that his daughter had to build it again from scratch. Hampered by lack of resources in the early part of her reign, Elizabeth had to wait until the 1570s before she could get construction underway under the leadership of her gallant sea captain, Jack Hawkins. It was Hawkins who was responsible for the design of the English broadsides that so successfully defeated the Spanish Armada in 1588. The significance of Drake's victory was that it demonstrated to any would-be conqueror of the British Isles that English sea power would have to be destroyed before a successful invasion could be launched. Henceforth, control of the sea lanes of the world was to become of increasing importance to England, if the basis of her commerce and eventual commercial supremacy were to be safeguarded. The role of the navy, whose foundations were laid in Tudor times, is difficult to exaggerate.

The third plank in Elizabeth's economic strategy was her social legislation. Tudor England witnessed a significant increase in the degree of regulation exercised by the state over the life of the nation. In the political sphere, this was part of the Tudor policy of strengthening the Crown in relation to the aristocracy and the church. In the economic sphere, it was occasioned by the realities of the times, the loss of overseas markets, land enclosure and industrial development. The destruction of the monasteries in 1536-9 undermined the ability of the church to minister to the needs of the indigent in English society. It was the towns whose population was being swollen by the steady influx of people from the land as the enclosure movement continued ahead, that had to bear the brunt of providing for those members of society who, for one reason or another, could not provide for themselves. The various pieces of Elizabethan legislation, which dealt with the problems and which culminated in the Poor Law of 1601, constitute one of the first attempts to deal with the issues of inflation, unemployment, apprenticeship training and wages at the national level. Most famous of these was the Statute of Artificers of 1563 which, in the words of S.T. Bindoff, the Tudor historian, *"set out to mobilize the resources of the nation."*[100] The intention was to ensure that there was work for all who wanted it, and for those who did not want to work, houses of correction were established. The most important provision of the Act, however, was its stipulation that every craftsmen should go through a seven year apprenticeship before he was qualified. In this way, it provided a nationally acceptable training scheme for English apprentices, and thereby laid a solid basis for the transmission of skills from master to

---

[100]   Bindoff, S.T., *Tudor England*, Penguin Books (1950), p.200.

apprentice in the following years. Elizabethan social legislation was a remarkable achievement. It provided England with a skilled workforce without which her industries could never have developed as they did. It also provided the groundwork for the administration of poor relief in England until the industrial era of the early nineteenth century compelled its modification. It was also the reason why English cities, for all their lack of hygiene, their dirt and their noise, did not suffer, as did European cities, from the problem of beggary.

The fourth plank in the Elizabethan economic strategy was the establishment of overseas colonies. The first attempts, however, by Raleigh in Virginia in 1585 and Gilbert in Newfoundland were a failure. The nation's resources were too heavily committed to the war with Spain in the latter part of Elizabeth's reign for such projects to be affordable. In 1609, however, the Virginia Company was founded. England's need for timber and the growing market for tobacco were the major reasons for the promoters' actions. English manufacturers regarded the new colony as a captive market for their wares; it was an attitude which was to characterise the establishment of all subsequent trading stations and colonies not only in North America, but in the West Indies, West Africa and India. Wherever colonies or trading posts were established, whether the prime motive was religious, as was the case with some of the North American settlements, or economic, they were always subject to the same commercial regulations, namely that trade was to be exclusively reserved to the Mother Country and other colonies belonging to the Mother Country.

Not all Elizabethan economic policies were successful, however. The principle of monopoly was not restricted by the Tudors to foreign trade. It was applied to everything, mining, manufacturing and internal trade. Letters patent were issued for every economic activity, much in the way in which licences are issued by the state today, with the important difference that in Tudor times they created monopolies. The Tudor intent was to secure revenue for the Crown. The result was high prices. The regulation of internal trade proved, however, to be short-lived. One of the first Acts of the Long Parliament, once it had asserted its own authority, was the abolition of domestic monopolies. Thereafter, English domestic trade was to be competitive. One aspect of the Elizabethan regulatory system, however, was destined both to be the forerunner of later legislation of a more comprehensive nature, and to remain on the statute book for some centuries to come, and that was the legislation forbidding foreign ships to enter the English coastal trade.

From Elizabethan times onwards, English governments were very sensitive to the need to protect English shipping.

While the achievements of the Elizabethan era provided some of the foundations on which later English rulers could build, the great turning point in English history came with the Puritan revolution in the mid-seventeenth century. The series of political upheavals that England went through between 1640 and 1702 were decisive for the subsequent history, political, religious and economic of the country.

In the political arena, the principle of Parliamentary government was established. Henceforward, every King of England would require Parliamentary support for the policies he wished to pursue, and ministers of the Crown would have to have the confidence of Parliament if they were to continue in office. The Stuart attempt to govern without Parliament, as Charles I had done, or behind Parliament's back, as Charles II attempted to do. was finished. The principle of limited or constitutional monarchy was established. The constitutional rights of the English people were secured. The powers of the Crown were restricted. English kings could not raise money without Parliamentary approval; any military or naval expeditions which they wished to engage in were on that account subject to Parliamentary consent. Englishmen could no longer be imprisoned without trial, nor English judges dismissed without the consent of both Houses of Parliament. Most importantly, the royal claim to govern by Divine Right lost its meaning when Parliament decreed the line of succession, thus ensuring that no Catholic ever became King of England again. The establishment of representative government in England in the seventeenth century was the direct outcome of the Puritan Revolution. England, and for that matter, America, owes its concept of freedom, of responsible freedom to the Puritans. Not only did England's system of government become a byword for liberty and the envy of Frenchmen in the eighteenth century, but it was to stand the country in good stead a century later when the Industrial Revolution threatened to undermine the social fabric of the nation. Whatever the shortcomings of the English Parliamentary system, and those familiar with the protests of John Wilkes in the early years of George III's reign will know that they were not inconsiderable, England managed to negotiate the reefs and shoals of social and economic turbulence without succumbing to the bloodbath into which her neighbour France was thrust by the collapse of the 'ancien regime'.

The victory of the Parliamentary party, supported as it was by the merchants of London, during the English Civil War, was, ipso facto, a victory for mercantile capitalism. The Puritan Revolution witnessed the union of the political and commercial classes in the government of the country, a union which was to be relatively little effected by the vicissitudes of the next fifty years. This is not to say that commercial interests now dominated Parliament; far from it. Maurice Ashley has observed that only 53 members of the Parliament of 1657 were merchants.[101] English Parliaments remained dominated by the landed interests, country squirearchy and nobility, until the end of the nineteenth century. Nevertheless, the presence of a significant body of merchants from 1640 onwards ensured that commercial interests received more attention than they had previously been given. As in Portugal in the thirteenth century and thereafter, so in Britain from the middle of the seventeenth century onwards, the alliance of political and commercial interests ensured the ultimate achievement of commercial and economic hegemony. Henceforth in England, commercial considerations would be paramount in the determination of English mercantile and naval policy. The days had gone when kings could set up rival trading organisations to the already existing chartered corporations, as the early Stuarts had done.

The significance of the politico-commercial alliance lies in the changed attitudes of governments towards commerce and industry from the mid-seventeenth century onwards. Christopher Hill has drawn our attention to the essentially mediaeval attitude of the Tudors and the early Stuarts; he observes that they were apt to look upon merchants as a repository of wealth and therefore as a source of funds whenever their own treasuries ran dry.[102] The practice, so beloved by Elizabeth and her two Stuart successors, James I and Charles I, of issuing monopolies for every industrial and commercial activity, reflected this attitude. The new approach was summed up by Thomas Mun in his tract on *"England's Treasure by Foreign Trade"*[103] published in 1664. Foreign trade, he argued, is the source of the nation's wealth. The state, therefore, should do all in its power to restrict imports and encourage exports, unless those imports were for re-export. Exports raised

---

[101] Ashley, Maurice, *Financial and Commercial Policy under the Cromwellian Protectorate*, Frank Cass (1934), Ch.1.

[102] Hill, Christopher, *Reformation to Industrial Revolution*, "Pelican Economic History of Britain", Vol.2. (1969), p.92-98.

[103] Mun, Thomas, *England's Treasure by Foreign Trade*, Blackwell (1967).

national output, thus benefiting the nation as a whole as well as the merchant. The export of specie - Mun was in advance of his times in this respect - was not to be frowned upon; on the contrary, if precious metals were not sent abroad, other countries could not buy our goods. A favourable balance of trade was an essential condition of a prosperous economy.

Mun's protectionist sentiments were out of keeping with the economic liberalism promulgated by Adam Smith a century later, and recently revived by his modern disciples, the monetarists. Nevertheless, in the course of the next century and a half of British history, Mun's doctrine prevailed, governments placing restrictions on the import of manufactured articles, in particular fashionable goods and luxuries, whilst doing all in their power to encourage exports. The import ban was extended to agrarian products if they were deemed to be in competition with domestic supply, hence the prohibition on the import of Irish cattle and Irish corn. The East India Company's trade was acceptable because a large proportion of it was re-exported to the continent of Europe, thus earning the country valuable bullion with which to buy its European imports. Even so, the British government became so alarmed at the volume of calico imports from India in the early eighteenth century that it prohibited them. It was therefore against the background of these restrictions that the cotton industry first became established in Britain. By an irony of fate, that same industry became one of the leading export manufactures at the end of the century, and did much, on account of the very low cost of cotton goods manufacture following the technical innovations in the industry after 1770, to undermine India's textile industry.

Ralph Davis has observed that English economic policy was far from consistent in the hundred years following the Puritan Revolution, that Parliaments did not always listen to the agitation of special interest groups.[104] It is hard, however, when looking at the evidence for the period to escape the general conclusion that protectionist policies were in the main followed, and that it was the steady, if not entirely consistent pursuit of policies designed to foster industry in the home country that enabled Britain to develop her manufacturing potential. From the time of Cromwell to Walpole, governments reduced duties on exports, in some cases abolishing them altogether, similarly duties on imported raw materials were steadily removed. As George I, speaking at the

---

[104]   Davis, Ralph, *English Overseas Trade 1500-1700*, Macmillan, London (1973).

behest of Walpole, put it in 1721, *"it is evident that nothing so much contributes to promote public well-being as the export of manufactured goods and the import of raw materials."*[105]

If modern sentiment is offended at Mun's treatise on protection, then it will most definitely be affronted by his notion that the nation's exports should be carried in ships belonging to the nation's mercantile marine. The very idea of placing restrictions on shipping sounds very foreign to modern ears. The seventeenth century, however, realised the immense importance of the possession of a mercantile marine, because they had the example of Dutch commercial supremacy before their very eyes. As Mun averred, the supremacy of Holland was due to her shipping, her fisheries and her trade. In the seventeenth century, that was the route to wealth, power and prosperity. Navigation Acts were by no means new to the English scene. Indeed, Parliament had first enacted them in the fifteenth century, but to no effect. English trade remained in the hands of the Hanseatic League and the Italians. William Cecil, Elizabeth's minister of state, enacted legislation to restrict the coastal trade of England to ships of English origin. In the person of Oliver Cromwell, however, England found a leader who was willing to put teeth into the Navigation Acts. The effect on England, as even Adam Smith was forced to admit, was stupendous. The shipbuilding industry became one of the great growth industries of the modern era in British history. Between 1560 and 1788, shipping tonnages multiplied by a factor of twenty at a time when population may have tripled or, at most even quadrupled. Even if allowance is made for the substantial number of ships being built in North America at the end of the eighteenth century, English shipbuilding was clearly a growth industry, probably the leading growth industry of the era. Indeed, the true significance of the shipbuilding industry can be gauged from the fact that whereas in 1560 the only ships that England built were those few which were required for the coastal trade, in 1850 half the world's shipbuilding was constructed in British shipyards. In the light of evidence such as this, the significance of the industry to the economic development of the nation takes on another hue. The role of the state in this development was critical. As we have already observed, Elizabeth's chief minister had made it policy to exclude foreign ships from the coastal trade. One hundred years later, the Restoration government, following Cromwell's lead, forbade the use of foreign built

---

[105]   List, Friedrich, *The National System of Political Economy*, Longmans Green & Co., London (1885), p.342

ships in the British fleet. The effect, significantly enough for those who argue that protection only leads to inefficiency and lower quality products, was that competition between England and Holland sharpened, so much so that by 1730 the English shipbuilders had a decisive advantage over their rivals.

The demand for ships, as J.U. Nef, the Dutch historian, observed some fifty years ago, increased the demand for several minerals, chief among them, lead, brass and copper. Since the processing of these metals required coal, shipbuilding, likewise, significantly boosted the growth of that industry too. Nef tells us that production rose from 210,000 tons per annum in the middle of Elizabeth's reign to three million tons at the time of the Glorious Revolution (1689), to fourteen million tons in 1780, and to 240 million tons per annum in the first decade of the twentieth century.[106] Demand for coal in turn had a circular flow effect on the economy inasmuch as ships were required to transport it from the coalfields which were in the north and west of the country to the main centres of industry which were in the south and east.

Shipbuilding also increased the demand for timber, a product the English reserves of which were steadily decreasing. Increasingly, shipbuilding materials such as timber, hemp, pitch and tar were imported from the Baltic States, thus giving an additional fillip to the demand for ships. The state itself, however, had an immediate interest in shipbuilding, inasmuch as it was always keen on the construction of large ships since these could be used by the navy in time of war. The state was also eager to ensure a ready supply of seamen for mercantile and naval operations. *"The expansion of the mercantile marine,"* says Christopher Hill, *"created a reserve of ships and seamen for the navy in time of war and so was supported by governments."*[107] A further side effect of maintaining a navy were the dockyards and arsenals which they required, for they were the largest manufacturing units of their day. Only the state had the resources to provide such facilities. The demands which they placed on the technical and administrative capabilities of the country were immense.

Shipbuilding was not the only industry to receive assistance from the state, however. As Ralph Davis has commented: *"The Navigation*

---

[106]   Nef. J.U., *The Rise of the British Coal Industry*, Vol.1. Frank Cass & Co., London (1966), p.172-4.

[107]   Hill, Christopher, *Reformation to Industrial Revolution*, p.30. "Pelican Economic History of Britain". Vol.2. (1969).

Acts were only the precursor of a great wave of discriminatory regulations and legislation in all economic fields, which were set in motion when the authority of Parliament was established after 1688. This found expression in a whole range of subsidies to individual industries, bounties for exports, prohibitions of imports, protective tariffs and so on, as Parliament warmed to the task of aiding English industry and raw material suppliers, inadvertently giving further privileges to English shipping. "[108] England was indeed a protectionist state, and it was behind the protectionist barrier that the nation built up its skills during the eighteenth century to overtake its erstwhile rival, France, to become the leading industrial nation. Nor did state involvement finish there! When Boulton and Watt placed the condenser on the steam engine, Parliament extended the patent from seventeen to thirty years to permit the owners of the licence a longer period in which to enjoy the fruits of their enterprise. Such practice is difficult to reconcile with the Classical Economists concept of *"laissez-faire"*.

Agriculture, likewise, was protected. Eric Kerridge's thesis that the Agricultural Revolution had already taken place in England before 1673 has acquired wide acceptance among historians. The role of the state in this process was far from negligible. As John Morrill has observed, *"it became a central concern of government to regulate the grain trade and to provide both local machinery and an administrative code, backed up by legal sanctions, to ensure that whenever there was a harvest failure, available stocks of grain and other produce were made widely available at the lowest extra cost which could be achieved."*[109] Parliamentary legislation restricted the import of cattle from Ireland and of corn from abroad. The English farmer was encouraged by means of a system of bounties to produce corn for export. A ban on the import of cloth into England destroyed the Irish cloth trade in the interests of its English counterpart. Henceforth, Ireland was to be treated as a colonial appendage of England, a fact which goes far to explain that country's increasing hostility towards the English.

The view that the Puritan Revolution marks the turning point in the commercial life of England is not as readily accepted among

---

[108]   Davis, R., *The Rise of the English Shipping Industry in the Seventeenth and Eighteenth Centuries*, David & Charles (1962).

[109]   Morrill, James, *The Oxford Illustrated History of Britain*, Oxford University Press (1984), p.289.

historians today as it was in the days of Ranke and Gardiner. Wilson[110], Minchinton[111] *et al* have identified the Restoration as the watershed in English commercial history. Certainly, the volume of commercial legislation which emanated from the early sittings of the Restoration Parliament can be used in defence of this view. Christopher Hill's observation that the Restoration saw the *"vigorous reconstruction of this apparatus of economic control and stimulation"*[112] is very pertinent. For the commercial and colonial policies of the post-Restoration era found their progenitors in the Puritan era. The whole apparatus of governmental policy and legislation in post-Restoration England was foreshadowed in the Navigation Acts, the Anglo-Dutch Wars, the Anglo-Portuguese treaties, the capture of Jamaica and the Spanish War that followed. It was Cromwell who put teeth into England's Navigation Acts, Cromwell who defied the Dutch when they refused to accept reciprocal commercial arrangements, Cromwell who defied Spain's claim to the New World, and Cromwell who negotiated the first of several treaties with Portugal in which the latter agreed to trade with England in return for English protection on the high seas. Cromwell's policy stands in marked contrast to that of James I who had Raleigh executed at the Spanish ambassador's behest. Cromwell's policy towards Holland and Spain fore-shadowed that of William III's against France. As Charles Wilson has reminded us: *"the rise of the British economy was based historically on the conscious and successful application of strength."*[113] Nobody demonstrated the truth of that axiom better than Cromwell himself.

Historians have argued about the role of foreign trade in the performance of the British economy in the pre-industrial era. Some have claimed that, since foreign trade was only a small proportion of total trade, its impact on the development of the economy has been overstated. This is to miss the point. An economy requires engines of growth, and the global commercial empire provided the impetus to expansion. W.E. Minchinton has argued that *"the processes of economic change in Britain have been more intimately moulded by*

---

[110]   Wilson, Charles, Quoted in Christopher Hill, *Reformation to Industrial Revolution*, p.159. "Pelican History of Britain", Vol. 2. (1969).

[111]   Minchinton, W.E., *The Growth of English Overseas Trade*, Methuen (1969), p.11.

[112]   Hill, Christopher, *Reformation to Industrial Revolution*, p.159. "Pelican Economic History of Britain", Vol.2. (1969).

[113]   Wilson, Charles, Quoted in Hill, Christopher, *Reformation to Industrial Revolution*, p.232. "Pelican History of Britain", Vol.2. (1969).

foreign trade than has been the case with any other major industrial economy excepting only perhaps Japan. "[114] Since mediaeval times, England had been a producer of raw materials, of which wool was then by far the most significant item. The manufacturing component of her export trade had never been significant. She was in the position of many Third World countries today, Australia included, a producer of raw materials and an importer of manufactured goods. Christopher Hill sees the process of change which occurred in England between the Tudor era and the reign of George III as taking place in five stages[115]. In the Tudor era, England sold the Old Draperies, broadcloths, as they were called, to the markets of Northern Europe. In the first half of the seventeenth century, she developed new products for a new market, namely the New Draperies for the markets of Southern Europe. In the second half of the seventeenth century, she exploited her colonial monopoly by exporting increasing quantities of goods to her fast growing colonial markets, and by importing goods from the Empire for re-export to Europe. In the eighteenth century, she concentrated on the sale of manufactured goods to the colonies until in the 1770s she achieved her great technological breakthrough, thereafter becoming the supplier of manufactured goods to the world.

The change in the geographical orientation of English trade was one of the most significant features in the economic development of the nation between the Tudor and the Hanoverian periods of English history. For whereas in 1621, only 7% of English imports came from non-European ports, by 1700 one-third of the nation's imports came from sources outside Europe, and one-third of all exports comprised goods imported from Asia and America. In the words of Charles Wilson[116], England had become an entrepôt. It was this dramatic shift in the direction of trade in the seventeenth century that provides the clue to England's subsequent development and confirms the view that it was the empire, albeit as yet relatively insignificant in size and population compared to Spain's, that provided the dynamic for economic growth. The subsequent increase in colonial territory after 1763 and the rapid expansion of trade which followed the end of the War of American Independence twenty years later, provide convincing evidence of the

---

[114] Minchinton, W.E., *The Growth of English Overseas Trade*, Methuen, (1969).
[115] Hill, Christopher, *Reformation to Industrial Revolution*, p.235. Pelican Economic History of Britain. Vol.2. (1969).
[116] Wilson, Charles, *England's Apprenticeship, 1603-1763*, Longman, London (1965).

importance of foreign trade in the economic development of Britain. Something of the significance of commerce may be seen when we compare the rate of growth of population with the rate of growth of foreign trade. The former increased by a factor of between three and four between 1560 and 1780, whereas the latter increased twelve-fold; indeed if we take the closing date for our period of study as 1800, foreign trade has increased thirty-six fold[117]. Of the two factors which Minchinton claims caused this, namely geographical expansion and commodity diversification, the former was by far the more important. For it was only as the colonies were opened up that commodity diversification became possible. It was the global commercial empires of the European nations that powered the European economies during the mercantilist era, and it was state policy that determined the direction of national effort.

It is against this background of the change in trade that the significance of the Navigation Acts can be seen. Efforts had been made in earlier decades, yea centuries, to restrict foreign involvement in English commerce, albeit to no avail. The successful enforcement of the act of 1651, while leading as it did to war, realised, in Hill's words, *"a Baconian vision to which men had long been groping, namely that state control and direction could stimulate material progress."*[118] The significance of the Dutch Republic's rise to economic hegemony of the world in the seventeenth century was not lost on perceptive Englishmen. The inconsistency of English commercial policy in the first half of the century contrasts most unfavourably with the Dutch States-General's systematic support for trade. As J.R. Jones observes, *"the Navigation Acts closed the British Empire to foreign shipping and established a monopoly area of privilege for British merchants."*[119] The British, in other words, were following identical policies to those which Spain, Portugal and Holland had followed in their day, albeit far more successfully. The British Empire, like its other European predecessors and counterparts was to be a trading monopoly. Only British ships were to be allowed to enter colonial ports, and foreign ships could only visit British ports if they were carrying merchandise from their own country. It is only true to assert, as A.H. John *et al* have

---

[117]   Minchinton, W.E., *The Growth of English Overseas Trade*, pp18-32., Methuen (1969).

[118]   Hill, Charles, *Reformation to Industrial Revolution*, p.157. "Pelican Economic History of Britain", Vol.2. (1969).

[119]   Jones, J.R., *Britain and the World 1649-1815*, Fontana Press (1980).

done, that *"The British Empire was the largest free trade area in the world in the eighteenth century"*,[120] if one means by that that trade *within* the empire was unrestricted. In no sense was trade between Britain and her colonies on the one hand and the rest of the world on the other in any way unrestricted until the middle of the nineteenth century. It is therefore more appropriate to regard The British Empire as a large captive market, the largest such market in the world.

While, however, the Navigation Acts closed the empire to foreign competition, they did open it up to internal competition. In Christopher Hill's words, *"the Act represented the victory of a national trading interest over the separate interests and privileges of the Company."*[121] The days of the monopolistic trading companies were, in other words, numbered, particularly the regulated companies. In 1689 the Merchant Adventurers was wound up and the Baltic trade declared open to any English ship that wished to pass into it. A similar policy of de-regulation effected other areas of privilege.

It is not without significance that historians have been so free with their use of the term 'revolution' to describe the changes which took place in England in the seventeenth and eighteenth centuries in the political, religious, commercial, fiscal, financial, agrarian, industrial, technological and scientific fields. Such was the scale of change in the country in those two centuries in almost every walk of life that it would be difficult to describe the nature and scope of the changes that did take place in any other terms. The changes, however, take on a new significance when we recognise the vital role played by the state in all departments of national life. In some cases, e.g. the political and religious settlements, the state engineered the changes that were made. In others, e.g. the commercial and agrarian fields, it acted as a motivator of the process of change. In the technological and industrial fields, it assisted the process by providing the conditions within which change could be achieved.

In the area of national finance, the state contributed in three very important ways to the development of a stable and effective system. The reign of the Dutchman, William III, saw two more pieces of legislation on the statute Book of England both of which were to have significant consequences for the nation. The first was the establishment

---

[120] John, A.H., *The Growth of English Overseas Trade*, Ed. W.E. Minchinton, Methuen (1969), Ch. 6. p.183.

[121] Hill, Christopher, *Reformation to Industrial Revolution*, p.157. "Pelican Economic History of Britain", Vol.2. (1969).

in 1694 of the Bank of England, whose prime function was to supply funds to the government for the conduct of the war. The institution of a central bank enhanced the confidence of the commercial classes in the effectiveness of the country's banking system as a whole. Although bankruptcy was part of life in eighteenth century Britain, the banking system was much stronger and far more able to cope with the needs of the commercial and industrial classes than it was in France where John Law's disastrous experiments with paper money undermined confidence in financial institutions and denied France the benefits of a central bank until Napoleon's time.

The second enactment of William's reign which had significant advantages for England was the Land Tax of the same year, 1694. Enacted during the first of the long series of conflicts between England and France, which historians have subsequently dubbed the second Hundred Years War, the Land Tax provided the means by which Britain's military and naval victories could be won. Once again, the superiority of British commercial institutions was demonstrated, this time by the soundness of the British fiscal system. Unhappily for France, Colbert's reforms did not adequately cover taxation; the power of the French nobility was too great even for Louis XIV to handle, consequently France lacked a uniform fiscal system until the Revolution swept away the privileges of the landowners, the aristocracy and the Church. Britain, thanks to Parliamentary government, had no such system. However much the landed gentry and the aristocracy might dislike paying taxes, they were, unlike their French counterparts, willing to put patriotism before business.

British commercial advantage was further strengthened by the legislation of the early Hanoverian period when Walpole was Prime Minister. In the wake of her first quarter century conflict with France (1689-1713), the British government found itself with an unprecedentedly large National Debt amounting to some £54 million. To bolster public confidence and guarantee the repayment of the loans, Walpole established the Sinking Fund. The consequence of these three measures, namely the setting up of the central bank, the enactment of the Land Tax and the establishment of the Sinking Fund, immensely strengthened Britain's hand against France. France's inability to wage war successfully in the eighteenth century was largely due to her incapacity to finance the effort required effectively. Britain, due to the strength of her commercial institutions, had no such disability.

No survey of the role played by the State in the economic development of England in modern times would be complete that did not take into account the country's policy of religious toleration. Christopher Hill has made out a good case for Cromwell as the author of policies of religious toleration in England.[122] In his defence, it must be said that the people who produced a disproportionate number of the industrial leadership of the country in the eighteenth and nineteenth centuries and who contributed most to the growth of science during the eighteenth century, were first given statutory protection to practice their faith in accordance with the dictates of conscience by Cromwell.

Cromwell's policy, and indeed English policy on religion after the English Revolution of 1689, stands in marked contrast to that of France. France had led the way in 1598 in Europe insofar as religious toleration was concerned with the Edict of Nantes by granting toleration to the Huguenots. The reversal of this policy by Louis XIV in 1685 is one of the greatest blunders that any nation has ever made. Banking, clock-making, the textile industry and scientific research had all benefited immensely from the contribution which the Huguenots had made. France's loss was Europe's gain, England's in particular, as the Spitalfields weavers demonstrated. It was in the field of scientific research, a field which has been traditionally a Protestant enclave in France, however, that the country was to suffer the most. For with the departure of Papin, France lost its leading mechanical engineer, as we would today describe him. Whether Papin would have produced an operational steam engine before Newcomen must remain one of the great unknowns of history. That France never developed a steam engine of her own until long after the British had been producing them in considerable number is due to the country's policy of religious intolerance. The expulsion of the Huguenots from France at the end of the seventeenth century deprived France of its opportunity to compete effectively with Britain in the field of technological development. The sheer ineptitude of the policy may be demonstrated by the fact that in the 1660s both countries, England and France, had seen the significance of science for the future of mankind and in both countries the State had furthered the pursuit of scientific knowledge by establishing an *"ad hoc"* institution, the Royal Society in England and the *"Academie des Sciences"* in France. In the eighteenth century, French science, nevertheless, did manage to establish a lead in the field of chemistry. In

---

[122]   Ibid.

engineering, however, it was the British who had the upper hand. France was to suffer accordingly at the end of the century when English cotton exports undermined French manufactures.

That Britain succeeded in becoming the first industrial nation on earth in the latter part of the eighteenth century was in no small measure due to the policies which English governments from the time of the Puritan revolution onwards followed. But for these policies, the conditions appropriate to the rise of Britain to world hegemony in the nineteenth century would not have been created, and Britain would not have witnessed that transformation of her social and economic life which historians have identified with the Industrial Revolution. English historians, as we have observed, have tended to play down the role of the State in this process. The myth that England's achievement was due in the main to private enterprise assisted by good fortune is one that dies hard. The time has now come to bury it!

5 The Cultural Factor

"Them that bless thee, I will bless; them that curse thee, I will curse."
Genesis 12:3

One of the questions which must inevitably be asked by any student of European History is why it was that Britain prospered so well under Mercantilism, whereas Spain fared so badly. In view of the obvious fact that Spain had acquired an empire long before England, the question is all the more deserving of our attention. Chronologically, Spain had an obvious advantage. In 1580, she not only controlled the whole of the Iberian peninsula - the union of the Crowns of Portugal and Spain becoming a reality that very year - but she also held sway over the whole of the Low Countries of Europe, an area along the Rhine known as Franche Comté and the Italian kingdoms of Naples and Sicily. To these very considerable European possessions, should be added the former territories of the Aztec and Incan Empires in Central and South America, and the string of trading stations which Portugal had acquired in the course of the previous eighty years which stretched from Brazil in the West to Macau in the East. At no previous time in history had any one nation ever controlled an empire of so great a geographical spread.

Potentially Spain was one of the wealthiest countries in Europe. In terms of natural resources, she had a sufficient supply of agricultural land; she was also well endowed with timber, though her woodlands had been significantly reduced in the Middle Ages. Her wine growing districts are renowned to this day. She also possessed a wealth of minerals, iron ore, gold, salt, oil, copper, lead, alum and mercury all being located within her borders. Additionally, control of the New World provided her with a steady supply of bullion with which to defray her expenditures as well as providing her with a market for any products which she might care to supply. With the acquisition of the

Portuguese Empire in 1580, she also gained access to the spices of the East Indies. A world empire lay at her feet. Yet, Spain, as historians are only too willing to acknowledge, lost her opportunity to become the world's leading mercantilist nation, to grasp the opportunities for economic development which her commanding position gave her.

Why was this? Antonio Ortiz has pointed out that the greatest weakness of the Spanish Empire was its lack of any centralised political institutions, other than the monarchy itself.[123] The union of the thrones of Castile and Aragon, for example, did not result in the union of government or administration. Each territory continued to be subject to its own Cortes, and therefore to be administered separately. Navarre even had its own currency, its own laws and its own Council. In consequence, the empire had no imperial institutions; there was no imperial bureaucracy, no imperial budget, and most significantly no economic unity. Indeed each of the five territories which constitute mainland Spain, Castile, Aragon, Navarre, Valencia and Catalonia had its own tariff arrangements. The empire, therefore, was never Spanish; it was only ever Castilian. Nevertheless, as Ortiz points out 6.6 million people out of a total population of 8.35 million lived in Castile. Castile therefore had by far the bulk of the population, and the bulk of the land area of peninsula Spain. Moreover, Castile controlled the New World possessions, and supplied them with food and manufactured goods. While, therefore, lack of a central unifying authority was a disadvantage insofar as it did impede the efficient utilisation of the nation's resources, it was certainly not a determining factor. The question therefore must certainly be asked whether Spain's situation in the sixteenth century was any different from that of Britain in the seventeenth century, England and Scotland being to all intents and purposes separately administered.

Why then did Spain fail to develop a dynamic capitalist economy based on mercantilist principles? Certainly the effort was made, as the string of decrees and regulations which emanated from the throne during the reign of Ferdinand and Isabella shows. J.H. Elliott tells us that no less than 128 ordinances governing Castile's economic life were enacted between 1479 and 1504.[124] In keeping with the economic thinking of the times, prohibitions were placed on the export of silver and gold. New legislation was passed to promote the growth of the

---

[123]   Ortiz, Antonio, *The Golden Age of Spain 1516-1659*, Basic Books, New York (1971).

[124]   Elliott, J.H., *Imperial Spain 1469-1716*, Penguin Books (1970), p.111.

shipbuilding industry, and Ortiz tells us that 100,000 tons were built each year, Spain producing one-eighth of Europe's total. The guild system of manufacture was re-organised and imports were restricted. Every effort was made to encourage the migration of Flemish and Italian artisans to Spain by giving them a ten year tax exemption. The Crown supported sheep farming and the woollen industry because it received substantial revenues from these sources. According to Ortiz,[125] industry did expand in the sixteenth century along with population, the soap, paper, glass and printing industries being organised on a large-scale basis. It was the poor quality of Spanish manufactures, coupled with their high prices, that made them uncompetitive on world markets. The consequence of this was that Spain remained a raw material supplier and an importer of finished goods. In 1550, Elliott tells us that one half of all Spanish exports of gold, wool and wine went to the Netherlands, while one-third of Dutch exports, mainly manufactured goods, went to Spain.[126]

It was this dependence on primary product exports and manufactured goods imports that was the great weakness of the Spanish economy, as indeed it must be of any economy which suffers that imbalance of trade. To finance her current account deficit, Spain relied on her supply of bullion from the New World. The failure of the nation to industrialise its economy, however, has been debated by historians within and without Spain over the centuries. Ortiz asks whether it had anything to do with guild regulations; it is a popular theme with historians, but it is doubtful whether there is any substance in the argument.[127] It has been advanced to explain the backwardness of industry in Italy in the seventeenth, and France in the eighteenth, century. It suffers from the weakness, however, that it ignores the fact that a sufficiently determined central government can always break the back of guild regulations.

The basic problem with the Spanish economy in the sixteenth century, as Ortiz has recognised, is the absence of an artisan class.[128] Spain was, in the sixteenth century what she has remained down to the twentieth century, the land of the rich and the poor. The rich were the

---

[125]   Ortiz, Antonio, *The Golden Age of Spain 1516-1659*, Basic Books, New York (1971).

[126]   Elliott, J.H., *Imperial Spain 1469-1716*, Penguin Books (1970), p.137.

[127]   Ortiz, Antonio, *The Golden Age of Spain 1516-1659*, Basic Books, New York (1971).

[128]   Ibid.

landowners, who relied on their incomes from land and its produce for their livelihood; the poor were the peasants whose means of subsistence was almost entirely provided by themselves. This absence of a middle class, for want of a better term, has impeded Spain's economic development, and is largely due, as Elliott points out, to the 'hidalgo' mentality which deems courage and honour as more important than trade and industry. That Spain should have acquired that outlook is perhaps not so very surprising as Lieberman observes in his *"Study of the Contemporary Spanish Economy"*.[129] For Spain is the result of a process of conquest, firstly by the north of the south, and secondly by the Mother Country of Latin America. The Spanish aristocracy consequently to this day regard wealth as something acquired by conquest, rather than the product of toil. Such attitudes as these go a long way towards explaining why modern Spain, (i.e. Spain since the time of the voyages of discovery) has declined economically, whereas mediaeval Spain was comparatively more affluent. For mediaeval Spain did have an artisan class in the Jews.

The expulsion of the Jews from Spain in 1492 and Portugal in 1497 has been regarded by historians as spelling the economic doom of those two countries. *"The same year, 1492, which saw the expulsion of the Jews, saw the successful voyage of Columbus. The wealth of Spain should have increased many times. It did not; and it did not because of the destruction of the class which was neither too ignorant nor too proud to engage in trade. Those who retained their Jewish religion went first; those who remained as "new Christians" were so fined and harried that their wealth was destroyed and many thousands of them also took the road to exile. In spite of the enormous wealth seized when the greatest and richest mediaeval Jewry was expelled with every refinement of cruelty, it profited the Spanish exchequer nothing, and the long decline of the Spanish economy dates from 1492."*[130]

At first sight, James Parkes' verdict might seem exaggerated. In 1492, Spain's acquisition of her American empire lay in the future, for the work of conquest of the Aztec and Incan empires so successfully executed by Cortes and Pizarro was not accomplished until 1519 and 1531 respectively. Nor was Spanish hegemony in Europe a reality before the accession of Charles V to the thrones of both empires, the Hapsburg and the Spanish, in 1519. The union with Portugal, which

[129] Lieberman, Sima, *The Contemporary Spanish Economy. An Historical Perspective,* Allen & Unwin, London (1982).

[130] Parkes, James, *A History of the Jewish People,* Penguin Books (1964), p.93.

united the two largest commercial maritime empires on earth at that time, was not achieved until 1580.But the writing was on the wall for the empire of Philip II, as subsequent events - the destruction of the Armada in 1588 by Sir Francis Drake (the English sea captain), and the failure of the Spanish Army under their ruthless leader, the Duke of Alva, to suppress their recalcitrant Dutch subjects - demonstrated only too well.

Parkes's verdict, however, does not stand alone. Werner Keller, the historian of the Diaspora, has this to say: *"Two days before 2nd. August 1492, the day of mourning for the destruction of Jerusalem, Spain was empty of all who professed the Jewish religion. Among the exiles were not only scholars and teachers, financiers and merchants, but also a great many of Spain vintners and successful farmers, artisans, armorers and metal workers. A significant portion of the middle class was gone. The economy soon felt the blow; in many once busy places, commercial life slowed to a standstill. Soon there was an acute shortage of doctors throughout Spain. The high degree of commercial and cultural achievement that the country had reached never returned after the expulsion of 1492. The sciences, philosophy and intellectual life in general never again reached the heights that had been attained during the Arab-Jewish period. The Spanish economy would have collapsed entirely had it not been for the baptised Jewish families who remained in the country. When toward the end of the sixteenth century a mass flight from the cruel toils of the Inquisition began among the marranos also, the economy of Spain was doomed. So was that of Portugal, where events followed a parallel course."*[131]

And the historian of Imperial Spain, J.H. Elliott adds his testimony. *"The departure of the Jews left a vacuum in the commercial and industrial sectors of the Spanish economy which only foreigners could fill. The expulsion of the Jews left the way open for the immigration of other foreigners less scrupulous than the Jews."*[132] Spain's mercantile activities, upon which the future of the realm depended, thus came under the control of men with little sense of loyalty to the country into which they had been wooed by its rulers, and even less commitment to its future. Not surprisingly, the Spanish

---

[131] Keller, W., *Diaspora: The Post-Biblical History of the Jews*, Pitman (1971), p.261.
[132] Elliott, J.H., *Imperial Spain 1469-1716*, Penguin Books (1970), p.110.

government found it difficult to enforce mercantile legislation. In consequence, Spain failed to become a leading economic power.

The Iberian peninsula is one area of Europe which enjoyed considerable prosperity throughout the Middle Ages. That it did so was in large measure due to the Jews. For it was they who did much to further the advance of agriculture, industry and commerce in the various kingdoms which governed the peninsula during that period of history. Moreover, as successful merchants, they were able to accumulate the funds needed for the undertaking of the transoceanic voyages of discovery. Additionally, it was the Jews who, in the three centuries before the voyages were undertaken, developed the knowledge of astronomy and the techniques of cartography which were to stand the Portuguese sailors in such good stead when they ventured forth into the unknown in the fifteenth century.

"Virtually all the nautical instruments and maps that Columbus took with him on his voyage had been made by Jews. Many of them were the creation of Jehuda Cresques, at one time head of the Nautical Academy of Palma on Majorca, later in Portuguese service under the name of Jacomo de Majorca, head of the School of Navigation at Sagres. Columbus also derived valuable information from Abraham Zacuto, the astronomer and mathematician."[133]

Spain's loss, however, was Turkey's gain. For it was *"The Great Turkish Empire boundless as the seas that wash its shores,"* that, in the words of Samuel Usque, a Jewish refugee from Portugal, *"opened wide before us."* Nor did it take the Turks long to discover just how valuable *"these hoards of Jewish immigrants were to the life of the country. Industry and trade boomed mightily. Sultan Bajazet II is said to have commented on Ferdinand of Spain; 'You are mistaken to call this king wise, for he has only ruined his own country and enriched ours.'"*

In the words of Keller, *"the international commerce of the young Ottoman Empire expanded significantly. The trade of the Levant ceased to be a monopoly of the Italians and Greeks. Ports on the Adriatic, Aegean, and Black Seas awoke from the sloth of ages and became thriving trade marts. Salonika, in particular, grew into the largest port of transhipment for the entire Mediterranean, and at the same time became a largely Jewish city. A rapidly expanding textile industry, created by the refugees, supplied the Turkish troops with*

---

[133]   Keller, W., *Diaspora: The Post-Biblical History of the Jews*, Pitman (1971), p.310.

uniforms. The mines in the vicinity of the city were worked by Jews. Jewish fishermen provided food for the population ; Jewish stevedores unloaded the ships."

"Never before had vocational opportunities been greater for the Jews, never had their religious liberty been more fully acknowledged than during this period in Turkey. The immigrants entered all fields, for they were freed at last of those occupational restrictions that had hampered them in the Christian countries. The government and population prospered also, for the Jews had brought varied experience and valuable knowledge with them. Some continued in their old professions as doctors and interpreters; but Jewish craftsmen also plied their trades. The metal workers were especially in demand, for they were familiar with the methods and craft secrets of the famous armorers of Saragossa and Toledo. Jewish refugees established printing plants, hitherto unknown in Turkey, and began printing not only Hebrew, but also Latin, Greek, Italian and Spanish texts. Could the fugitives from Spain and Portugal and other Christian countries be blamed if they also instructed the Turks in the latest military developments? They established a modern armaments industry, set about manufacturing gunpowder, and made firearms and heavy artillery.[134]

The influence of the Jews on the economic life of Europe has not been given the attention which it has deserved by historians. In view of the treatment which has been meted out to these people down through history, in view of the appalling prejudices which have beset them, this should not surprise us. Yet if we are to understand the economic development process, as it has taken place in Europe, we must take account of the remarkable contribution which the Jews have made. Time does not permit a detailed analysis of their impact on Carolingian France, on Norman England, Spain under the Caliphate, Mediaeval Poland, Modern Germany or the United States of America. Suffice it to say that wherever communities of Jews have become established and have been permitted to practise their arts and perform their skills, the life of the nation has been enhanced and the economy has flourished.

"Israel passes over Europe like the sun. Where it shines, new life springs up; where it departs, everything that had previously flourished moulders."[135] Without exception, history demonstrates the

---

[134]   Ibid. p.270-1.
[135]   Sombart, Werner, *The Jews and Modern Capitalism*, Transaction Books, London
      & New Brunswick (1982), p.13.

truth of Sombart's axiom. Another writer, McCandlish Phillips, has this to say: *"Jews play a more critical role in history than Gentiles generally do. That is always true in the long run, if not in the short. More than that, Jews are socially and culturally influential. They cannot avoid being influential as a people. In any society in which they are found, Jews are influential out of proportion to their numbers. They affect the history of the nation they are in and they affect its culture. To a significant extent, the history and culture of the nation will turn on what some Jews do."* [136]

Why have the Jews been so influential in the economic life of the countries in which they have been domiciled? Why is it that Jews exercise influence out of all proportion to their numbers? Why is it that a nation that has only 1% of the world's population carries off 13% of all Nobel prizes awarded?

The rationalist and scientist, C.P. Snow, argued that the Jews must have a superior genetic structure to that of the Gentiles. Evidence to confirm that hypothesis has not, however, been forthcoming. An entirely different explanation is offered here, one which takes seriously the principal influence moulding the lives of Jews down through the ages, namely the monotheistic and teleological character of their faith. For it was the Jewish conviction that the invisible was more important than the visible, the eternal more value than the transitory, the spiritual more important than the temporal, the moral more significant than the material that sustained them through the long and bitter years of persecution which they had to face. It was these values which, when they permeated European civilisation either directly or through the aegis of Christianity, moulded its whole outlook and culture.

The great contribution which the Jews made to the world was the Bible, and it was the Bible which gave them the distinctive character of their faith, namely monotheism. The conviction that God is One, that there is one sovereign power in the Universe who is creator and sustainer of all things was unique to Judaism, although it is now shared by Christianity and Islam. In the Judaeo-Christian tradition, God is separate from His creation; He therefore exists apart from nature; creation, however, came into existence through His Sovereign Will. This conception of the origin of material existence gave rise to the notion that, as the Psalmist expressed it, *"the earth is the Lord's and*

---

[136] McCandlish Phillip, *The Bible, the Supernatural and the Jews*, Bethany Press, Chicago (1984), p.279.

the fullness thereof"[137], and that man's function as a steward of Divine resources was to utilise those resources in such a way that his own needs and desires were satisfied, whilst at the same time ensuring that the earth was adequately replenished. The Land of Palestine was to be the Jewish homeland, and it was to be a land *"flowing with milk and honey"*[138]. Significantly, when the Jews have cultivated it, the land has flourished; when they have not been in residence, it has deteriorated. Significantly, when Jews have been allowed to take up agricultural activities in those countries to which they have been exiled, e.g. Mediaeval Spain and Poland, agriculture in those countries has flourished. Jews are quite capable of working with their hands when they are permitted to do so. Why is this?

At the heart of the Jewish faith lies the Torah, the teaching, obedience to which is the essence of Judaism; it covers all aspects of human life, the Jew's relationship to God, to his family, to fellow Jews and to those outside the faith. The Torah enjoins the worship of God and Him alone, respect for parents, monogamous relationships and fidelity within marriage, respect for human life, liberty and property, concern for the poor and those outside the faith, concern for the health and hygiene of the community, the sanctity of labour and the dignity of man. It is outside the scope of this book to detail the impact which all of these ordinances have had on the social and economic life of the Jews and, *ipso facto,* of Europe. Some aspects of the Torah, however, merit special consideration.

At the centre of Jewish life lies the family; the family is the basic unit in the Jewish social system. It is within the context of the family that the child is taught the basic doctrines of the Jewish faith, learns the significance of the various Jewish festivals and acquires that knowledge of what is expected of him as a Jew later in life. The family is thus the basic social and educational unit within which he is nurtured. Without the monogamous relationships which the Judaeo-Christian tradition teaches, there can be no satisfactory family life, as anyone familiar with polygamous societies is aware, and without family life, society collapses. The present breakdown of family life, as an American sociologist has observed, is a prelude to the breakdown of society. No society can survive when the family unit is destroyed.

The emphasis placed on education in Judaism to a very large extent explains why Jews have been so successful wherever they have

---

137   Psalm 24:1.
138   Exodus 3:8.

gone, and why today Jews still tend to occupy the upper echelons of society. Education first received its major impetus under Ezra, the Jewish leader who led the exiles back to Palestine after the Babylonian Captivity. The recognition that the exile was the consequence of disobedience to the Divine Law provided a powerful stimulus both to learn and to obey that Law. According to Roth, the Jewish historian, it was then that education became the order of the day for Jewish siblings.[139] The importance thus attached to passing on the faith from generation to generation explains why Jews were generally much better educated than Gentiles, and 'ipso facto' why they tended to fulfil middle class vocations in Europe. In Roman times, Jews were expected to learn a trade and to pass that knowledge on to their children. Later, in mediaeval and modern Europe, it was the Jews who dominated such professions as medicine and surgery. No explanation of Jewish dominance in economic life and culture can be complete that does not take into account the very real part played by education in the Jewish home.

Respect for life, liberty and property are valuable contributions which the Jews have made to European culture and which have been embodied in numerous constitutional documents in modern times. Respect for life is reflected in the Jewish attitude to justice, which in Jewish Law is to be even-handed. In modern terminology, all are equal before the law; there is to be no distinction on grounds of class, creed or race between contestants at a law suit. The Jewish judge is enjoined to *"give justice to the weak and the fatherless; to maintain the right of the afflicted and the destitute, and to rescue the weak and needy and deliver them from the hand of the wicked"*.[140] The Anglo-Saxon world today takes for granted the existence of an impartial and therefore incorrupt judiciary; the phenomenon, however, is something of a luxury outside countries which have not been imbued with the Judaeo-Christian tradition. Yet, commercial life cannot function effectively without it. The slow advance of so many countries' economies in the world today can be attributed, at least in part, to their corrupt judiciaries.

Respect for the liberty of the person was enjoined on the Jews after their experience of slavery in Egypt. The Deuteronomic code restricted the practice of servitude very considerably and encouraged

---

139   Roth, Cecil, *A Short History of the Jewish People*, East & West Library, London
       (1969), Ch. VI, "The Return from Exile".
140   Psalm 82:3,4.

manumission.[141] The provisions of the law in this respect were not always observed by the Jews, with disastrous consequences for the nation. Solomon's use of forced labour to build the Temple, not only provoked strong hostility among the Israelites but resulted in the division of the kingdom.[142] The southern kingdom's refusal to comply with the commandment resulted in its extermination. Respect for the individual was yet another aspect in which ancient Israel was to be different from the nations which surrounded her.

It is significant that the Bible, under whose influence so much has happened to relieve the shackles of servitude for so much of mankind, was written against the background of the slave-owning empires of the Ancient World, Egypt, Assyria, Persia. Greece and Rome. During that era, as the historians of technology have observed, the world made very little technological progress. Slavery reduces the incentive to develop labour efficient techniques; consequently technical innovations during this period were few. When a society can solve its economic problems by using slave labour, marginal cost is zero and technique becomes insignificant.

It is frequently said today that slavery is the result of a shortage of labour.[143] The implications of this view are that the slave-owning empires adopted slavery as the solution to an economic problem - namely the insufficiency of the labour force in their own societies to do all the work that was required of them. This view requires examination. A far more likely explanation is that nations resorted to slavery as a means of fulfilling their labour requirements because they regarded manual labour as demeaning. This was clearly the case with the Ancient Egyptians who regarded shepherding as beneath them. Hooykaas, in his study of *"Religion and the Rise of Modern Science"* has this to say about the Greeks: *"The great idealistic philosophers especially were of the opinion that the intellectual and spiritual development that was necessary for exercising the duties of the citizen could not take place in conjunction with manual work. The free artisan is barely given a place in Aristotle's ideal state; he does the work of a slave, without having the right attitude of obedience, so that in fact he is inferior to a slave."*[144]

---

[141]   Deuteronomy 16:12-18.
[142]   I Kings 12.
[143]   Hopkins, Anthony, *An Economic History of West Africa*, Longmans (1973).
[144]   Hooykaas, R., *Religion and the Rise of Modern Science*, Scottish Academic Press, Edinburgh (1972), pp 76,78.

It should not surprise us, therefore, that the steady disappearance of slavery from Europe from the third century onwards was followed by a very slow but steady increase in the number of technological innovations. As historians are only too well aware now, the so-called Dark Ages were anything but dark from the point of view of technical invention. The researches of Lynn White *et al* have resulted in a radical revision of our perception of the first millennium of the Christian Era. Progress in Europe, however, was severely inhibited from the ninth to the fourteenth centuries by the growth of serfdom, an institution which was almost as demeaning as slavery in its nature. The disappearance of serfdom in Western Europe after the Black Death facilitated the steady economic progression of that region. The increasing tendency for the landed nobility in Eastern Europe to convert their free peasantry into serfs from the fifteenth century onwards contributed markedly to the economic retardation of those regions.

Throughout the Middle Ages, however, as Hooykaas has observed, Greek ideas exercised a strong influence on the minds of educated people with the result that mediaeval society tended to disparage manual labour, and therefore to set much less store on technical invention than moderns do. It was not until the Reformation completely supplanted Greek thinking with the Biblical view that manual labour was an honourable activity for men to engage in, that men were once again able to give their time and talents to scientific and technological questions. It is no accident, therefore, that modern technology had its origins in those countries that were strongly influenced by the Protestant faith. For the Protestant faith, like Judaism before it, had sanctified work, manual labour in particular.

In England, there was a world of difference between attitudes towards technological innovation in the Tudor and Hanoverian Eras. Tudor England was still very largely influenced by the notion, current in Roman times, that technical invention which displaced workers was bad. Hence the Reverend William Lee, who invented the knitting machine, died a pauper. The Luddite mentality won the day. Two centuries later, an entirely different story can be told. Newcomen, Watts and Arkwright all reaped rich rewards from their inventions in their lifetimes. The cultural environment had changed. Labour saving, efficiency devices had become acceptable. Men were able to take the long-term view, to realise that any short-term disadvantages that might arise as a result of technological innovation would be offset by the longer term benefits to society. Modern society has yet to realise that unemployment arises because governments do not push ahead rapidly enough with technological innovation.

Nor were the Greeks alone in their attitude towards manual labour. Similar views were to be found among Hindus. The whole caste system works on the principle that priestly activity, the martial arts and commercial life are of more significance than manual labour. Those who engage in a craft occupy the lowest rung on the caste ladder in Hindu society. Those whose vocation is manual labour are the untouchables, the most despised elements in Hindu society. Even today, the backward state of Indian society can be attributed to the refusal of high caste Indians to engage either in the nursing profession or in manual occupations. Caste was much more heavily entrenched in Indian culture than in Japanese society with the consequence that Japan was able, much more easily than India, to cast off the shackles of her past in the second half of the nineteenth century than was India. A society that despises manual labour is not a society which will make much technical or economic progress.

The two major movements in modern times to liberate slaves, firstly in the British Empire and later in the United States of America, both owe much to the Judaeo-Christian tradition. In both cases, the Protestant influence was powerful. In England, the crusade in favour of abolition was led by an evangelical, William Wilberforce. In America, Abraham Lincoln, an equally pious and God-fearing man, successfully led the struggle against the secession of the Southern States, thereby outlawing slavery throughout the union, at the same time, giving a greater measure of credence to America's commitment to human rights.

Judaism, and Christianity too, when it remained true to its Biblical heritage, sanctified labour. All work, other than that which was expressly forbidden in the moral law, was considered honourable before God. The injunction to labour is a basic pillar of the Judaeo-Christian tradition and is enshrined in the Commandment: *"Six days shall you labour and do all your work; but the seventh day is a Sabbath to the Lord your God."*[145] A society which dignifies work will therefore consider the invention of labour-saving devices both sensible and fair, sensible because they improve efficiency, and fair because they alleviate the burden of toil and drudgery.

Respect for property was a further tenet of Judaism and one which was well illustrated by the Old Testament story of Naboth's

---

[145]   Exodus 20:8.

vineyard.[146] Property rights have been an important part of the European tradition since the demise of feudalism in mediaeval times. Indeed, the capitalist economy is contingent on the existence of property rights, a fundamental assumption of the system being the private ownership of the factors of production. There is undoubtedly an element of irony in the fact that it is to the Jews that Europe owes this all-important institution, for it was the Jews who suffered more from the arbitrary sequestration of property at the hands of European governments than any other group of people. Property rights are the backbone of the modern world economic system. The existence of property rights is a bulwark against arbitrary government, for it is always property that is endangered by tyrants. Tyranny, indeed, usually begins with attacks on property. It not infrequently proceeds through an attack on the liberty of the subject, usually in the form of arbitrary imprisonment, to loss of life. Modern forms of totalitarianism illustrate, only too well, the fact that, once property rights are undermined, it is not long before liberty and life are endangered.

Another important feature of Jewish thought and belief is the notion that the poor, the disadvantaged and the unfortunate should not be exploited. No Jewish creditor was entitled to dispossess a fellow Jew of his personal property if in so doing, he placed him in a situation of acute need or desperation. The Biblical injunctions relating to usury were framed with that in mind: *"if your brother becomes poor, and cannot maintain himself with you, you shall maintain him; as a stranger and as a sojourner he shall live with you. Take no interest from him, but fear God, that your brother may live beside you."*[147] Aristotle failed to comprehend this, and accordingly placed an outright prohibition on usury, a prohibition which bedevilled the Catholic Church in mediaeval times and bedevils Islamic fundamentalists to this day.[148] It was left to Calvin to rescue the church from the authority of Aristotelianism, and to validate the lending of money with interest.[149]

A similar concern underlay the enactment of the Jubilee Year, which ordained that all land was to be restored to its original owner every fifty years. Land was the basis of wealth in Ancient Judah, as indeed it has been in almost all human societies. The provisions of the

---

[146]   I Kings 21.
[147]   Leviticus 25:35,36.
[148]   Galbraith, John Kenneth, *A History of Economics. The Past as the Present*, Hamish Hamilton (1987), p.12.
[149]   Tawney, R.H., *Religion and the Rise of Capitalism*, Penguin Books (1938).

Mosaic Law ensured that every Jew had a sufficient supply of land to cultivate to meet his family's needs. The inalienability of land was a legal provision designed to ensure that no Israelite would find himself in a position where he could not meet his own and his family's requirements. Any sale of land undertaken to meet urgent financial need was never permanent. The buyer only had ownership of the land until the next Jubilee year. Like so many of the provisions of the Mosaic Law, the enactment relating to social justice was ignored, with the result that Ancient Israel became the land of the rich and the poor, with the rich acting, as they are so wont to do, as oppressors. It was against this kind of oppression that the Prophet Amos inveighed so heavily.

There was, therefore, never any assumption in Jewish thought that the pursuit of self-interest would automatically ensure social optimality. Perfectibilist market systems are a product of eighteenth century rationalism, and rationalism, as Hooykaas observes, is always guilty of oversimplification, as indeed was Adam Smith when he made his case for the market economy. The provision which governments down through the ages have had to make to ensure that the indigent are adequately provided for are symptomatic of the inability of market systems, when left to operate freely of their own accord without any interference from the political authority, to provide adequately for the needs of every member of society. The Judaeo-Christian tradition answers the question: *Am I my brother's keeper?"* affirmatively.[150]

Another very significant aspect of the Torah was the prohibition on the borrowing of money from foreigners. Lending was permitted, but not borrowing. Why was this? Quite simply, money is a form of power, and whenever money is borrowed, other influences are exerted on the borrower. Since Israel was surrounded by nations whose practices were *"an abomination to the Lord"*, these influences, would have been detrimental to her well-being, which was *"to be a light to lighten the Gentiles"*. The Deuteronomic monetary injunctions, however, were to serve the Jews well after the Diaspora, which culminated in the establishment of Jewish communities throughout most of the Roman world. It is this migration of the Jewish people that gives Judaism its international character, and it is the international character of Judaism that has facilitated the development and operation of international commercial activities from early times, long before the name of Rothschild had been heard. Jews were renowned as merchants

---

150   Genesis 4:9.

94

in many countries of Europe, simply because in many instances that was the only profession that they were permitted to follow. Not surprisingly, it is the Jews that we have to thank for the development of many of the techniques of modern capitalism. Bills of exchange, stocks and shares, banknotes and bonds were all personal instruments of commerce before the Jews transposed them into public facilities. The whole securities industry Sombart attributes to Jewish initiative. The Jews, moreover, were influential in breaking down much of the antipathy felt in the mediaeval world to commerce. Competition, and the much vaunted profit motive, owe their origin to Jewish influence. That the Jews were able to do this, was due to their confidence in one another's honesty and fair dealing. The backbone of much modern commercial activity is confidence in the honesty, trustworthiness and fidelity of those with whom one does business. It is not surprising that modern banking, insurance and the stock markets grew up in countries in which the Judaeo-Protestant ethic was the dominant factor. Jewish preoccupation with efficiency, an economic technique which the Protestant dissenters readily adopted, in large measure explains why business has been so highly successful in those countries which have enjoyed a Protestant culture.

Perhaps the greatest contribution which the Jews made to the development of European civilisation was their invention of history. It seems strange to us who live in a society which is so strongly conscious of its history, to talk of history being invented, but invented it was. It is an error to assume, as Herbert Butterfield has demonstrated in his masterly analysis of the origins of history that all people have been conscious of their past, let alone allowed the events of the past to influence their approach to the present and the future.[151] This is a uniquely Jewish phenomenon, but it is one which has had an immense impact on European history and civilisation. For it is the sense of history which gives to European culture its teleological character.

The Bible is a record, *inter alia*, of God's sovereign acts in history, of his deliverance of the Jewish people from slavery in Egypt that they might become a nation dedicated to the worship of Yahweh, obeying his commandments and living in a covenant relationship with Him. The Biblical record, however, tells us that the Jews did not remain faithful to their calling and consequently experienced civil war, the division of the kingdom and finally captivity in Babylon as a

---

[151]   Butterfield, Herbert, *The Origins of History*, Basic Books, New York (1981).

punishment for failure to observe the Torah. Restoration to the Promised Land was accompanied by the conviction that if these evils were not to befall the nation again, the Torah must be observed in its entirety. Always in Jewish history, the consciousness of the past not only influences the present but it also influences the future. The sense that God has redeemed the Jews for a purpose obtrudes throughout Jewish history, and it is this teleological orientation of Judaism and subsequently Christianity, with its belief in the Messiah, the Christ, who came to save not only the Jews, but the rest of mankind from the consequences of their rebellion and alienation from God, which has so strongly influenced the course of European history. Europe could never have expanded beyond its shores to occupy two other continents, had the cultural influence of Judaism and Christianity been opposed to it. Demographic expansion, teleological orientation and technological inventiveness are the principal characteristics of European history and it is these which have moulded European history and civilisation. Europe owes them to the Jews.

The command to *"Be fruitful and multiply"* is yet another Biblical admonition which the Jews have fulfilled whenever the Gentile nations have allowed them to.[152] The Jewish emphasis on good eating habits, on hygiene and health generally, for which the Torah made comprehensive provision, accounts for their capacity to fulfil the Biblical injunction successfully. We who live in the second half of the twentieth century have become obsessed with the problem of the "population explosion", as we are wont to describe it. We view the statistics on demographic increase with alarm, even though the statistical evidence now points to a lowering of the birth rate in every part of the world, and ask ourselves how long it will be before the shades of Malthus descend upon our planet yet again. We all too easily overlook the fact that population growth has been a necessary concomitant of economic growth throughout history, and that without it economic growth could not have taken place. Demographic expansion lies behind the territorial expansion of every nation in history, including the Chinese, the Japanese, the Arabs, the Persians, the Greeks and the Romans. The history of Europe is the history of the consecutive expansion of small nations, and that history can be written in demographic terms. For demographic expansion lies behind the maritime explorations of Portugal in the fifteenth century, the

---

[152]   Genesis 1:26.

commercial expansion of the Dutch Republic in the sixteenth and seventeenth centuries, the imperial conquests of the British in the eighteenth and nineteenth centuries, and the territorial expansion of the United States of America in the nineteenth and twentieth centuries. Similarly, Spain's bid for European hegemony in the sixteenth century, France's counter attempt in the seventeenth and eighteenth centuries and Germany's effort in the nineteenth and twentieth centuries were all accompanied by significant increases in population.

Nor should it surprise us that Europe was not only able to expand demographically and subdue the rest of the world, but that it discovered, through the aegis of modern science, the means to do so. For Modern Science, as R.K. Merton has informed us, is a product of the Puritan era in English history,[153] and few Christians have held the Bible in higher esteem than the Puritans. That Puritanism should have produced modern science should not surprise us. There is undoubtedly much truth in Merton's contention that all the great intellects of a period tend to devote their time and talents to one particular field of endeavour. Elizabethan England, in consequence, produced a galaxy of dramatists, Ben Jonson, Dekker, Marlowe and, greatest of all, Shakespeare. The closure of the theatres by the Puritans in 1642 closed that avenue of opportunity, though not before its best practitioners were dead. The genius of the age thereupon turned its attention to science to fulfil its ambitions, though Merton fails to explain adequately why that should be the case. His suggestion that the attitude of the time was conducive to the development of modern science is undoubtedly true. Men were looking for more effective ways of doing things. They were looking for techniques which would enable them to pump water out of mines, determine longitude at sea, improve the performance of sailing ships and the effectiveness of cannon, and it was to science and the scientists that they turned for the answers. The scientists were not always able to oblige, but they did develop that attitude of rational enquiry into the workings of the universe which was fundamental to the development of modern science. The creation of this atmosphere of openness to a consideration of the possibilities and alternatives available to man was one which the study of Scripture assisted. For the God of the Bible was a God of Order, and the task of science was to understand the principles on which the universe functioned. The Puritans facilitated that task by their ability to reject Aristotelian science which, for almost two

---

[153]   Merton, R.K., *Science, Technology and Society in Seventeenth Century England*, Fertig, New York (1970).

millennia, had held the world in its grip. For the Reformers had already rejected the Thomist synthesis of Christianity and Classicism, and they had no difficulty rejecting the authority of the ancients in the field of science. The Puritans, therefore, were not bound by the findings of the idealistic philosophers of the Ancient World; in consequence, they were free to observe, to investigate, to experiment for themselves, and this they did with impunity. Modern technology, and all that goes with it, is the product of modern science. The early scientists were men of the Bible, men who were anxious to think God's thoughts after Him.

The debt which the western world owes to the spiritual legacy of the Protestant Reformation is well recognised in our culture today. The Puritan work ethic, the Quaker tradition of absolute honesty in business dealings, the Scotsmen's propensity to thrift, hard work and willingness to sacrifice short term goals to achieve longer term objectives, the Dutchman's industry and the Swiss reputation for dealing with the greatest of all temptations, money, have had a profound impact on the development of European culture. The Protestant ethic has done much to transform the values and life-style of the world in which we live.

The German economic historian and sociologist, Max Weber, drew the attention of the academic world to the connection between Protestantism and economic development in his celebrated monograph, "The Protestant Ethic and the Spirit of Capitalism",[154] almost a century ago. The theme was developed by R.H. Tawney in "Religion and the Rise of Capitalism"[155] twenty years later. The Weber-Tawney thesis, as it was subsequently referred to, argued that the more rapid economic development of Northern Europe was attributable to the alleged moral approbation which Protestantism gave to the acquisition of wealth. Weber's instinct with regard to the importance of religious values in the development of European civilisation was sound. His use of religious values to justify the capitalist system has provoked strong dissent, not surprisingly in view of the very plain teaching of the New Testament on the dangers of a life spent in the service of Mammon. A more critical evaluation of the thesis, however, should take account of the fact that Capitalism was not only by no means a new phenomenon in Europe in the sixteenth century - it had flourished in the Italian city states in the later Middle Ages - but that it was very much alive in the Roman Empire before Christ's time, as anyone familiar with the parables of the

---

[154]   Weber, Max, *The Protestant Ethic and the Spirit of Capitalism*, Unwin Uni Books, London (1930).

[155]   Tawney, R.H., *Religion and the Rise of Capitalism*, Penguin Books (1938).

Nazarene will realise. The empirical, to say nothing of the moral, objections to the Weber-Tawney thesis, are not insignificant.

The principal of short-coming of Weber's thesis, however, is that it treats the Biblical ethic much too narrowly. Commercialism, in the sense of profit-making, never was unique to Europe; the ancient civilisations of the Orient provide numerous examples of commercial life in varying degrees of sophistication. Industrialism was originally unique to Europe, specifically to Britain, though it was since been copied by the rest of the world. Industrialism, however, cannot be explained simply in terms of commercialism, the latter involves trade principally, the former manufacture. The growth of industrialism in Europe, can only be adequately explained in terms of the rise of technology, and this, as we have seen, is conditioned by cultural considerations. To understand the impact which the Biblical ethic has had on European culture and history, it is necessary to examine it in its totality. It is not only the injunction to labour that is important as Weber implies, but the whole ethical system which the Jews gave to the world, a system which encompassed the family, procreation, education, justice, human rights, property rights and protection of the poor and disadvantaged members of society. Europe's teleological orientation, demographic expansionism, technological innovativeness, cultural creativeness and former economic superiority may be attributed to the religious values on which her civilisation was based. Other societies have been influenced by certain aspects of this ethic, and the extent to which that ethic has influenced them determines the magnitude of the economic progress which they have made. Europe alone has imbibed something of the totality of the ethic and to her accordingly has gone the accolade for economic achievement.

6 China and Europe

"I assure you that this river runs for such a distance and through so many regions and there are so many cities on its banks that, truth to tell, in the amount of shipping it carries and the total volume and value of its traffic, it exceeds all the rivers of the Christians put together and their seas into the bargain. I give you my word that I have seen fully 5,000 ships at once, all afloat on this river. Then you may reflect, since this city which is not so very big, has so many ships, how many there must be in the others. For I assure you that the river flows through sixteen provinces, and there are on its banks more than 200 cities, all having more ships than this."[156]

One of the first Europeans to reach China was Marco Polo, and he arrived just as the first Mongol Emperor, Khublai Khan, was establishing the authority of the short lived Mongol dynasty over the length and breadth of China. The stories which he brought back to Europe on his return in 1295 about China's wealth and power seemed to his contemporaries so incredible that, on his deathbed twenty years later, they urged him to recant. The intrepid Italian explorer refused. He had told the truth, which, quite simply, was that China completely outstripped Europe in the thirteenth century in administrative, cultural, scientific and technical performance. The splendour of the capital city of Peking, the luxury of the court, the effectiveness of the administrative system, the wealth and diversity of the craftsmen, and the generally high level of opulence which Chinese of all classes appeared to enjoy made a tremendous impression on him. What also impressed him strongly was the extent of China's technical achievement, for not only did the Chinese boast some remarkable architectural accomplishments

---

[156]   Elvin, Mark, *The Pattern of the Chinese Past*, Stanford University Press (1973), p.145.

which rivalled, if they did not surpass, the great cathedrals of Europe in magnificence, but they also had discovered gunpowder, invented paper, and produced the world's first printing press. China was, without doubt, what she claimed to be - the most magnificent civilisation on earth, and nobody was more conscious of this fact than the Chinese themselves. Tales of men, such as Marco Polo, continued to inflame the imaginations of European explorers for the next two hundred and fifty years, until the Portuguese had rounded the horn of Africa, voyaged to the Far East and discovered the truth of Marco Polo's observations for themselves.

Historical research has more than justified Marco Polo's eloquent testimony to Chinese achievements. Archaeological and literary evidence abundantly supports the claims which the Venetian merchant adventurer made about the size and splendour of China's greatest cities. Palaces and temples which have survived the intervening years witness to the ingenuity and skill of a people who for many centuries led the world technically and commercially. Libraries of printed literature testify to the high level of culture which these people enjoyed. A communications network of roads and canals on a scale unsurpassed in any other Continent of the world until modern times, provide abundant evidence that China was all that Marco Polo said she was, the leading commercial and technological empire on the face of the earth in the thirteenth century. If further testimony was required, historians would have no difficulty supplying it, for China had possessed for close on two millennia the greatest military fortification in the world in the form of the Great Wall. Built at a cost in human labour which the Chinese peasant to this day only speaks of in funereal tones, the Great Wall stretches some six thousand miles in length from the Pacific Ocean to the gorges of the Yangtze river deep in the mountains of central Asia - a phenomenal testimony to the determination of China's rulers that, on no account, was her territory to be invaded by tribesmen from beyond the pale of civilisation. China, however, did not rely solely on fortifications for her defence. In the eleventh century, China could boast an army of one and a quarter million men, a crossbow department which produced 16.5 million arrowheads per annum and an Imperial Armaments office capable of producing 3.25 million weapons per annum.[157]

---

[157]   Ibid. p.84.

Perhaps the final proof of the nation's remarkable capacity to impress the outside world of her magnificent achievements came in the fifteenth century when the Ming dynasty decided to equip a fleet to voyage to India, Persia, Arabia and East Africa. At the time when the Ming Emperor made his decision to build the flotilla of 130 ships in 1403, Timur the Great was still alive, destroying all in his path in much the same way as his predecessors, the Mongols, had done two centuries earlier. The Ming rulers decided that the world needed to know that mighty China was still as great as she had always been and that Timur could still be defied. The expedition which sailed from China in 1405 was the first of seven which, in the course of the next twenty-eight years, were to travel to the Indian Ocean regions. *"These spectacular voyages proved that China was a superior world seapower whose shipbuilding techniques and navigational abilities were unmatched by any other nation."*[158] Bruce Swanson's words are a fitting tribute to China's first attempt to sail the oceans of the world. The task of building, equipping, manning and sailing a force of such size was a remarkable testimony to the ingenuity, discipline, technical capability and managerial capacity of the Chinese people. Europe was not to see anything comparable to the Chinese Armada until 1588.

The value of the study of comparative economic history lies in the facility with which historians can analyse the impact of the variable factors of production as they are called - such elements as natural resources, population growth, the character and resourcefulness of the people themselves, their capacity both for capital accumulation and for technical innovation and, most important of all, the quality of their political leadership - on the performance of their respective continents, empires or states.

Insofar as natural resources are concerned, China was no more advantaged than Europe. Both continents possessed and exploited their not inconsiderable reserves of timber - for the construction of houses and boats, of silver, - to facilitate the development of a monetary economy, and of salt as a food preservative. Neither was lacking in coal or iron ore, China's use of them being greater than Europe's on account of her more advanced technique. China's lack of stone, moreover, did not prevent her from constructing some of the most remarkable edifices that mankind has ever seen. Europe's possession of a longer coastline than China's cannot, however, be regarded as in any way more

---

[158] Swanson, Brian, *A History of China's Quest for Seapower*, Naval Institute Press, Annanpolis (1982), p.28.

advantageous, as R.M. Hartwell argues, for it was China and not Europe that first undertook transoceanic voyages of discovery. It would be difficult to argue too that China benefited in any way from her terrain, only 7% of which is cultivable, or from her riverine system. Europe probably had minor advantage in both respects. Nor was the development of fisheries a differential factor in either continent. Climatically, China may have suffered a slight disadvantage, the Chinese landmass suffering from greater extremes of heat in summer and cold in winter.

Both Europe and China experienced secular increases in population between the seventh and the thirteenth centuries, and both suffered from the ravages of plague in the fourteenth century as the Black Death, which originated in China, swept across Asia to Europe. In both continents population growth was accompanied by economic growth. As in China, so in Europe, cities began to flourish in river valleys increasingly from the tenth century onwards, while the manorial system of agriculture dominated the countryside. In both continents, mercantile communities expanded in number and size, precious metals replaced barter as the means of exchange and banking became institutionalised. In neither continent, however, were the standards of health and hygiene sufficiently developed to avert the spread of plague. In neither continent, however, was the decrease in population in the fourteenth century an impediment to transoceanic voyages of discovery in the fifteenth century.

Economists have long realised that the character of the people themselves, their capacity for work, their willingness to discipline themselves, their resourcefulness are important factors in the economic development process. There is, however, no reason for supposing that the Chinese were more virtuous or more willing to work harder than their European counterparts. In both societies religious and philosophical precepts enjoined the virtues of labour. Judged by their fruits, it would be hard to argue that Chinese were any more or less diligent than Europeans.

In terms of technical resourcefulness, however, the Chinese did manifest some advances over Europe. *"Cast iron was invented in China eighteen centuries before it became known and used in Europe,"*[159] according to Raymond Dawson. Iron was used in the construction of bridges one thousand years before Europe adopted such

---

[159]   Dawson, Raymond, *The Chinese Experience*, Chas. Scribner's Sons, New York (1978), pp.181,2.

techniques. It was also used extensively in the production of swords, bows, arrows, spades, hoes, ploughshares and also ships, where the demand for iron nails, anchors and armour was high. In the use of paper China was well ahead of Europe. Wood-block printing was another area in which the Chinese had an advantage over Europe, China having invented the device in the ninth century. Printing greatly stimulated the spread of ideas in all fields, agriculture in particular. Shipbuilding in China was also more advanced than in Europe, as Dawson shows. Three devices which appeared on ships in China long before they did in Europe were the water-tight compartment, the stern-post rudder and paddle-wheels. Kaofeng, the capital of the Sung dynasty, became in the twelfth and thirteenth centuries one of the most advanced industrial areas in the whole world, with iron and steel complexes unsurpassed until the nineteenth century in Europe.

China's technical advantages, however, were demonstrated to greatest effect in the field of capital works. The Great Wall far surpassed anything that Europe ever produced in that field either under the Romans or later. So did China's cities, whose splendour and magnificence so captured the imagination of Marco Polo. Her temples and palaces matched the cathedrals and castles of mediaeval Europe. It was in the field of communication that China really scored over Europe. For the canal system which she developed one millennium before Europe was the means by which she acquired that commercial and industrial advantage which set her ahead of Europe in the Middle Ages. It was the canal system which enabled her to site her capital in the northern part of the country whilst at the same time continuing to enjoy the very considerable benefits of trade with the south. It was her canal system that enabled her to create an inter-regional, indeed a national market long before a commercial empire of similar size could be developed by the European Powers. Europe had nothing comparable. In consequence, commerce in Europe was never as well developed as it was in China.

Europe's principal disadvantage, however, was not the lack of a canal system, important as that was to become in the histories of the various nation states in the eighteenth and nineteenth centuries. Europe's greatest weakness was her lack of political unity. Europe's riverine system could well have substituted for China's canal system, had the continent enjoyed the benefits of political unification. Europe throughout the Middle Ages, and indeed until comparatively modern times, had to live, not only with acute political division but with its consequence, namely economic dislocation caused by the presence of customs barriers, tolls and tariffs which every city state and every feudal state reserved the right to levy. Eli Hecksher, the historian of mercantilism, tells us that the Rhine had no less than 77 toll points on its banks in the fifteenth century, whilst the Loire had 128.[160] It was this lack of economic unification which restricted the economic growth and development of Europe during the Middle Ages.

China's more spectacular achievements are attributable to the more advanced state of her political organisation. China had acquired economic pre-eminence in the thirteenth century because she had enjoyed a greater degree of effective political leadership. That is why the work of the great unifiers in Chinese history, the first Emperor, Cheng and his prime minister, Li Shih Ti, and the first emperor of the Sui dynasty, Yang Cheng, and his ministers, is so important. It was these men who provided the framework within which the economic development of the country could take place. Without their preparatory work, the construction of such defence facilities as the Great Wall or the 130 forts which the first Ming emperor built along the coast during the fourteenth century to safeguard China from piratical attack, could never have been undertaken. Likewise, the remarkable commercial development which followed the construction of the canal network by the Sui dynasty would never have taken place. Technological innovation does not take place in a vacuum; it occurs in response to perceived need. Its success, however, depends on the cultural and political environment of the time. China's era of technical development occurred between the seventh and the fifteenth centuries, a time when both the cultural and the political environment was right.

Also instructive is the fact that it was during the Sung dynasty that China made the greatest progress, for of all the dynasties which have ruled China during her two millennia the Sung was probably the most commercially minded. The location of the capital Kaofeng, which had previously been a commercial city, indicated a willingness on the part of China's rulers to give greater recognition to the role which commerce and the mercantile class played in the development of the empire. There is considerable debate among scholars about the significance for China's economic development of society's alleged attitudes towards merchants. The closer relationship, however, which developed between the political and commercial leadership of the

---

160   Hecksher, Eli, *Mercantilism*. Garland, New York & London (1983), Vol.1. p.80.

country in Sung times prefigures the politico-commercial alliance which lies at the heart of the successful expansion of the European city and nation states from the twelfth century onwards.

Sinologists traditionally have given much attention to the attitudes adopted by Chinese toward commerce and in particular to those who made their living from it. It has frequently been observed that merchants stood fourth in the hierarchy of social esteem in China, ranking behind the mandarins, the scholarly group of officials who governed the country, whom the Chinese held in the highest regard, and behind farmers and artisans, who occupied the second and third positions respectively. Only entertainers ranked lower in Chinese society. Certainly, Confucianism did not rate the pursuit of profit highly, and the Legalist tradition did not consider that merchants made any worthy contribution to the state. It should not be forgotten, however, that merchants were not well thought of in many other societies which, notwithstanding, enjoyed a measure of economic growth. India, for example, ranked merchants behind priests and warriors. R.W. Southern has argued that mediaeval European society adopted a similar ranking system, placing monks and priests in first place and soldiers in second. China, India and Europe have nevertheless recorded significant economic progress during the Christian era, such attitudes towards commerce notwithstanding.

Width is as crucial a part of historical understanding as depth," argues Mark Elvins in his study entitled *"The Pattern of China's Past". "Many patterns only show themselves at a distance."*[161]

The comparative study of the economic development of Europe and China is one of the more illuminating undertakings on which historians can embark. The similarities and dissimilarities between the political and economic progress of the two Continents, if such a term can be used to describe China, are most instructive. For it is only as we place Europe and China alongside one another and strive to understand the impact of the variable factors upon their respective development that we can truly appreciate the significance of the role of the state, of the political leadership, in the whole process.

The early history of both China and Europe had significant political similarities, for in both continents the city state was the mode of political, social and economic organisation in the first millennium BC and in both continents in the third century BC, one city state, Rome in

---

[161]   Elvin, Mark, *The Pattern of the Chinese Past*, Standford University Press (1973), p.139.

the West, and the Ch'in state in the East, began the process of military conquest of its neighbouring lands which was to culminate in the establishment of the two empires. The process of empire building was much more rapid in China, whose first ruler, the Tiger of Ch'in, as he has been described, accomplished the task in his own lifetime, than it was in Europe, where it took three centuries or more before the Roman empire reached its full size. In both states, new political machinery came into existence to administer the various lands under imperial control. Economic life was given an impetus as a result of the state's political and military policies and a level of culture was achieved which went unsurpassed in China for half a millennium until the advent of the Tang dynasty in the seventh century and in Europe for one millennium until the Renaissance of classical art and learning in the thirteenth, fourteenth and fifteenth centuries. Comparing the Roman Empire with China under the Han dynasty, Latourette has this to say: *"It was not as populous, and it may not have been as wealthy as the Roman domain, but it had a high and creative civilisation."[162]*

Neither empire, however, solved the long-term problem of political unification effectively. Rome early succumbed to military dictatorship. The empire's principal problem was its cultural bifurcation, and the late fourth century division of the empire into two political segments with one emperor at Rome and another at Constantinople, reflected the essentially Roman character of the western half of the empire, and the essentially Greek character of the eastern half. Whilst the destruction of Rome is usually attributed to the barbarians who invaded the empire at the beginning of the fifth century AD, there is much to be said for the view that Rome was destroyed in the same manner as her Chinese counterpart, namely from within.

The political development of Europe and China thereafter diverged. In the west, the empire, Charlesmagne's efforts notwithstanding, remained nothing but a phantom, preserved only in the empty title *"The Holy Roman Empire"* until its abolition by Napoleon in 1806. The basis of political and economic power in mediaeval Europe was the city state, the feudal barony and the feudal monarchy. With the arrival of the modern era in the latter part of the fifteenth century, the feudal monarchies of Western Europe evolved into nation states.

---

[162]   Latourette, K.S., *A History of Modern China*, Penguin books (1954), p.33.

In China, however, the imperial institution which had been virtually destroyed when the Han Empire collapsed in 220 AD, was revived by the founder of the Sui dynasty, Yang Chi'en in 581 AD China thereafter was governed by an emperor. Continuity was broken on several occasions during the next 1500 years as dynasties came and went. The area under central government control varied with the dynasty in power and the character of the ruler. China was most successfully administered when the Emperor, or, as occasionally happened, the Empress, was a strong, powerful and effective ruler, capable of crushing provincial warlordism and establishing the authority of the central government. An ineffective ruler weakened the state and permitted the rise of a powerful gentry class unwilling to pay taxes; political disintegration was usually accompanied by the rise of provincial warlordism. Each new dynasty that came to power provided a succession of capable, energetic, powerful men who made the authority of the central government effective throughout the entire country. As the dynasty came under the pressure of an effete court life, of luxurious and often scandalous living, it weakened until the central government was no longer able to control the country or to withstand attack from without.

The explanation for China's remarkable achievements between the seventh and the thirteenth centuries is to be found in the significant accomplishments of the short-lived Sui dynasty. To attribute to the Sui so much of what happened later, may seem unrealistic at first sight, yet it was during that epoch in China's history that the foundations of the empire's later greatness was laid. In describing Sui as *"a brief, but crucial era"* in Chinese history, the historian of the dynasty, Arthur Wright, puts his finger on the nub of the matter[163]. The re-organisation of government which Yang Chi'en and his successor undertook was essential if the re-unification of north and south was to enjoy any political permanency. The abolition of gentry power in the provinces, in particular at local governmental level, and its replacement by a two tier system based on Han precedents, was a decisive step in the right direction in a country which was apt to succumb to centrifugal forces whenever the central authority showed a tendency to weaken. As Wright has put it, *"the system of recruitment, examination, appointment and surveillance was a bold and thoroughly ruthless*

---

[163]   Wright, A., *The Sui Dynasty*, Knopf, New York (1978).

108

effort to neutralize entrenched privilege and to discipline local officials only to be responsible to local government. "[164]

Sui's political achievements had their counterpart in the dynasty's economic achievements, the most important of which was canal construction. As Raymond Dawson tells us, *"canal construction had started in the pre-imperial period, and much work had been done during the Ch'in and Han Dynasties; but all earlier achievements were dwarfed by the great Sui and T'ang canal network which linked the capital at Changan with both the Peking area in the north and the Yang'tze valley and Hangchow in the south."*[165] The impact of canalisation on the subsequent economic development of China is hard to over-estimate. As Brian McKnight tells us: *"In the eighth and ninth centuries, the Chinese economy began to develop with unprecedented rapidity. From a society within which barter had dominated rural exchange, China was transformed by the middle of the Sung into a society within which money circulated in all regions and among all levels of people."*[166] John Haeger reinforces the point when he says that *"the beginning of 'modern' Chinese history can be traced back to the so-called T'ang-Sung transition in the eighth, ninth and tenth centuries. A necessary condition of this effervescence of commercial and economic activity was that China witnessed a major demographic revolution in the eighth century as Chinese migrated from the North China Plain to the Yangtze valley."*[167] Yoshinobu Shiba, the Japanese historian, tells us that whereas only 23% of China's total population was located in the south at the beginning of the seventh century; by the middle of the eighth century, that figure had increased to 43%.[168] Migration, moreover, was accompanied by a steady increase in urbanisation, as trade increased and a monetary economy based on silver as its mode of exchange came into existence.

The great cities of the south were, moreover, *"primarily commercial cities, not predominantly administrative centres,"* as Dennis Twitchett tells us.[169] Such a development was new in Chinese history, cities having been principally political creations rather than

---

[164] Ibid.
[165] Dawson, Raymond, *The Chinese Experience*, Chas. Scribner's Sons, New York (1978), p.191.
[166] McKnight, Brian, Quoted in Haeger, J.W., *Crisis and Prosperity in Sung China*, University of Arizona Press (1975), p.96.
[167] Ibid. p.4.
[168] Shiba, Yoshinubu, Ibid. p.16.
[169] Twitchett, D., *Cambridge History of China*, Vol. 3., (1978-80), C.U.P.

economic ones. Urbanisation led to a steady increase in the number of towns. As markets increased in size, so too did the number of trade guilds which artisans and merchants established. Governments were slow to appreciate the significance of the commercial revolution of the eighth century and taxation in consequence remained much heavier on the rural population than on the urban. Change was effected, however, as governments came to realise that merchants, far from being the execrable class of parasites which Confucius and the Legalists had portrayed them, could indeed be regarded as sources of state income.

The demographic revolution, which itself was the result of a political revolution - the coming of the Sui dynasty - and a series of technical innovations - the construction of the canal network - was accompanied by a revolution in agriculture. For, between the eighth and the twelfth centuries, agriculture was transformed by the introduction of improved milling machinery, which led to the replacement of millet by wheat in the north, and by the steady increase in wet-field rice cultivation in the south, the main area of progress. Mark Elvin[170] identifies four major areas of improvement, the first of which were the methods used by farmers to prepare the soil through the extraction of weeds and the planting of crops. The second improvement came with the use of new seeds and multiple cropping, an innovation which increased production of food significantly and permitted a doubling of population in the period. Improved hydraulic and irrigation techniques constituted the third avenue of improvement, while the increased commercial activity which agricultural improvements engendered, itself led to greater specialisation of industry - the fourth area of improvement. The principal technical innovations which made this revolution possible were the dam, the sluice-gate, the peripheral pot-wheel and the treadless water-pump. The extensive use of cast iron, an invention which, according to Dawson was made eighteen centuries earlier in China than in Europe, facilitated the large-scale production of such agricultural implements as spades, hoes and ploughshares.[171] As in Europe, so in China, from the ninth century onwards, the manor which, as Elvins says, alone had the resources for change, was the basis of the country's agricultural revolution. While, however, serfdom did exist in China for several centuries, *"increased contact with markets*

---

[170]   Elvin, Mark, *The Pattern of the Chinese*, Stanford University Press (1973), p.113.

[171]   Dawson, Raymond, *The Chinese Experience*, Chas. Scribner's Sons, New York (1978).

made the Chinese peasantry into a class of adaptable, rational, profit-orientated petty entrepreneurs. "[172]

Most new Chinese dynasties established a new capital city for themselves. Yang Ch'ien, the founder of the Sui dynasty, founded Chang'an, a city which, under his T'ang successors, became the largest in China and one of the most resplendent on earth at that time. The Sung dynasty (960-1279) established its capital in the south at Kao-feng, hitherto a commercial centre, thus, as we've seen, recognising the supreme importance of commerce in the life of the nation. Nevertheless, the Sung dynasty was less stable politically than its predecessors, a feature which has led one of its historians to assert that *"the supreme irony of Sung history"* is *"that a period of towering achievement in material culture and intellectual subtlety should also have been shaken by a crippling succession of political and military crises."*[173] John Haeger continues his support for his claims by arguing that it was only in Sung times that China finally developed a national market and consequently a national use of labour. Wealth, under the Sung, became the sole basis of prestige in the countryside, and the means by which merchants could buy their sons' education and hence their entry into the much coveted scholar classes.

The major development of the Sung dynasty, however, was the shipping industry. Shipping did not originate with the Sung, indeed it had become increasingly important under the T'ang dynasty. Under the Sung, however, it was to become big business as, not only domestic trade, but international trade flourished. Maritime commerce between China and India, Persia and Arabia had been a reality since the third century A.D. Until the era of the Sung, however, it had generally been undertaken by foreigners. The closure of the silk route to the west under the Northern Sung gave an impetus to the development of China's maritime trade. Shipbuilding, as in Europe at a later date, provided a stimulus to the economy, in particular to the demand for timber on the one hand, and for hemp, pitch, tar, as well as nails and other iron implements on the other. The use of the stern-post rudder, the compass and the water-tight compartment made the Chinese junk of the Sung era a very much safer ship than most contemporary bottoms. Also the integration of national and international commerce made the Sung era

---

[172]   Elvin, Mark, *The Pattern of the Chinese Past*, Stanford University Press (1973), p.167.

[173]   Haegar, J.W., *Crisis and Prosperity in Sung, China*, University of Arisona Press (1975), p.6.

one of the most prosperous in the history of China. Under the Sung, *"the Yangtze valley really became an integral market"*.[174] The commercialisation of the region with its wealth of waterways owed much to the expansion of the shipping industry, and the specialisation of agriculture and industry which both precipitated it and followed it. The development of markets in China, as in Europe at a later date, was the direct outcome of improvements in transport technology. *"Southern Sung was, in every sense of that term, a financial state"*, to use John Haeger's expression.[175]

While there is much to be learned from China's successes in the millennium or so that preceded the transoceanic voyages of discovery, there is as much to learn from her failure in the fifteenth century to grasp the opportunity to establish a commercial maritime empire similar to that which the Europeans developed between the fifteenth and the nineteenth centuries. For the failure of the Chinese after the death of the eunuch admiral, Cheng-Ho, in 1435 to seize the opportunity which his voyages had opened up and establish firmly and authoritatively China's control of world trade, was one of the greatest examples of lost opportunities in history. It was that decision on the part of the Ming governments that opened the way for the European nations one hundred years later to establish their maritime hegemony and, through the aegis of the mercantilist system, their monopolistic control of world commerce and industry which culminated in Great Britain's remarkable domination of the world in the nineteenth century.

Historians have gone to some length to explain why the Chinese behaved as they did. Mark Elvin has observed that the only justification which the Chinese government considered they had for a navy was for coastal defence purposes.[176] With the completion of the Grand Canal to Peking in 1411 and the consequent disappearance of sea transport between North and South China, any justification in the eyes of the government for a navy disappeared. The navy, thereafter, came to be looked upon as an expensive luxury which the state could well do without. Its only other function, that of demonstrating to the world that

---

[174]   Shiba, Y., Quoted in *Crisis and Prosperity in Sung* China, University of Arisona Press (1975).

[175]   Haegar, J.W., Quoted in *Crisis and Prosperity in Sung* China, University of Arisona Press (1975), p.11.

[176]   Elvin, Mark, *The Pattern of the Chinese Past*, Stanford University Press (1973), p.220.

China was still, despite the ravages of the Mongol invasions, an important political power, could be achieved in less expensive ways.

It was not only the navy that suffered, however, but foreign trade as well, and with the demise in foreign trade, China suffered a severe economic recession. Already, in the fourteenth century, Chinese governments had turned to paper money as a means of overcoming the problems caused by an insufficient supply of currency. All might have been well had they respected the rules regarding the printing of paper money, but they did not, with disastrous consequences! Money was printed until it became worthless. China's experience was a tragic precursor of Germany's in 1923. The Chinese people lost confidence in the capacity of their governments to manage their currency effectively. The cessation of foreign trade in the following century only exacerbated the currency problem and precipitated a severe depression. *"It is apparent,"* concludes Elvin, *"that government policy caused China's overseas and coastal trade to go into a profound depression beginning in the fourteenth century and ending in the sixteenth century"*, when the Europeans opened up China's trade with the outside world once again.[177] Thereafter, trade between China and Europe became strictly a one way affair, with China as the principal beneficiary. In exchange for the silver which Europe acquired from South America, China supplied the manufactured goods, porcelain, textiles and silks. It was an arrangement which was to cause the European nations, with their nervous preoccupation with the balance of payments, a considerable degree of anxiety. Not unjustifiably, the Chinese thought of themselves as superior to the rest of the world as the remark of Ch'ien Lung, the great eighteenth century Chinese emperor, to Lord Macartney in 1795 illustrates: *"Our celestial empire possesses all things in abundance."*[178]

Other historians have drawn attention to the Chinese government's decision to re-locate the capital at Peking near the troublesome northern frontier. They argue that it was China's obsession with security on that front that forced the court to give up any ideas it may have entertained of grandiose maritime ventures. Whilst it is true that the grim memories of the Mongol invasions were still relatively fresh in the minds of the Chinese - two hundred years is a comparatively short time in their history - China had had to live with the

---

[177]   Ibid. p.224.
[178]   Fairbank, J.K., Reischauer, E.O., Craig, A.M., Quoted in *East Asia - Tradition and Transformation*, Allen & Unwin, New York (1973).

problem of the northern frontier for well over a millennium and had done so reasonably successfully. The fears of the Ming dynasty, however, were not groundless. The next dynasty, the Manchus, entered the country from the north; the ease with which they did so, however, was facilitated by the treachery of a Chinese.

Events, however, were to show that China had far more to fear from the ocean than she did from the steppe. Japanese pirates and Portuguese men-of-war were to make that point painfully clear in the sixteenth century. With the benefit of hindsight it is easy to condemn the Chinese for their short-sighted behaviour. It is, perhaps, pertinent to observe, however, that if Europeans could make the journey to China overland, as many were increasingly doing after Marco Polo's adventure in the thirteenth century, then the Chinese should have realised that the day might well come when they could make the journey by sea.

Dun J. Li in his study entitled *"The Ageless Chinese"* invokes what has become a familiar argument when he says that China's problem was essentially one of cultural superiority.[179] The Chinese people, Li maintains, were averse to commercialism, merchants being given little esteem by society at large, a view which he reinforces by citing the case of China's seafaring merchants, most of whom came from the lower orders of society and tended to be poorly educated. Commerce, maintains Li, had a poor reputation in Chinese society. Migration, moreover, was complete taboo, being seen as an act of disloyalty to one's ancestors. Cheng-Ho's voyages were seen as useful only insofar as they impressed upon the world China's cultural superiority. The fact that the admiral only brought back curiosities further reinforced court thinking on the essentially useless nature of these expeditions. Even more derogatory was the description of them as *"eunuch's enterprises"*.

It is perhaps worth observing at this stage that significant numbers of Chinese, at the risk of being regarded as betrayers of their ancestors - a serious crime whose punishment was death - did migrate to South East Asia from the fifteenth century onwards. Such people could easily have become, as the Europeans did later, the vanguard of a movement towards commercial maritime expansion. The Chinese government, however, unlike its European counterparts, was not interested in overseas expansion. As long as China could behave as an

---

[179] Dun J.Li , *The Ageless Chinese*, J.M.Dent and Sons, London (1965). Ch. 9 on the Ming dynasty.

Asian overlord and collect tribute from the states on her borders, she was content to remain as she was. Hence, China lost her opportunity not only to expand commercially, but to maintain her technological leadership. Once more the critical nature of the role of the state in the economic development process is highlighted.

There is one other factor, however, to which historians of this era in China's history have repeatedly drawn attention, and that is the change which came over Chinese society in the fourteenth century. Dun J. Li has argued that the Ming era was noted for the barbarity of its behaviour, and he adduces as evidence the use of corporal punishment on court officials. This he attributes to the brutalisation of Chinese society which occurred after the Mongol invasions.

Of equal concern to Li, however, is the aridity of much of the intellectual thought of the period.[180] It is a theme which Elvin[181] echoes. Philosophy and art, he argues, became introspective, intuitive and subjective in the fourteenth century. Scientific objectivity ceased to count; the analytical approach was given credence no longer. Chinese philosophy became pantheistic. The whole social and organisational matrix of Chinese society after the fourteenth century differed from earlier times, he argues. China's era of technological innovation was over. It had *"stopped progressing well before the point at which a lack of scientific knowledge had become a serious obstacle,"* claims Elvin.[182]

Elvin then goes on to offer a further explanation why China ceased to be technologically innovative. China, he argues, was caught in a high-level equilibrium trap. *"With falling surplus in agriculture and declining per capita income and per capita demand, with cheapening labour but increasingly expensive resources and capital, with farming and transport technology so good that no simple improvements could be made, the rational strategy for peasant and merchant alike tended in the direction not so much of labour-saving machinery as of economy on resources and fixed capital. Huge, but static, markets created no bottlenecks in the production system that might have prompted creativity. When temporary shortages arose, mercantile*

---

180   Ibid.
181   Elvin, Mark, *The Pattern of the Chinese Past*, Stanford University Press (1973), p.225-234.
182   Ibid, p.314.

versatility, based on cheap transport, was a faster and surer remedy than the invention of machines."[183]

The high-level equilibrium trap theory raises as many questions, as it answers. Machinery, it should not be forgotten, fulfils other vital functions besides economising on labour. The first use of the steam engine in Britain was to pump water out of mines, a task which could not be done effectively any other way. Moreover, as Elvin is aware, the Chinese did make some technological innovations in the eighteenth century. The real question that has to be asked is why they did not make more. The answer is that China, unlike her European contemporaries, failed to establish a commercial empire. *"The Manchus brought what we usually know as the Chinese Empire to its widest extent. Under them it included all of China proper and what we have called the outlying dependencies, Manchuria, Mongolia, Sinkiang and Tibet. In addition several states were in a subordinate position...Of these the chief were Korea, Annam, Burma and Nepal."*[184] But the Chinese never practised mercantilism. So long as their underlings paid tribute to the Chinese throne, all was well. The Chinese never came to look upon their tributary peoples as a potential source of trade. Once again, the conclusion that China suffered on account of her government's ambivalent attitude to trade is inescapable.

China's attitude toward scientific discovery and technological invention is all the more difficult to understand in view of contemporary developments in European society at the time, developments the nature of which they were well informed, thanks to the presence at the court in Peking of the Jesuit Fathers after 1644. Fairbank's conclusion, however, that: *"alien rule inspired hostility to alien things in general"*, provides the answer to that conundrum.[185] Having developed a civilisation which was superior to anything else in the world in the thirteenth century and was still regarded among eighteenth century Europeans, such as Adam Smith, Leibniz, Spinoza, Goethe and Voltaire, as a mighty achievement, the Chinese naturally came to see themselves for what they were, or had been, namely the greatest nation on the face of the earth. Not until the middle of the nineteenth century, when British ironclads sank Chinese junks with an ease which surprised and mortified the Chinese, did the latter even begin to appreciate the

---

[183]   Ibid, p.314.
[184]   Ibid.
[185]   Fairbank & Reischauer, *China: Tradition and Transformation*, George Allen & Unwin, Sydney (1979).

extent to which Europe's scientific discoveries and technological innovations had given the West an advantage. Even then, as we shall see from reading the next chapter, China's response showed much less appreciation of the true situation than did Japan's.

7 Japan and China

Only one Asian nation has, at the time of writing, succeeded in breaking out of the pre-industrial age to become one of the world's leading industrial nations, though others are well on the way. That nation is Japan. Bequeathed a small island, or more, correctly, series of islands, with very little in the way of natural resources other than volcanic soil, the Japanese have, nevertheless, succeeded in overcoming the manifest disadvantages of their geographic location, to rise to the top of the world's production league table. Their achievement, in emerging from semi-feudal isolation to become within the short space of one hundred years, the leading technological power on earth, is one of the most remarkable stories of modern times. Just how the Japanese did it, what were the factors that made this possible, what strategies were pursued, are questions it behoves us to answer. For Japan's approach to industrialisation and economic modernisation is of value to us in the lessons which it provides. Theirs was no slavish imitation of western methods; on the contrary, after an initial period in which everything western was copied, they recognised that much of their culture was of value and refused to jettison it for the untried methods and ways of the west. Nevertheless, they were quick to recognise the West's superiority in the 1860s and to adapt themselves to the advantages which it offered.

Japan's first contact with Europeans occurred in 1542 when the Portuguese first reached the Far East. The European gift to Japan was twofold - Christianity and science. The first the Japanese were to reject, the second they accepted. It was the Jesuits under the leadership of St. Francis Xavier who brought Christianity to Japan, and who, in the brief space of seventy years, were instrumental in converting around 5% of the population to Christ. Traditionally minded Japanese objected. Christianity, they argued, was foreign to their way of life and culture and should not therefore be tolerated. Accordingly, the decision was taken to extirpate the new religion entirely from the nation and to shut

Japan off from all contact with the outside world. For the next 250 years (1603-1853) Japan remained isolated in her island fortress, all communication with the West being forbidden. European ships that visited the islands of Japan were turned away at gun point, Japanese who came into contact with the hated foreigners were forbidden on pain of death to return to their homeland. Only one trading post out of the many that the Europeans had established in the sixteenth century remained, the Dutch port at Deshima in Nagasaki Bay. Such knowledge and information that the Japanese did acquire of the advances of western science in the seventeenth and eighteenth centuries filtered through this entrepôt.

Japan's isolation was rudely shattered in 1853 when Commodore Perry of the United States Navy entered Tokyo Bay with a flotilla of ironclads and a letter from President Fillimore of America demanding, interalia, that Japan open her doors to commerce with Western nations. The Americans had a number of objectives not the least of which was the desire, having now spread across the continent of North America, to extend their power and influence in the Pacific Ocean. Their immediate goal, however, was the procurement of coal from Japan for their steamships en route to China, together with guarantees that any American sailors who were picked up at sea by Japanese fishing vessels, would receive humane treatment. Perry's arrival, the exceedingly brusque manner of his approach, the impressive technology of the steamship and the iron horse, as the Japanese described the railway, resulted in the concession of his first and immediate requirement, namely the stationing of an American envoy in Tokyo and the signing of the 'unequal' treaties, as Japanese historians have subsequently described them. Similar treaties were subsequently signed with other European nations.

For the next fifteen years Japan fomented. On the one hand were the conservatives who were determined at all costs to keep the country closed to outsiders on the ground that the nation would be contaminated by influences alien to Shintoism and the Japanese pantheon of divinities. On the other hand, there was an increasingly powerful group of men who, having become aware, through their contacts with the Dutch, of the immense scientific and technological strides that Europe had made in the preceding two centuries, realised that Japan could not remain in isolation for ever, and that her future security and well-being as a nation depended on her willingness to trade with foreign countries, and to acquire the knowledge and techniques that the scientific and industrial revolutions had conferred on Europe. A number of these men, in complete defiance of the long-standing taboo on foreign travel, journeyed to Europe and America to see for themselves what the West had accomplished. What they saw had an immense impact on their outlook, thinking and behaviour. Determined that Japan would one day aspire to similar cultural and economic heights, they set about the task of convincing their compatriots of the need for modernisation. The task was not easy, for it involved a complete about turn in the direction in which the country was going, and this could only be accomplished by a virtual political revolution.

The details of the story of that revolution, which climaxed fifteen years of internal conflict and erupted in 1867 into a brief Civil War, need not concern us here. Suffice it to say that the Shogunate, the system of government under which Japan had been ruled for the better part of six centuries, was brought to an end with the suicide of the last holder of that office, following his failure to evict the hated westerners from Japan. The reforming party within the nation was now free to restore the Emperor to his rightful position as the leader of the nation and the head of the government, but not before an event unique in Japan's long history had taken place, namely the poisoning of the Emperor Komei, a renowned traditionalist, at his palace in the old capital of Kyoto.

The accession of the Emperor Mitsuhito, the enlightened One, as he became known, heralded the new era. Japan's attempt to catch up the West and to overtake her, in short, to become a leading military power, was beginning. Unification, modernisation and military strength were the slogans which the Choshu clans of the western isles had given the nation. They were the goals to which the Japanese were to strive in the course of the next century. Her economic development strategies were devised with these objectives in view. Once strong at home, the Japanese mission was nothing less than the complete ejection of the European nations from the Far East, a goal which, in large measure, they achieved ironically during and after the Second World War, but at a price which no Japanese would have been prepared to pay had they known beforehand the cost. For the immediate future, however, their aim was to obtain the abrogation of the unequal treaties, two clauses of which caused the Japanese the greatest offence and humiliation. The first related to the opening of the country to foreign trade and the fixing of the tariff at a rate not in excess of 5% of the imported value of the merchandise. The second related to the treatment of westerners found guilty of violating Japanese law. The Western Powers had insisted that all such persons should be handed over to them and tried according to their law. Japan was too weak to refuse. Initial attempts to secure the abrogation of the treaties by diplomatic means in the 1870s were met with a rebuff. It was not until after her victory in the war against China in 1894-5 that Japan was able to secure some amelioration of the offensive clauses. Final dissolution of the terms of the treaties did not come until 1911, six years after Japan's victory over Tsarist Russia. The Japanese were obliged to prove themselves militarily before the West was prepared to treat with them on equal terms.

The abolition of the Shogunate and the restoration of the emperor were only the first steps in the political modernisation of Japan. The political changes that followed were of far greater significance and consequence for the nation, for without the abolition of all the ancient feudal practices according to which Japan had been governed for centuries, the country could not have entered the modern era. In the first three years of the new reign, the new rulers of Japan, the young emperor assisted by his close advisers, accomplished a complete revolution in the administration of the country. The whole clan system of government, according to which the feudal lords had been able to wield effective power in their own territories, was replaced by a modern prefectural system based on the French model. Along with this move went the abolition of the old feudal dues whereby the peasant was required to pay in kind a rice quota to his overlord each year in return for his protection. At the same time, the old caste system of Japan, according to which all Japanese were categorised as warriors, farmers, craftsmen or merchants, was abolished, and freedom to choose one's occupation, to own property, to marry a person of another caste, to move from one's village to another village or to a city, was granted. Moreover, the clan lords who, throughout the period of the Tokugawa Shogunate, had been required to spend every other year in Tokyo, were free to move around the country or travel abroad as they pleased.

The economic and social consequences of these decrees were profound. Japanese of all classes were now free to travel as they wished. They were no longer obliged to work on the same land as their forefathers had done for centuries. They were free to buy whatever goods they wanted to; indeed, all restriction on the movement of merchandise were lifted, thus facilitating a far greater degree of trade between the different areas of the country.

Along with the abolition of the feudal system went several other developments which were vital to Japan's modernisation. The first of these was the establishment of the Imperial Civil Service, to which entry was to be made on the basis of merit rather than social position. The Civil Service, being the organ by which the country was to be administered, replaced the former feudal system of the hereditary clan lords. The new Japan was to be governed by men who had earned their way to the top, rather than by those who had been born into it. The second was the creation of a modern army. In 1873, the new government decreed military conscription for all citizens, thus overthrowing the existing military system whereby the defence of the nation was entrusted to a special class of persons, namely the samurai or warrior caste. Military and naval academies for the training of officers for the new conscript defence forces were established. The success of the new scheme was first tested in 1877 when the Satsuma clans in the western provinces rebelled against the modernisation policies of the Meiji government. The effectiveness with which the rebellion was defeated demonstrated the merits of the new modernised conscript force. The third and vitally important measure from the point of view of the new government , was its decision albeit at a very early stage in the modernisation process, to make education compulsory for everyone. This, the Japanese did in 1872, only two years after Britain had introduced her own Education Act. In addition, they established a number of special schools at which science and technology were the principal subjects taught. That the Japanese were prepared so early in the process of modernisation to embark on such a vast project as universal literacy showed amazing courage. Admittedly, under the Shogunate, Japan had enjoyed a much higher level of education and consequently of cultural homogeneity than any other Asian nation. Nevertheless the decree to universalise education demonstrated a remarkable act of faith in the nation's future.

For most nations in Japan's position, the task of staffing the schools and the civil service with personnel who not only had the right training for the job, but also were imbued with the requisite spirit of service, would have been almost impossible. The Japanese government solved the problem in a unique manner. The warrior class, or 'samurai' as they were known, were no longer required to perform their traditional duties now that the new citizen army had been established. Accordingly in 1870, they were compensated to the tune of £2.4 million for the loss of their income by the government. A few of them took up business as an outlet for their energies, but the majority invested their money in the newly emerging western style banks and re-entered government service as teachers, civil servants or members of the recently created police force. Indeed, it has been calculated that 78% of all holders of government offices were former 'samurai'. This fact is all the more important in view of the high degree of dependence which post-Revolution governments have shown towards these organs of administrative convenience. The bureaucracy is still a major factor in Japanese government to-day, as the role of the Ministry of International Trade and Industry has demonstrated.

It is also significant that Japan did little about the writing of a modern Constitution until the gains of the revolution had been well and truly consolidated. Not until 1889, by which time the 'samurai' were securely established in their positions of power within the bureaucracy did Japan promulgate a constitution, the adoption of which saw the virtual completion of Japan's political revolution. It is also significant from the point of view of this work that Japan, in promulgating her administrative and constitutional changes, should have looked, not to the United States of America or Britain, the home of constitutional government, but to France and Germany, both of whom emphasised the importance of a strong centralised government. From the French, the Japanese had derived the nation-wide prefecture system of administration based on the division of the country into departments. From the Germans, Japan was to be given the lessons in 'realpolitik' which were to govern her relations with the European Powers ever after. Bismarck's advice to the Japanese delegation which visited Berlin - *"that the only way for a small country like Japan is to strengthen and protect herself with all her own might and set no reliance on other nations. When International Law is not to a nation's advantage, it is ignored and resort is made to war."* - did not fall on deaf ears.[186]

For the time being, however, the Japanese were satisfied that the only style of government that would suit them was autocracy. The Meiji Revolution of 1868 had seen the restoration of the emperor to his former imperial power, and it was a constitution based on autocracy and the hereditary power of the ruling family that the Meiji reformers wanted. At no stage were their reforms imbued with a true spirit of liberalism, whether in the political or the economic sense. Traditionally government in Japan had been feudal; modernisation demanded that the

---

[186]   Bergamini, David, *Japan's Imperial Conspiracy*, Granada, London (1976), p.256.

nation unite first, and unity, it was believed, could only be won and preserved by restoring Japan's ancient figure-head emperor to his rightful position of power within the State.

Other steps were taken to strengthen the imperial position in the Meiji era. The Diet was based on the German Bundestag. Representation was limited to the propertied classes of Japan, amongst whom the old *samurai*, now enriched by the state's decree to commute their old feudal incomes, were a dominant group. The Upper House was restricted in its membership to those titled persons whose landholdings and wealth conferred on them the dignity of holding high office in the state. The system went a long way towards ensuring that compliance with, in some cases, complicity in, the Imperial Will, which the framers of the constitution wished to secure. A Privy Council, selected by the Meiji Rulers, was the essential organ of government and remained so until Japan's defeat in 1945. It was this body, more than any other, that ruled Japan, with the consequence that ministers of state, including prime ministers, could come and go without in any way effecting the consistency of policy. It was the Emperor who ruled, as Bergamini has tried to show in his remarkable study of modern Japan, *"The Imperial Japanese Conspiracy"*,[187] and it was the duty of his ministers to ensure that the Imperial Will was carried out. To the extent that they were able to do this without arousing opposition either in the Diet, the press or the nation, they were retained. When they failed, they were replaced by men who could achieve the Imperial goals more effectively. Constitutional liberalism was never adopted in Japan, though a few men, such as Saionji, continued to espouse it. The achievement of the Imperial goal of unity, modernisation and expulsion of the foreigners from the Far East could only have been achieved with the adoption of a strong, centralised, autocratic government.

The Meiji Reformers took one further step to enhance the Emperor's position and make him sovereign in reality as well as in name. Following the revolution, the land belonging to the Tokugawa Shogunate was expropriated by the emperor and thereafter administered by him. In the course of the next thirty years, the emperor increased the area of land held either by himself personally or by the state until over half of all land in Japan was either owned or controlled by him. The object of the reformers was to counter any revolutionary tendency that might manifest itself. The Meiji were not, as the Satsuma

---

[187]   Ibid.

rebellion of 1877 showed, without their opponents, and any weakening of their resolve to carry through the modernisation program, could well have led to their overthrow. With half the country under the direct control of the emperor, counter-revolutionary activity was rendered much more difficult. The avowed purpose of the reformers was to provide the emperor with sufficient income to be able to pay the army and the police out of his own pocket without recourse to the Diet. The strengthening of the Imperial position not only rendered the government independent of the Diet, but enabled the emperor to pursue policies which met with little favour in the nation at large.

The consolidation of political power in the hands of the Imperial government of Japan, a task which was readily achieved by the Meiji reformers, facilitated the job of economic modernisation. In spite of the fact that Japan had been cut off from Europe and European scientific developments for a quarter of a millennium, she had, nevertheless, developed some of the basic skills required for industrialisation. Although 85% of her population was still employed in agriculture, 5% were classed as *samurai*, and a further 5% as priests, she still had a town population of some 5%, many of whom were engaged in industrial and commercial activities. Building construction, ship design and fabrication, cloth-dyeing and sword making were all skills which, under the Tokugawa shogunate, were well-developed. The Japanese were also conversant with the water mill and with the techniques of warehousing. Edo, as Tokyo was formerly known, was a city with an estimated population of over one million people, and although this represented only about one-thirtieth of Japan's total population of thirty million, it has been estimated that the city controlled approximately a quarter of the national purchasing power. Osaka, too, was well established as a mercantile centre in Tokugawa Japan. Urbanisation on this scale necessitated the development of a transport and communications system to provide the basic requirements of city life. In a country of mountainous terrain, heavy reliance was placed on coastal shipping as a means of moving food and goods from city to city. Monetary systems for the exchange of goods were well established and credit transactions extensively practised. Japan's relative isolation - she did maintain some contact with Korea and China during the Tokugawa period - together with the feudal restraints that were placed on her economic growth and development inhibited advance along western lines.

It was the signing of the treaties that forced the Japanese to abandon their policy of seclusion and enter into commercial relations with the European Powers. The admission of machine made products from Lancashire and Yorkshire at prices well below those at which the Japanese could produce them themselves using the old techniques of handcraft, destroyed the old handloom cloth industry. The Japanese were not slow to appreciate that, if they were to preserve any form of textile industry in the country, they would have to purchase machinery from abroad and establish modern style factories. This the government readily did. To pay for the import of the new machinery and for the skills of the foreign technicians whom the Japanese employed to assist them in setting up their new ventures, the Japanese exported tea, locally produced porcelain and silk, demand for which in the west was growing with the destruction of French supplies due to disease.

The establishment of factories in the early years of Japan's economic resurgence was almost solely a government inspired activity. Having been isolated from western developments for so long, few Japanese had any conception at all of the steps to take to establish modern style businesses. The merchants had only had experience of buying and selling and profiteering. Investment, risk capital and technology were completely alien concepts to the Japanese businessman of the early Meiji era; accordingly they were unwilling in many cases to take the risks involved. Most, therefore, of the heavy industrial enterprises that were established in the 1870s, the shipyards, the railways, the cement plants, the glass works, and the iron and steel works, were financed and managed by the state. Some of the *samurai* did establish small-scale factories for the production of textiles. Even in the field of silk and cotton manufacture, the government found it necessary to set up model factories as a means of demonstrating what could be done.

The early years of the reform period also saw the establishment of a large number of banks. In 1872, the Bank of Japan was established and the subsequent decade saw another one hundred and fifty banks set up. The mobilisation of funds for the establishment of factories, the opening up of coal mines, and the commencement of heavy industry, was an essential part of the Meiji Reformers economic modernisation program. Deeply suspicious of the intentions of the foreign powers and distrustful of their economic ambitions with regard to Japan, the reformers made it their business to avoid any reliance on foreign capital whenever possible. Accordingly, in the first twenty-five years of

Japan's economic modernisation, only two foreign loans were contracted. The first of these, signed in 1870, for £1 million, was used to finance the construction of the Tokyo-Yokohama railway. The second, contracted in 1873, for £2.4 million was used to finance the payment of bonds to the samurai to compensate them for the loss of their income as military retainers. Apart from these two foreign loans, Japan relied on her own resources for the funding of her earlier economic development program. Heaviest reliance in this respect was placed on the Land Tax which, in 1871, provided 85% of government revenue.

In their early efforts at modernisation, the Japanese gave little attention to agriculture. The decree in 1868, abolishing the payment of feudal dues and entitling the peasantry to take up the ownership of land, nevertheless accomplished a major step in the right direction so far as agriculture was concerned. The government's attempt to persuade ex-samurai to take up land in the island of Hokkaido was unsuccessful. It was not until 1877, after the Satsuma rebellion had been crushed, that the government took positive steps to modernise agriculture. Experiments were undertaken with western techniques of dry land farming and animal husbandry, but Japan's climatic conditions favoured the paddy fields. A dai-Nippon Agricultural society was established in 1881 to provide information on the best practices and techniques to adopt when farming in Japan. The Ministry for Agriculture and Commerce was set up with wide ranging authority over veterinary schools, agricultural experimental stations, silk worm and mulberry experimental stations, stockbreeding centres and nurseries. The Ministry was also responsible for the education of the farmer and the adoption of the most appropriate farming techniques. A number of plants were set up for the processing of fish meal and oil. Japan's early neglect of agriculture was all the more reprehensible in view of her dependence on it for the success of the industrialisation program. For not only did agriculture supply the bulk of the capital in the form of taxes for many of the government inspired initiatives in heavy industry, but it also provided the products, silk, cotton and tea, which were Japan's principal exports in the early period of industrialisation.

The second stage of Japan's modernisation program, extending from the early eighties through to the mid-nineties, saw the steady extension of those policies of economic development which had been deemed to be successful in the earlier period. Railways, mileage of which totalled 385 in 1885, increased sixfold in the course of the next decade. The tonnage of modern ships constructed at the shipyards increased from 60,000 to 210,000. The electric telegraph and the telephone were also introduced into the country, the latter very soon after its invention in America. The textile industry continued to grow until by the turn of the century it was employing over 200,000 workers. One significant change, however, did occur. While the government continued to be responsible for the construction and operation of the railways, all forms of telecommunication, the arsenal and the mint, as well as such heavy industries as shipyards, cement works, glass works and similar engineering establishments were sold to private enterprise, thus paving the way for the development of that specifically Japanese capitalist institution, the *zaibatsus*.

The population also continued to grow, in part due to the abolition of the ancient Japanese custom of female infanticide, thus ensuring a ready supply of labour for the newly developing industries. Agricultural output, thanks to the government's initiatives in the late seventies and early eighties, increased in line with population growth, thus ensuring the nation's self-sufficiency in foodstuffs. Three factors contributed to the growth of agriculture: the use of better fertilisers, the use of improved seeds and seedlings and the systematic experimentation with new methods and techniques designed to make the most appropriate use of the land. The heavy dependence of the government on Land Tax in the seventies was to some extent obviated by the introduction of a liquor tax which, by 1884, was providing one-fifth of the state revenues, as against the two-thirds yielded by the Land Tax.

The success of Japan's economic modernisation program was evidenced by the desire of the Meiji Rulers to put the country to its first test. Korea had been a focal point for Japanese expansion for several decades. Indeed, some Japanese had urged an attack on the country in 1873, but more prudent counsels prevailed. In 1895, however, internal rebellion provided the Japanese with their opportunity. China, regarding the peninsula as a tributary state, also intervened. The resulting war saw Japan victorious. The intervention of the European Powers, however, deprived Japan of the most important of her gains, the Liaotang peninsula. Winning the war and losing the peace was a feat Japan was to repeat again ten years later, though this time the enemy was Russia. Japan's victories, however, bore fruit; for the first time, she was seen to be a rapidly growing industrial power in the Far East, with whom one day, other European Powers would have to reckon. More importantly,

Japan's successes brought about the revision of the unequal treaties which the country so strongly detested. Already, in 1894, in recognition of the formulation by the Japanese of a civil and criminal code which was more acceptable to western standards of morality and law, Britain had agreed to waive the extraterritoriality clause in the treaties. Foreigners in Japan were henceforth subject to Japanese law. It was not until 1911, however, that Japan was free to raise tariff barriers at will on any and all goods imported into the country, a measure which went far to safeguarding those industries that were weak and could not stand foreign competition. The wars had other advantages for Japan, not least of which was the opening by China and Korea of their countries to trade with Japan. The success of the Japanese navy, most of whose ships had been supplied by the west, provided the government with an additional reason for boosting domestic shipbuilding. A naval construction program was commenced, designed to provide the Japanese with their own defence force. The success of this new measure may be seen from a comparison of the shipbuilding figures of 1895, when they were 210,000 tons, with those of 1915, by which time they had reached 1,530,000 tons. By no means all of this effort was expended on the navy; a considerable portion of it was devoted to the construction of a modern merchant fleet.

The wars, however, provided Japan with a much needed impetus to become self-sufficient in many more aspects of industrial life than she had so far been. The intervention of the foreign powers after the wars with China and Russia only strengthened Japanese resolve to become less dependent on them for the supply of her military, naval and railway equipment. Accordingly, the government nationalised the railways and then set about the construction of railway workshops with the intention of supplying all the nation's needs for coaching stock, wagons and locomotives. This decision was followed by a further significant expansion of the rail network; another 4,000 miles of track was completed between 1895 and 1915 thus providing additional stimulus to the growth of the national economy.

Although the Japanese were anxious to become economically as self-sufficient as possible, they were not averse during this stage of their development to the use of foreign capital to finance major industrial projects. Confident of the ability to manage their fortunes successfully, to expand their economy and to develop their resources, the Japanese, in the period from 1900 to 1914, years in which the expansion of their heavy industries continued apace, came to rely more and more on foreign investment for their industrialisation program. The third stage of Japan's development program also saw much less reliance placed on the Land Tax as a source of revenue, a variety of other taxes, such as the liquor tax, taxes on incomes and profits and customs duties, having taken its place.

It was the Great War, however, that provided the Japanese with their opportunity to expand their economy more rapidly than at any previous time in their history, as the labour force statistics so eloquently demonstrate. The principal reason for this rapid acceleration of production was the opening up of markets in Asia which until 1914 had been virtually captive to the European trade. The dislocation of traditional trading patterns engendered by the war provided the Japanese with their opportunity. Some idea of the growth of foreign trade can be gleaned from the fact that silk exports, which had long been the mainstay of Japanese exports, increased threefold between 1913 and 1929. Cotton goods, on the other hand, had multiplied eightfold, a fact which illustrates only too clearly Japan's increasing tendency to rely on manufactured goods as her main source of export income. Not all of the new business came from the opening up of new markets in Asia. Some of it was the result of increasing trade with America, with whom the Japanese drew up a substantial level of credit.

The war, however, was particularly beneficial to those industries which the Japanese had been struggling since the beginning of the century to establish on an indigenous basis, machine tool manufacture, chemical production, fabrication of electrical equipment, and electrical power generating plant. All of these nascent industries, which Japan had found difficulty nurturing while the unequal treaties were in force, now expanded rapidly, in part due to the erection of tariff barriers, but in the main due to the war.

To facilitate this rapid growth, Japan became increasingly dependent on the import of raw materials. In her early years, Japan had not only produced enough coal to meet her own needs, but had been able to export a surplus to pay for the import of her manufacturing equipment. But Japan's lack of raw materials put her in a position where she had no alternative but to import increasing quantities of coal, iron ore and the other metallurgical requirements of modern industry.

The growth in the industrial sector of the economy meant that the State was no longer so heavily dependent on the agricultural sector for its revenue. Industrial growth had now reached the point at which business expansion could quite successfully be provided for out of the profits of industrial and commercial enterprises. The nature of the *zaibatsus* - the inclusion of a financial institution within the umbrella of business enterprises of which they were constituted - ensured that they always had access to funds for expansion whenever they wanted them. The Great War meant that foreign sources of funds were no longer available, and the enormous income which the nation was able to earn from its increased exports during the war enabled it to pay for the loans which it had incurred in the pre-war era of debt-financed expansion.

Nor did expansion cease with the signing of the peace treaty. The American consumer boom of the 1920s benefited Japan inasmuch as she was able to find increasing scope in the United States for her exports. In return, American companies, particularly the automobile firms of General Motors and Ford, invested in Japan, thus starting that era of close association between the two nations which, with the brief interlude of the war years, has continued to this day. The Japanese, however, were careful this time not to permit foreign investment to exceed one-fifth of total investment.

Japan was much less seriously affected by the Great Depression than either Europe or America for several reasons. The construction boom which followed the Great Earthquake of 1923 resulted in a serious banking crisis which forced the government to intervene to put the monetary system in order. Secondly, in the person of her young Emperor, Hirohito, Japan had found a leader who was determined to oust the European Powers from the Far East in fulfilment of the Meiji Reformers goals for the nation. Accordingly, Japan made every effort from 1926 onwards to strengthen herself economically and industrially for the conflict which lay ahead. The extent to which Japan expanded her economy in the thirties may be seen from the fact that whereas during the twenties the number of workers employed in industry remained fairly close to the 1.8 million mark, between 1930 and 1936, the figure rose to 2.8 million. This does not imply that the twenties were a static period in Japan's history; on the contrary, consumption of electric power trebled and manufacturing output increased 70%. The comparison between Japan's economic performance in the twenties and thirties only serves to underline the indisputable fact that, once a country has its objectives clarified, its rate of economic progress multiplies dramatically. Production of such basic materials of the modern industrial world as steel, cement, electricity, soda ash, dyes, and caustic soda increased two, three and sometimes fourfold. There was an increase in consumer goods production of one-third; the output of heavy industrial goods increased by 83%, the sectors experiencing the greatest rate of expansion being the metallurgical, engineering and chemical industries. Japan's intentions to put the economy on a war footing were obvious. During the 1930s, the power of the *zaibatsus* increased dramatically. The close association between the government and the leaders of industry, an association which was cemented by the extensive imperial shareholdings in the *zaibatsus*, was further strengthened by the increasing number of government contracts which were let in the early thirties, after the Manchurian campaign.

Japan's lack of raw materials, however, continued to pose problems for her. For the country was dependent on foreign suppliers for all her rubber, cotton and wool, for well over half of her iron ore, and a substantial portion of her bauxite and nickel requirements. An increasing portion of her foodstuffs was also imported, as population expansion exceeded the nation's capacity to supply its own needs, a fact which added further justification, in Japanese eyes, for the imperial program of territorial expansion. To pay for the increased imports, the country had to continue its export drive in a big way. The deterioration in export prices in the 1930s for manufactured goods following the Depression meant that Japan had to increase her exports by 50% to compensate for the increased cost of imports. Cheap Japanese articles found their way increasingly into the markets of America, the south-east Asian nations, and even to Africa and South America. Japan's heavy military expenditures were to a large extent financed by foreign loans. State revenues became increasingly financed from income and business taxes, the Land Tax having dwindled to a mere 1% of total government income by 1940. Manufactured goods became increasingly important as a source of export income, while raw silk continued to decline in importance with the production of synthetics.

In spite of the immense importance given by the state to military objectives and the consequent emphasis on heavy industry which marked Japan's economic growth in the 1930s, the standard of living continued to rise. Only about 15% of production was exported, the remainder being consumed by the domestic market. The increasing urbanisation of the country was, as elsewhere, a product of industrialisation. Conditions among the lower classes in the country nevertheless remained poor. The government's policy of taxing land as the means to finance its early industrialisation programs certainly placed a very heavy burden on agriculture. It was, however, a more prudent policy than foreign borrowing would have been, even though it meant that the lot of the average Japanese farmer improved but little before 1900.

Conditions in Japan's factories, particularly in the early years of industrialisation, were appalling. As in Britain, heavy reliance was placed on female and child labour. Until 1913, the country had no industrial legislation worth the name, and, even after that date, much of it was never effectively enforced. The leaders of the *zaibatsus* were free to exploit their workers in a totally merciless manner. Women were herded into dormitories and not allowed away from the factory site for months at a time. When they did escape from their barrack room conditions, many or them never returned. In the event of a dispute between an employer and his employees, the latter never had any means of redress whatsoever. Trades Unions, being contrary to the consensus mentality of the Japanese, did not exist. Many employers paid their workers late, very often in the form of vouchers expendable only in the company's shops on goods the prices of which were determined by the employer. Such practice makes nonsense of any theory that Japan was an example of liberal capitalism with its theory of the free market, competitive enterprise and employer-employee bargaining, just as the constitutional arrangements deny the validity of any claim which Japan might make to being a liberal democracy.

Defeat in war together with the destruction of much of the nation's capital stock provided the leaders of Japan with a new challenge, one which the resourceful Japanese were not slow to seize. An observer of the Japanese scene in 1945 could have been forgiven for thinking that Japan as a nation was finished. A small island with a population in excess of seventy million, with very little in the way of natural resources, the country's future looked bleak indeed. But the Japanese leadership saw it otherwise. Acutely conscious of the disastrous miscalculation which they had made in 1941, they set about the reconstruction of the nation's economy. Capitalising on their pre-war experiences, they determined their objectives. Japan was to become one of the world's leading industrial nations, and within the astonishingly short period of twenty-five years, she succeeded in achieving that objective. The task was made a little easier for her by the foreign policies of her erstwhile conqueror, the United States of America, whose government saw in a rejuvenated Japan a bulwark against Communism, as represented by the combined might of Russia and China. Moreover, American business interests saw in Japan's economic recovery the opportunity for economic expansion. For their part, the Japanese continued to exercise considerable caution with regard to foreign investment; only in 1971 did they relax their very tight restrictions on capital inflow into the country and permit a higher percentage of foreign investment. Their success, however measured, testifies to their vision, courage, energy, self-discipline and, above all, the quality of their leadership.

The Japanese continued the old tradition of close association between the leaders of government and the captains of industry which had marked the pre-war period. The Ministry of International Trade and Industry together with the Ministry of Finance have been the principal agents of Japan's remarkable recovery. These two government departments have been responsible for the preparation and co-ordination of the nation's economic development program. It is they who lay down the guidelines for economic growth and thereby influence the direction in which the economy is going. Japanese planning has never been imperative in the Russian style, but indicative and thus more in line with French practice. Planners are highly respected by the nation at large, a fact which stands in stark contrast to British attitudes towards Whitehall or American attitudes towards Washington. The relevant departmental ministers, whose functions are co-ordinated by MITI lay down the sectoral targets which it is believed the nation should be able to achieve. It is the task of the *kereitsu*, the *zaibatsus'* successors, to meet these targets. The Japanese have always been great believers in the virtues of competition, so each kereitsu then competes for its share of the market. The result in Japan's case has been a constant over-shooting of the target with the result that the Japanese economy has expanded at a much greater rate than even the planners anticipated. Planning is integrated; both public and private sectors being accounted for. Implementation is dependent upon *"the announcement effect"*.

In addition to these five and ten year plans, the government has many other weapons with which to influence economic performance, the promotion of competition between the *kereitsu*, the thirteen or so conglomerates which account for over 90% of the national output, being the first. Competition for market share within a particular sector and even within a particular industry of the economy is very real but it is competition between giants, each of whom knows that their survival is essential to the well-being of the nation. The development of large-scale oligopolistic enterprises, each having under its umbrella such diverse activities as banking, insurance, shipping, mining, ocean-going transport, automobile manufacturing, chemical manufacturing, and iron and steel production, all competing one with another, is a feature of capitalism which is unique to Japan. Industrial enterprise in America and Europe knows nothing of it.

Government influence over and control of industry is not limited to the central planning function or to the promotion of competition. The government may decide for reasons of national security that a particular industry should be encouraged, in which case it has a wide range of options available to it. It may exercise its authority to purchase shares in the company. It may content itself with the supply of credit on easy terms. It may make available depreciation allowances, or it may restrict the quantity of similar goods imported by means of tariff duties. Japanese practice and performance is very different from that of the Anglo-Saxon countries with their traditional *'laissez-faire'* conditioning. Japan knows nothing of the inhibitions with which two centuries of classical economic theory have bedevilled the West's attempts to manage their economies successfully.

In the field of agriculture, the Japanese government has had a further resounding success with the major land reform of 1946, when absentee landlordism was abolished by governmental decree and tenants became the owners of the land. The success of the act may be gleaned from the fact that whereas after the war approximately half the land was let out to tenants, in 1950 this figure had been reduced to 10%. This agrarian reform facilitated the mechanisation of Japanese agriculture in the 1950s. Japan has not been self-sufficient in foodstuffs since the 1930s, with the consequence that she has absorbed more and more of the surpluses of the American farmer. The government's policy of being self-sufficient in rice production has resulted in over-kill and the export of the surplus.

The tremendous success of the Japanese economy is in evidence in just about every country of the world today. Japanese built motor cars, computers, electrical goods, such as dishwashers, washing machines, vacuum cleaners, stereo-record players, tape-recorders, clocks, digital watches, pocket calculators, witness to the superb genius of a people who have through diligent and painstaking imitation of western ways of scientific thinking and behaviour, pulled themselves up very largely by their bootstraps to the point where they have taken their place amongst the world's advanced nations. Japan's emergence from a state of semi-feudalism one hundred and twenty years ago to become a modern industrial power provides us with an excellent example of the principles of managerial macro-economics in action. The Meiji Reformers approach to the modernisation of their country was an essentially pragmatic one, and it highlights very appropriately the steps which a country must take if it is to utilise its resources effectively for the benefit of the nation as a whole. For the Japanese, like most other nations that came late to industrialisation, followed a course that had certain recognisable features. Like the Germans, who in the 1860s, were taking their final steps towards political unification as a prelude to industrialisation, and the Russians who, in the 1930s, went through one of the most rapid surges in industrialisation that the world has ever seen, the Japanese were faced in the 1850s with the task of coming to terms with the world in which they lived, of recognising the distinct advantages which those nations which had preceded them in the economic development stakes had acquired. The almost brutal way in which the world forced Japan to open her doors, to recognise the existence of other nations and to trade with them, compelled the Japanese people to re-appraise their own situation in the light of the scientific and industrial revolutions which had occurred in the West. It was this extremely painful task of arriving at a clear understanding of where they stood in relation to the outside world that finally shook the Japanese out of their lethargy. The manner in which the British had treated their neighbours, the Manchu rulers of China in 1842 was not lost on the observant Japanese, and, although they did not suffer the same degree of humiliation as the Chinese, the unequal treaties were a sufficient goad to Japanese national honour and prestige. The extent of the West's cultural and scientific progress, however, never sunk right home until Japan abandoned her policy of seclusion. When in the 1860s Japanese began to travel to America and Europe, the door to modernisation was opened. For only then were they able to comprehend the extent of the developments which the West had undertaken. The recognition that their country had no commercial centres like London, Amsterdam or Paris, and no industrial centres like Birmingham, Lyons or Pittsburg, brought home to the observant Japanese the extent of western advance. The cultural shock was traumatic, and it was some time before the progressives were able to convince their reluctant clansmen that, unless the country united and modernised, it would be subjected to the same kind of treatment as China had received, or worse, become a colonial territory as India, Ceylon and Annam had. Coming to terms with the world in which they lived, understanding where they stood in relation to the outside world, accepting the harsh realities that they were, as a result of the exclusionist policy which they had followed for the past two hundred and fifty years, a backward nation, scientifically, technologically, industrially, militarily and culturally, was the first step in the right direction for the Japanese.

The second step in the process of economic modernisation was the development of the vision of their country as a modern industrial state. Having come to terms with their relative backwardness, the Meiji Rulers were in little doubt at all about the role which they saw Japan fulfilling in the world and most notably in the Far East. The objectives were not difficult to specify, and specified they were by the Choshu clan of the western isles when they adjured the Meiji Reformers firstly to unite the country, secondly to modernise it, and thirdly to expel the hated westerners from the colonial territories which they had seized. It was a task to which the Japanese, with their gift for the practical, were to seize on and perform only too well. They saw no reason why their country should not rank amongst the foremost industrial and military powers, and it was to this end that they bent their efforts in the course of the next seventy years.

The Meiji Reformers had a number of factors on their side. The first was their geographic position. Located on a series of islands at the far eastern extremity of the Asian mainland, the Japanese had developed the necessary degree of homogeneity and national self-consciousness which was to stand them in good stead in the years that followed the Revolution. They enjoyed the distinction of being one of the most educated people in Asia. Their clan lords, to whom the real government of the country at local level had belonged, spent every other year in residence in Old Edo, thus forming a relatively stable governing class. The warrior class, the *samurai*, to whom the defence of the country was entrusted, was not a homogeneous group. The major cause of division within the state was the feudal system of government and society coupled with a relatively mild caste system of social organisation which classified people into four major categories, warriors, farmers, craftsmen and merchants. The restrictions which these antiquated laws placed on social mobility were readily abolished by the reformers to Japan's lasting benefit. In respect of the caste system, Japan was more fortunate than India, where the abolition of caste has been a very much more traumatic process on account of its close association with religion in the mind of the average Indian. Japan was able to abolish her caste system and at the same time revive her ancient religion of Shintoism, a fact which contributed in no small way to the reformers' success in reviving the imperial institution.

The Japanese, moreover, enjoyed the good fortune of having come from one single racial stock, with the sole exception of the Ainu people in Hokkaido, who were only a small minority of the total population. The Japanese, therefore have not had to wrestle with the problem of a subject people, as have the rulers of the Latin American states, where a master race, the Europeans created a culture totally different from the Indian peoples over whom they ruled. The Japanese have not had that type of cultural disunity to overcome and have accordingly managed to develop a sense of unity much more readily.

The Meiji Reformers also inherited a level of technique which was quite advanced by Asian standards. Sword-making, cloth dyeing and weaving were all skills which Japanese craftsmen had mastered some centuries earlier. Porcelain of good quality was also produced. The art of musket manufacture the Japanese had learned from the English in the sixteenth century. When the time came for the industrialisation of the country, the Japanese had the basic requirements of a skilled and disciplined workforce ready to hand.

The psychology of the Japanese people was a further factor insofar as the speed with which modernisation could be effected was concerned. As a people they were able to reach a consensus of opinion on the importance of political unification and economic modernisation much more readily than a group of warring tribes could have done. The willingness of the average Japanese, to-day, to abide by the wishes of the group is very strong indeed. Individualism, which is so pronounced a feature of Anglo-Saxon society, is not encouraged in Japan.

The Japanese place much more emphasis on conformity and co-operation. This did not, however, prevent the Japanese from setting up their own business undertakings, because they were encouraged to do so by the Meiji Rulers, who recognised the importance of the entrepreneurial spirit in the West and were anxious to encourage its development in Japan.

A group psychology which stresses consensus and co-operation and condemns individualism is one which yields readily to strong leadership. In any community, the leadership factor is important, but nowhere is it more so than in Japan where the emphasis is placed on working towards a common goal. The task of the reformers was made very much easier by the willingness of the people to accept the need for reform and to undertake that reform in the spirit in which it was intended. Meiji Japan did experience several revolts amongst its subjects, but they were easily suppressed by the new conscript army. Considering the enormous risks which the reformers took when they put the country through its vast political and social revolution, this was no mean achievement.

Given the objectives which the Choshu clans had laid down for the new Meiji rulers, the reformers then had to decide what strategy to adopt to achieve the goals. All observers, whether professional historians or economists, have remarked on the importance of the role played by the government in Japan's drive toward industrialisation. Japanese economic historians, none of whom have any time for theories of *"laissez-faire"*, fully accept that the State's role in the economic development process was critical.

The State's role was felt most strongly in the early years of the Meiji era, for it was then that the basic decisions to modernise Japan were taken. It was then that the Japanese determined that, come what may, they would not be subjected to the foreign yoke, that they would unite behind their political leaders, thus ensuring the unity of the country, and resist all attempts at foreign subjugation. The edicts of the early years of the Meiji era indicate clearly the dominant role played by the State in the modernisation of the country. The decrees abolishing the old feudal system with its clan government, its division of society into castes, its restrictions on the ownership of property, on marriage, and the movement of people around the country, not to mention business activity in general, laid the groundwork for modernisation. The political decrees which legalised the restoration of the Imperial system of government, the abolition of the Shogunate, and the establishment of a strong centralised governmental system along the lines of the French *departmentes*, provided the foundation for the creation of a modern state. The edicts which followed, establishing a modern system of taxation, a system of universal, compulsory education and a modern currency concluded the government's preparatory period.

Thereafter, the nature of the government's role changed and the task of industrialisation became uppermost. Having no experience of the problems, let alone the pitfalls of such a program, the Meiji reformers decided that it would be unwise for the government to entrust heavy industry and the capitalisation which it required to private enterprise, which, in any case, had no experience of such activities. Accordingly, these functions were handled exclusively by the government in the first decade of modernisation. As T.C. Smith observes, *"Government ownership and management of industry was a salient feature of the early Meiji period and was partly the result of the new government's inheriting the enterprises developed by its predecessors; in extending the principle to new fields of industry the Meiji Government was following Tokugawa example."*[188] The Japanese experience was not unlike that of many governments that have entrusted business activities to their own employees; corruption and bribery rapidly showed their ugly heads. It was for this reason that the government abandoned its early attempt at running business enterprises and handed them over to the Sumitomo, Mitsubishi and Mitsui families, to name but three, to operate.

The sale of these industries to the families who eventually became the controllers of Japan's *zaibatsus* did not see the end of the government's involvement in industry. It was in fact the beginning of that very close association between government and industry which has characterised Japanese history ever since. For the government was still instrumental in directing the overall thrust of the development program, and government contracts for defence equipment and government policies for railway expansion, had a decisive influence on the way in which the zaibatsus developed and the rate at which they developed. As G.C. Allen has remarked: *"The importance of communication had early impressed itself on the minds of Japanese leaders, and by its control of the railways the government provided itself with a powerful means of guiding economic development."*[189]

Lockwood identified three factors in Japan's economic modernisation program which have had great influence on the way in which Japan developed. The first of these is the persistence of the family pattern in the industrial organisation which employs the most advanced technology. The second is the firm grip which the Meiji Rulers exercised in directing the national development towards military expansion. The third was the formation of the ruling oligarchy of *zaibatsus* who inherited a tradition of clan and guild monopoly and thus dominated trade and industry from the start.

The State's role has continued since World War II to be a very important factor in Japan's ascendancy to industrial hegemony of the world. The Ministry for International Trade and Industry and the

---

[188]   Smith, Thomas C., *Political Change and Industrial Development in Japan: Government Enterprise (1868-80)*, Stanford University Press (1955).

[189]   Allen, G.C., *A Short Economic History of Modern Japan (1867-1937)*, MacMillan, London (1981).

Ministry of Finance have continued to spearhead the country's economic development program and to guide the *kereitsu* in their choice of investment. Japan's economic recovery since the war owes much to the concerted efforts of the planners and the industrial leadership of the country. Western observers have commented, almost without exception, on the uniformity of purpose within the nation. The impression given to visitors to Japan is that the country is steadily working towards one goal, namely the greatness of Japan Incorporated. It is this characteristic of the Japanese psyche to co-operate in the pursuit of common objectives that has distinguished Japan's approach to industrialisation from the beginning of the Meiji era.

The second and very significant feature of Japan's modernisation program was her philosophy of self-reliance. The Japanese, as we've seen, were taught by Bismarck at an early stage in their history that the only way by which they could make up the leeway between themselves and the West was by utilising their own resources to the full. The Japanese leadership heeded the German statesman's warning and determined thereafter not to place more reliance than was absolutely necessary on foreign finance. For this reason the Meiji Reformers only contracted two foreign loans during the first twenty-five years of their era of economic modernisation. Japan, in point of fact, relied on funds supplied from local sources, and it was the peasantry who bore the brunt of the costs of the economic modernisation program in the form of the Land Tax. Such was the determination of the Japanese not to be sucked into the vortex of international capitalism. The unequal treaties, with their implied designation of Japanese citizens as second class persons (inasmuch as they did not abide by normally acceptable civilised standards of conduct), was a sufficient insult to Japanese pride. Having been forced to open their doors to trade with the West on terms which the intruders laid down, the Japanese did everything in their power to avoid becoming more embroiled with the hated foreigner than they absolutely had to. This posed a serious problem for them, but it was one which they were able to overcome by relying almost wholly on internal sources of revenue for their modernisation projects.

Japan demonstrated only too well the ability of a people, when given the right leadership, to improve their own material well-being without becoming dependent on foreign investment. The Japanese people did not have all the skills required for modernisation, and so they, like the British, the French, the Germans and the Russians before them, borrowed them from the West and paid for them as they received them. They were not, however, prepared to sacrifice their own independence by heavy borrowing in foreign money markets. Japanese history demonstrates the important principle that a nation can pull itself up by its bootstraps if it has the will to do so. Japan was able to do that because her farmers produced enough food not only to meet their own increasing needs, but the increasing needs of a steadily expanding workforce. The 33% improvement in agricultural output between 1886 and 1913 was due in large measure to the reforms which the government had promulgated between 1877 and 1881. These reforms ensured that Japan was able to feed her steadily expanding population at a time when many of her workers were required to man the new industries. What determines what a nation can do is the level of skill of its people, their willingness to put those skills to work for the good of the community and the capacity of the leadership to direct the energies of the people into mutually constructive channels. Foreign capital is not required.

Japan's refusal to utilise foreign aid in the early years of industrialisation was both prudent and necessary in view of the extremely expansionist attitude of the European Powers. That she felt strong enough after 1894/5 to risk contracting foreign loans, was due to her increasing self-confidence as a nation. Indeed, in the years leading up to the Great War, Japan relied very heavily on foreign sources of capital to finance the development of her heavy industries. The war saved her from economic dependency, not only because foreign investment virtually dried up, but because it enabled Japan to enter markets which had hitherto been a European preserve and thus generate the funds to pay her debts. Never since then have the Japanese allowed themselves to become heavily indebted to foreign nations. During the 1920s, foreign investment was restricted to one-twentieth of national investment. The military rearmament program of the 1930s was funded to a large extent from foreign sources, but Japan was now strong enough to be able to afford this method of finance. Similar policies of self-reliance have marked Japan's post-war recovery, the funds for which have been largely supplied internally.

Japan's policy in regard to foreign investment has served her well. It has enabled her to keep at arms length the foreign powers whose predatory commercial instincts she had every reason to fear. It has also enabled her to prove to herself that she could modernise her economy without external financial aid from countries that had already trodden the path of industrialisation.

In view of the problems which have beset those nations which have depended heavily on overseas funds for the development of their economic potential, Japanese policy appears to have been very wise. It is significant that, with the exception of the United States of America, a substantial portion of whose capital investment was supplied from Europe, most countries that have industrialised successfully have done so without heavy dependence on foreign loans. Britain, France and Germany to a large extent shouldered the burden themselves. The Soviet Union, having repudiated the debts of the Tsarist government, was obliged to go it alone. China, since 1949, has trodden a similar path. The history of the Latin American countries in this respect offers considerable evidence in support of the contention that reliance on foreign investment is a highly dangerous policy, which is fraught with problems for the borrower as well as having uncertain risks for the lender.

A further factor in Japan's modernisation program which deserves examination was her desire to see the unequal treaties repudiated. The tariff restriction clauses in those treaties the Japanese found most galling, and they did all in their power to get them abolished as soon as they could. Nevertheless, in spite of the fact that they were not permitted by the western powers to impose duties in excess of 5% on imported merchandise, Japan was able during the Meiji period to lay the foundations of her modern economy. Whether she would have been able to do this more rapidly if she had been able to erect higher tariff barriers, is a matter for conjecture. It may well be argued that low tariffs stimulated her businessmen to buy foreign machinery so that they could compete with the cheap imported products on even terms. Certainly it was the textile industry that provided one of the major pillars of Japanese commerce in the first fifty years of industrialisation. A quarter of the Japanese industrial work-force was employed in textile manufacture in the first two decades of the twentieth century, a factor which contributed in no small way to Japan's ability to seize markets, hitherto closed to them during, the Great War.

Protectionism, however, certainly did assist the growth of Japan's heavy industry from 1911 onwards. The latter had been established in response to the government's desire to make the country self-sufficient in the production of defence equipment. It was therefore very largely maintained at government behest. Moreover, because a number of heavy industries continued to be state owned and controlled, the government was able to insist on all contracts for heavy plant and equipment being placed with local business enterprises when the latter had the capacity to produce the goods. Moreover, the close association between the government and the *zaibatsus* ensured that no contracts were placed with foreign firms if the work could be done by Japanese business houses. The principles of *"laissez-faire"* capitalism, of buying in the cheapest market and selling in the dearest, did not interest the Japanese. Considerations of national honour, national pride and the national economy over-rode economic theory. Politics was more important than economics insofar as the Japanese were concerned. Heavy industry in Japan increasingly owed its successful expansion to the government's tariff policy. In this respect, Japan was no different from America, Germany, France, Russia and Britain during the Mercantilist period, all of whom had gone through the process of industrialisation behind high tariff barriers.

From the earliest stages in their modernisation epoch the Japanese recognised the importance of education. Two years after Gladstone's government belatedly made education in Britain universal and compulsory the Japanese did the same. Inheriting from the Tokugawa period a substantial degree of literacy in the community at large, the Japanese set about the task of making the nation literate. This remarkable decision for a country as isolated and backward as Japan then was and as lacking in appropriately trained personnel, not to mention facilities, says much about the character of the leadership in Japan during the Meiji Revolution.

The Japanese have always been a very curious people, ready and willing to imitate other nations when they consider it to be to their advantage. Throughout history, Japanese cultural and intellectual life owed much to China. Indeed, many of the skills which the Japanese had learned before the coming of the Europeans, they had acquired from the Chinese, namely writing, porcelain manufacture, silk processing and sword making. When the Europeans arrived in the seventeenth century, the Japanese acquired the art of making firearms from them. When in 1868, the young emperor, Mitsuhito, came to the throne, he quickly told his people that: *"Intellect and learning should be sought for throughout the world in order to establish the foundation of Empire."*[190] Japan's modern day success is in no small measure due to the readiness with which her people have heeded his advice. In the early days of modernisation, the Japanese engaged many European

---

[190]   Bergamini, David, *Japan's Imperial Conspiracy*, Granada, London (1976).

technicians and engineers to assist them with the development of their industry, agriculture, banking and commerce. Some of the assistance given proved unsatisfactory, particularly in the field of agriculture, where European experts sent out to advise the Japanese had very little experience of paddy field farming. Gradually, however, the Japanese acquired the scientific techniques of the Europeans and soon established their own expertise in such areas as wet land farming. In the field of machinery manufacture, they were not slow to develop their own equipment, some of which they even sold to the British. Their subsequent record in the field of technological development needs no elaboration.

Early in her modern history, Japan had to come to terms with the fact that her islands were not well endowed with natural resources, minerals in particular. Coal and copper made up the bulk of the nation's mineral deposits. Zinc, lead and silver deposits were also found. Japan, however, has almost no nickel, cobalt, bauxite, nitrates, rock salt, potash, phosphates or oil. Her lack of natural resources, however, has been more than compensated for by the resourcefulness of her people and has therefore never acted as a brake on her determination to modernise her economy. The Japanese simply took a leaf out of Britain's book, and became an importer of raw materials and an exporter of manufactured goods. In so doing they demonstrated to the world that natural resource deficiencies are no impediment to national economic development.

Japan's economic modernisation is an excellent example of managerial macro-economics in action. Understanding the world in which they lived, visualising the role which they wanted their country to play in the modern world, developing the goals towards which they wished to aspire were the initial tasks in the process of development. Having determined where they were going, the next task was to delineate a strategy according to which they could modernise the nation and industrialise the economy. By identifying and concentrating on the key tasks, agriculture, education and transport, Japan was able to raise herself within the short space of one hundred years from a state of semi-feudal isolation to become a modern industrial economy. No mean feat!

The fundamental question must now be both asked: Why did Japan succeed where China failed?

Economic historians have searched for reasons to explain China's failure to modernise. Where Japan succeeded so well, China failed so miserably. Moulder argues that China had been brought into the world economy at an earlier stage than Japan and that therefore she ceased to be able to exercise effective control over her own economic development.[191] The hypothesis, however, lacks credibility. Nations do not suddenly lose control of their own affairs or their own destiny, because they trade with other nations. The fact that China had been trading with the West for longer than Japan simply proves that China had been open to foreign influences for longer.

Feuerwerker in his study of China's early industrialisation program identifies seven reasons for her failure:[192]

1) China did not develop an agricultural surplus as did Japan.

2) The Chinese merchant and bureaucratic classes were not motivated to embark on risk-taking, entrepreneurial activity of the kind that Japan engaged in so successfully.

3) Chinese domestic industry was unable to win back the domestic market from foreign domination as Japanese manufacturers had done.

4) Western technology and organisational forms were successfully taken over by Japan but not by China.

5) The role of the Ch'ing (Manchu) government was largely ineffective so far as modernisation was concerned, whereas in Japan it was critical.

6) The Meiji Reformers' Land Tax was crucial to ensure the effective flow of funds to the central government for the latter to carry out its program of industrialisation.

7) In Japan, the silk industry was controlled and standardised by the government through various agencies. In China, no such centralised control was attempted. China's peasant economy remained backward and tradition bound, consequently her share of world markets declined, whereas Japan's increased.

Immanuel H.Y. Hsu in his study of Modern China considers that there were six factors which led to the failure of the Self-Strengthening movement, China's early attempt at reform.[193]

---

[191]   Moulder, F.V., *Japan, China and the Modern World Economy. Towards a Re-interpretation of East Asian Development*, C.U.P. (1977).

[192]   Feuerwerker, Albert, *China's Early Industrialization*, Harvard University Press (1958).

1)   The lack of co-ordination between the provinces and the central authority. Regionalism, he argues, was stronger than the central government, a sign of the decay of the empire. A man such as Li Hung Cheng, who was only a provincial governor, was responsible for more reforms in the early days than any other official of either the central or the provincial governments.

2)   The limited vision of the reformers, whose aim was to strengthen the existing order, not to modernise the nation.

3)   Shortage of capital.

4)   The imperialist escapades of the foreign powers which forced China to engage in expensive defensive efforts.

5)   Only men of second rate ability were associated with modernisation. Traditional Chinese attitudes of superiority towards the outside world prevented the nation from taking stock of its own position objectively.

6)   Technical backwardness and moral degradation.

Both Feuerwerker and Hsu put their fingers on the fundamental malady of China in the latter part of the nineteenth century. Feuerwerker sees it as the lack of positive direction by government. Hsu describes it as a lack of real vision on the part of the leadership which resulted in a desire to strengthen the old order, rather than to modernise the nation, a deficiency which owed its strength to traditional Chinese attitudes of superiority to the rest of the world.

The striking fact about the Japanese was that the progressives, who realised that Japan could no longer continue to resist the efforts of the European Powers to force her to enter into commercial and diplomatic relations with them, and who, therefore, decided that the country must unite and modernise its political, economic and military structure, managed to secure power and to retain it. In China, the men of progressive stamp, men such as Prince Chung, who was the leader of the government in the 1860s, and Tseng Kuo Fang, the high-minded, public-spirited Confucian official who was very largely responsible for the suppression of the T'ai P'ing rebellion, never succeeded in acquiring total control of the reins of power and directing the nation towards the goals of modernisation and industrialisation.

---

[193]   Hsu, Immanuel Chung-Yueh, *The Rise of Modern China*, Oxford University Press, New York (1970).

The fundamental reason for China's failure, however, must be laid at the feet of its *de facto* ruler, the Dowager Empress Tzu Hsi, whose infant son assumed the throne in 1860. Thereafter, for the next forty-eight years, Tzu Hsi was the effective ruler of the country. It was she who decided which of the imperial offspring was to succeed to the throne, and she who, either overtly or covertly, dominated the government of China for the better part of half a century. Born in 1835, she was only twenty-five years of age when she took effective control of the country. Guided by men of real vision and perception of world affairs, her reign might have become as noted for its brilliance as that of her Japanese counterpart, Mitsuhito. Tragically for China the men of progressive stamp, who recognised that some measure of reform was necessary, lacked the breadth of vision and the depth of understanding of the vast changes which had taken place in the western world, and, consequently , were unable to put China on the road to economic advancement. Imbued with the spirit of Confucianism, convinced of the superiority of Chinese institutions of government, and of the importance of the Confucian ethic, they were too blind to see the need for a radical approach to the process of modernisation such as Japan underwent in the first five years of the Meiji era.

It was this total lack of real understanding of the problem that prevented China from developing in the way that Japan did. Occupying the land mass of eastern Asia as they had done for centuries, enclosed behind their protective fortress, the Great Wall, from the invasion of less civilised peoples, enjoying a level of culture and civilisation which, until the middle of the eighteenth century, rivalled that of any other in the world, it was very difficult for them to appreciate the vast strides which scientific discovery and the acquisition of technological power had conferred on the western nations. Their initial appreciation, that the West had stolen the advantage militarily, and all that China had to do was to modernise her armed forces and equip them with up-to-date weapons, fell far short of the mark. When in the 1870s, it was increasingly recognised that commercial and industrial might lay behind the West's rise to ascendancy, the Chinese leadership continued to show a marked reluctance to adopt any measures of reform, let alone a root and branch modernisation of the kind which Japan underwent so successfully.

As the history of Japan shows, it would have been quite possible for the Chinese to have retained the old institutions of their society, the emperor, the bureaucracy, and the principles of government according to which their country had been governed for two millennia. For the Japanese not only retained their emperor, but made him the centre of power in the new state. Japan, moreover, suffered the added disadvantage of having to abolish her feudal system of government. The Chinese, thanks to their first emperor, had stolen the march on the Japanese in that regard, having abolished feudalism some two millennia previously and established a central government which, when it functioned effectively, was unsurpassed by any other administration in the world. The principal problem with China in the nineteenth century was that the imperial system of government was once again in decline. Corruption was rampant at all levels of the bureaucracy. The competitive examination system continued to supply men of ability, and in some cases men of integrity, for the senior posts in government, but the world of learning was quite incapable of producing another Confucius, another Mencius or another Lao Tzu. So far as the Chinese were concerned, these men had said all that needed to be said on such subjects as philosophy, politics and government. Little, if anything, of real ingenuity or originality had been said since. The great movements of European culture had passed the Chinese by. When the clash between the two civilisations really made itself felt and Chinese inferiority was so clearly demonstrated, the Chinese failed to appreciate its true significance.

Worse still for China, the dynasty was unable to provide men of the calibre of K'ang-hsi or Ch'ien Lung, the two great emperors which China had produced in the seventeenth and eighteenth centuries, to rule the nation in that critical second half of the nineteenth century. The Dowager Empress, for all her considerable ability and force of personality, lacked the self-assurance and the conviction to lead the country forward in the direction in which it should have gone. Shrewd, cunning and unscrupulous in her dealings with the members of her court and her government, she was content, so long as the dynasty and her own personage were safe, to play the progressive element in Chinese society - those who were willing to adopt western science and technology whilst preserving the system of government and the ethics of traditional Confucian Chinese society - against the conservatives - those who resisted any kind of modernisation. For thirty-five years, she presided over a China which was steadily, under her malign influence, becoming more and more corrupt and decadent, a fact which was forcefully brought home to the Chinese when the nation suffered its worst humiliation ever at the hands of the Japanese in 1895. Even after that fiasco, the Empress continued to play her old game of Machiavellian power politics, oblivious of the real needs of the nation. Not until the disaster of the Boxer Rebellion reinforced the appalling weakness of the nation, and western warships appeared on China's inland waterways, did the empress see the folly of her ways. By then it was too late! The reforms which should have been carried through forty years previously were finally authorised and China moved forward toward modern nationhood. But the revolutionary movement was gaining ground fast and the Empress had made no provision for anyone of real ability to succeed her, with the result that when the dynasty collapsed, China once again entered a period of warlordism from which she only finally escaped when Mao Tse Tsung took over the helm in 1949.

Feuerwerker cites a number of other factors in Japan's favour and against China, but none of these has any real weight when compared to the failure of the Chinese government to appreciate the real significance of the situation in the 1860s.[194] For if China had had the men of vision and perception that Japan had in positions of power, she would have enjoyed the same quality of leadership that Japan experienced and her merchants, who showed themselves quite resourceful in the 1880s and 90s in setting up modern textile mills, developing coal mines and providing the basis of an engineering industry, would have moved into the modern manufacturing sector sooner. But the lack of support given to industry, both psychologically and financially, was a serious blow to Chinese entrepreneurs, on top of which the attitude of the bureaucracy, which regarded the industrial enterprise as an alien import unworthy of a great nation such as China, was a further impediment to progress. Given the kind of entrepreneurial spirit which the Chinese have shown, both in their homeland and in the countries of south-east Asia to which they have migrated, there was no reason why the nation should not have been able, given sound government support, to supplant imported textiles with locally produced goods and take over the market from overseas suppliers, as, indeed, China did when the Great War broke out in Europe. There was intrinsically no reason why the Chinese, any more than any other Asian nation, should not have taken over western science and technology successfully. The Chinese were just as capable of doing this, as indeed they have shown since 1949, as any other nation. China's fundamental

---

[194]   Feuerwerker, Albert, *China's Early Industrialization*, Harvard University Press (1958).

weakness was the paralysis of her government. Given the kind of leadership which Japan had in the latter part of the nineteenth century, China would have re-established her position in the world much sooner.

In the middle of the nineteenth century the economies of China and Japan had reached approximately the same level of technical advance, Japan having borrowed from China when it suited her purposes. Neither had had much contact with the western world, though a few able men in both countries were aware that the West had stolen the march on them. Both countries were made forcibly aware of that fact, China through defeat in the Opium War, Japan through Commodore Perry's mission. Both countries went through a period of intense ferment and even Civil War, though the latter was a far more serious affair in China than in Japan. But whereas in Japan the men of perception and vision, the men who understood the extent of the gulf which the progress of science and technology had opened up between industrialised societies and pre-industrialised societies, came to power determined to close the gap, in China, no such men came to the fore. Those progressives who did appreciate that their country was no longer the world's cultural and technical leader, failed to appreciate the immense advantage which the industrial revolution had made to the West. Their failure led to China's becoming one of the most backward nations on earth in the twentieth century.

China's failure to modernise her economy in the late nineteenth century is further proof of the basic premise of this work, namely, that what determines what a nation can do is the level of skill and technical advancement which its people have reached or have the capacity to reach given the existing state of knowledge. What determines whether they will utilise their energies to obtain optimum performance is the quality of the leadership of the nation as a whole. There are only two requirements for leadership, character and performance. In China's case, both were lacking. In Japan's case, the capacity of the nation to accomplish the remarkable transition from the feudal era of the Tokugawa Shogunate to the industrial society of the later years of the Emperor Meiji's reign demonstrated beyond doubt the ability of the leaders to perform. There was intrinsically no reason why China, properly led, should not have performed just as well as, indeed, even better than, her rival, Japan. What China lacked was leadership, and for that she paid very dearly.

If anything, China's natural resources placed her at a far greater advantage to Japan insofar as industrialisation was concerned. Had she begun the task of development thirty years earlier, she would easily have outstripped Japan in the race towards modernisation. She failed, not for lack of capital. No nation ever suffers from a shortage of capital, for the real capital of a country is its assets, and its greatest assets are not its natural resources, but its people. The Japanese tackled the problem of financing industrialisation by means of the Land Tax. If the Chinese had carried out the same far-reaching agricultural reforms as the Japanese, they would not only have been able to feed the rural masses satisfactorily, but would have had a sufficient surplus to meet the needs of their industrial workers. China had the people and had she tackled the problem of education at the same early stage as the Japanese, she would have progressed towards economic maturity at a much greater rate than she did. China's sad fate was determined by the ineptitude and follies of her leadership.

8 The Jewish Influence on Economic Thought

"The Jews have a singular ability to take hold of history and of ideas and to shake them profoundly .... Moses ... Jesus ... Marx ... Freud ... Einstein ... such Jews have had a vast impact and influence on the affairs of mankind. That influence has endured, as with Moses and Jesus, over millennia. Because of what the Jews were meant to be some Jews touch history and culture and ideas in ways that affect the lives of millions. "[195] McCandlish Phillips

Kenneth Galbraith once remarked that the Economics profession was dominated by Jews and Scotsmen.[196] The economic theory of the most influential Scotsman, Adam Smith, specifically that relating to the role of the State in the economic development process has been the subject of much of the criticism of this work. The purpose of this chapter is to examine the ideas of four of the most influential economists: Ricardo, Marx, Friedman and Samuelson, all of whom are Jewish by lineage if not by religious conviction.

DAVID RICARDO

Ricardo's Principles of Economics still enjoys considerable repute among academic economists today as one of the first attempts to reduce economic thought to a set of principles.[197] Many of Ricardo's ideas, however, have been discarded with the lapse of time, the Iron Law of

---

195   McCandlish Phillips, *The Bible, the Supernatural and the Jews*, Bethany Press, Chicago (1984), p.281.

196   Galbraith, John Kenneth, *Prophets and Priests of Capitalism*, Film.

197   Ricardo, David, *The Principles of Political Economy and Taxation*, Dent, London (1969).

Wages being one of them. The pessimism which beclouds so much of the thinking of the early nineteenth century Classical Economists has not been justified by history. As Roger Waud has phrased it: *"No one really believes in the Iron Law of Wages today in the advanced industrial countries, for a variety of reasons, wage levels are well above subsistence level for the great majority of workers."*[198]

Ricardo's theory of comparative advantage, however, still occupies pride of place in the modern economic textbook, as Waud demonstrates: *"The argument for free trade based on the principle of comparative advantage is one of the most solid cornerstones of economic analysis. No other issue seems to command such unanimous agreement among economists as the case for free trade."*[199] Yet no economic theory has been more freely breached by nations than the Classical Economists' doctrine of Free Trade. The realities of life are that - city states excepted since they have to take the world as they find it - no nation in history has ever industrialised other than behind high tariff barriers.

Great Britain raised duties on a series of imported goods during the Marlborough Wars against France as a means of raising revenue to defray the expenses of the War. When, however, the Treaty of Utrecht was signed in 1713, the British government did not ratify the commercial clauses in the document because they realised that France enjoyed a technological and, therefore, a cost advantage in the manufacturing field. Accordingly, tariffs between the two countries remained in place, until, in the wake of the wave of liberalisation which swept Britain and France seventy years later, the Eden Treaty was signed. By 1786, the boot was on the other foot. Great Britain, owing to the remarkable technological breakthrough which her artisans and mechanics had made in the previous fifteen years, had established a significant economic advantage, particularly in the field of cotton goods which were of higher quality and lower price than their French counterparts. The consequence of the significant tariff reductions which accompanied the signing of the Eden Treaty, was the destruction of a significant portion of the French manufacturing industry. Yet one more group of malcontents was added to the flames of discontent which were to engulf France in Revolution three years later. The quarter century of conflict which followed saw the re-imposition of trade barriers between

---

[198] Waud, Hocking, Maxwell & Bonnici, *Economics*, Harper & Row, Sydney (1992), p.849.
[199] Ibid.

the two countries, the most notable of which was Napoleon's Continental System in 1806.

In 1820, however, there occurred an event which would have shaken Adam Smith to his marrow, an event which David Thomson, the English historian of nineteenth century Britain records in the following words:

"The London Merchants presented Parliament with a petition which embodied principles that were to win ascendancy in economic policy during the next forty years. Two of the most important of these were: That freedom from restraint is calculated to give the utmost extension to foreign trade, and the best direction to the capital and industry of the country; that the maxim of buying in the cheapest market and selling in the dearest which regulated every merchant in his individual dealings, is strictly applicable as the best rule for the trade of the whole nation. These principles which had been laid down forty-four years previously by Adam Smith in "The Wealth of Nations" were now to reform British commercial and fiscal policy. Their results, in combination are usually called 'the free trade movement'." [200] Throughout the 1820s and 30s successive Chancellors of the Exchequer gradually reduced and finally abolished many of the impediments that Britain hitherto had contended with.

The great era of Free Trade in British history, however, was not ushered in until the 1840s, when the British Parliament abolished three statutes which up to that time had placed severe restrictions on trade and industry. The first of these legislative rescindments was the act prohibiting the export of machinery. Parliament repealed the legislation in 1842. The significance of this step has not been sufficiently appreciated, for it was the invention of machinery which more than any other development had given the British the lead in the field of engineering. By legalising the export of machinery, the British were denying themselves the benefits of the unique advantage which they had acquired for themselves by being first in the field. It now became possible for other nations to import the latest British technology and compete with the British at their own game. British machinery manufacturers, however, saw no reason why trade liberalisation should not benefit them as much as it had their counterparts in the textile industry. Accordingly, they campaigned for repeal and won the day.

---

[200]   Thomson, David, *England in the Nineteenth Century*, Penguin Books (1950), p.77.

The second legislative rescindment which heralded the dawn of Free Trade was the abolition of the Corn Laws by Parliament in 1846. In spite of the Agrarian Revolution which England experienced in the eighteenth century and the improvement in crop yields which rotation, the abolition of strip farming and the introduction of new seeds brought, Britain was unable to feed herself. A rapidly growing population on an island with limited resources had placed the British in a position of dependence on foreign producers. The landed interest in the country, aware of the threat to their livelihood if unrestrained competition was permitted, enacted the Corn Laws in 1815. The legislation provided an elaborate mechanism for the control of the import of corn when food was scarce, and for its restriction in years of plenty. A sliding scale of tariffs permitted imports when domestic prices rose; when they fell, imports were restricted and in some cases prohibited altogether. The Act, however, was readily circumvented, not least by the merchants whose propensity to hoard corn when it was cheap, and only release it on to the market when it would fetch a high price was a feature of pre-industrial society. The creation of these local monopolies, with which readers of Thomas Hardy's novel, *"The Mayor of Casterbridge"*, will be familiar, would only be effectively overcome once railways covered the island and national markets were truly integrated. It was malpractices such as these, together with the growing conviction in the manufacturing communities that liberalisation would be better for all concerned, that led to the formation in 1839 of the Anti-Corn Law League. The event which triggered the repeal of the Corn Laws, however, was the Irish potato famine which began in 1845. The Free Traders, however, did not win a complete victory, for a duty of one shilling a bushel continued to be levied on all imported corn.

The third piece of legislation whose repeal may be cited as marking the end of the Mercantilist era were the Navigation Acts. More than any other legislative enactment, the Navigation Acts embodied the principles and ideas on which the Mercantilist philosophy was based. First effectively enacted in the Cromwellian era, and then re-enacted in the reign of Charles II, when the English were experiencing significant competition from Dutch commerce, the legislation was designed to protect English shipping by ensuring that, in time of peace, the nation could handle its own trade in its own vessels, and that in time of war, it would have available a fleet which it could use for military purposes. At the time of enactment, the commercial clauses in the legislation were considered to be of equal importance to the military ones. For over a century, the legislation was enforced as rigidly as governmental capability permitted. Britain's increasing wealth, along with the desire on the part of the commercial classes in the country for their relaxation, led eventually to their final abrogation in 1849 and 1854.

It is vitally important from the point of view of this argument that we should understand why it was that Britain, in the middle of the nineteenth century should have opted for the liberalisation of trade. In formulating his great thesis in the 1770s, Smith had entertained considerable doubts about the willingness of the mercantile and manufacturing interests in the nation to agree to an open door trading policy. Yet, fifty years later, as we've seen, these same groups were petitioning Parliament to abolish those very restrictions on trade which their forefathers so strongly defended. The answer is to be found in the rapid strides which British industry took in the last quarter of the eighteenth century and the first quarter of the nineteenth century. This economic advance was achieved, as we've seen, against the background of Mercantilist policies, and had nothing to do with the principles of *"laissez-faire"* capitalism as embodied in the liberal creed espoused by Adam Smith and the Classical Economists. It was not ideological commitment to the doctrine of Free Trade which made Britain great, but her mastery of technology. It was technological innovation that placed Britain ahead of her European and American rivals and that led to that vast economic expansion in the nineteenth century that resulted in 1897 in the British Empire covering a quarter of the globe. It is important to realise here that Britain only became a free trading nation once the initial impetus of industrialisation, symbolised by the Great Exhibition of 1851, had provided the nation with a very comfortable advantage over its rivals. Britain did not adopt the classical economic doctrine, as espoused by Smith, until her economic hegemony was well established, and she did so then only because it was in her interests to do so.

It has been remarked, in reference to the theory of comparative advantage, that: *"it is believed in only by those who will gain an advantage from it. In each era the rules for international economic relations are moulded to suit the views of the country that is the most powerful."*[201] These words exactly describe the position which Great Britain, then the Workshop of the World, enjoyed in the middle of the nineteenth century. No other nation in history, not even the United

---

[201]   Robinson, Joan, *The New Mercantilism, Collected Economic Papers*, Vol.4., Basil Blackwell, Oxford (1973), p.1.

States of America in 1945 enjoyed such an immense advantage as the British did in 1850. They were, without any doubt, the leading industrial nation, the leading commercial and economic power on earth, and they could dictate the terms on which they conducted trade with the rest of the world. Free Trade suited them. It was to their advantage, and for that reason they adopted it and kept to it long after the 1880s when the other nations of Europe had given up their very mediocre effort at liberalisation. The British had the technology, they had the markets and they exploited them to their advantage.

Other nations knew that they did not enjoy such advantages and therefore did not adopt similar policies. The United States of America industrialised her economy between the two wars, the American Civil War and the Great War. America enacted tariffs to protect her nascent industries soon after gaining independence in 1783. During the Civil War, duties were raised to 47% on all imported goods. In 1890, President McKinley, a member of the Republican Party, the party of Big Business, increased them to 50%, and seven years later, they were raised once again to 60%. It was the Democrats who, aware that the United States of America had little to lose now that its level of industrialisation enabled Americans to compete with their rivals, the British and the Germans, on more or less equal terms, initiated the process of tariff reduction early in the twentieth century in an attempt to reduce the cost of living. As Paul Samuelson has observed, the United States of America has traditionally been a high tariff barrier country.[202]

Germany, likewise, industrialised behind high tariff barriers. The Zollverein, the German Customs Union, was formed in 1818 to keep British goods out of the still severely politically fragmented German territories. Some reduction of duties did accompany the wave of economic liberalisation which swept Europe in the middle of the nineteenth century. Traditionally, however, economic historians have tended to exaggerate the significance of this so-called 'liberal' epoch in European history. Protectionism, however, returned to Germany in 1879 when Bismarck jettisoned the liberals in the Reichstag in support of the Conservatives. It was to remain the order of the day until the Great War. France and Italy, both of whom were modernising their economies from 1880 onwards, also did so behind high tariff barriers. Russia likewise.

---

[202]   Samuelson, Paul, *Economics*, 13th.ed., McGraw Hill, New York (1989).

Only one country did not erect tariff barriers during the latter part of the nineteenth century. That nation was Japan. The Japanese did not do so because they were not permitted to do so by the terms of the treaties which they had been compelled to sign with the European nations in the 1850s. Those treaties required the Japanese to trade with the world on the terms which the then all-powerful European nations laid down, namely that all goods entering Japan from the outside world were to be subject to a customs duty which was not to exceed 5% of the landed value of the goods. The Japanese chafed under the burden of the *"unequal treaties"*, as they have subsequently described them in their textbooks, but there was nothing that they could do about them until the end of the century. Just as soon as they could secure their abolition, they did so; and Japan, thereafter, industrialised her economy behind tariff barriers. Being the leading industrial nation today, Japan is in a position to adopt economic liberal trading policies. The Japanese, however, have displayed considerable intransigence in adopting such policies. A knowledge of their history, in particular of the way in which they were treated by the European powers in the nineteenth century, goes a long way towards explaining their attitude.

Nor is there any evidence to support the contention that world trade was in any way inhibited by protectionism. Between 1865 and 1913, the era when America, Germany, France, Italy and Russia were all busy modernising their heavily protected economies, world trade increased fivefold. At no time in history had such an unprecedented explosion of commercial activity taken place.

The Great War inevitably caused some dislocation of commercial activity, but trade recovered in the 1920s, and continued to improve until 1929, tariff barriers notwithstanding. It was the Great Depression, as it is commonly called, that witnessed the collapse of international trade. Between 1929 and 1931, world trade fell by 80%, to one-fifth of what it had been before the Depression. Recovery thereafter was steady, and 1929 levels were once again attained in 1939. There is no justification, however, for the view that the *"beggar my neighbour policies"*, adopted by the industrial nations in the wake of the Great Depression, inhibited recovery. Galbraith et al, however, who criticise the Smoot-Hartley tariff which the United States of America imposed in 1930, are justified in their criticism, for the United States of America was the world's leading creditor nation in 1930, and the only way by which her creditors could pay back their debts was by trading with her.[203] It ill behoves the *leading* commercial and industrial power to restrict trade, since it has everything to gain from a relaxation of restrictions.

It is frequently alleged that the post-World War II era has seen a liberalisation of world trade, with GATT -the General Agreement on Tariffs and Trade - being heralded as evidence of this. Milton Friedman correctly observes, however, that the post-war era has also seen a significant increase in the quota system of control. More pertinent is the growth on a world-wide scale of trading blocs, the most renowned of which is the European Economic community, the original *"raison d'etre"* for which was fear of America's domination of Western Europe's industry. A similar fear motivated the formation of that very much less successful bloc in the 1960s, the Latin American Free Trade Association. ASEAN, the Association of South-East Asian Nations, is another economic trading bloc, and one which Australia must inevitably take notice of, on account of its proximity to her shores. Trading Blocs, therefore, have become the order of the day in the post-war era, not Free Trade, and it is against that background that the nations of the Third World must formulate their trade policies. Being exporters of raw materials and importers of manufactured goods, they can ill afford the luxury of the theory of comparative advantage.

The history of Australia, which, although not a Third World country in terms of her living standards, nevertheless enjoys a similar trading configuration to that experienced by Third World nations, demonstrates the disadvantages of trading in situations where the terms of trade continually go against the trader. The decline in Australia's terms of trade since 1953 when the index stood at 174 to 1975 when it stood at 100, to 1987 when it stood at 62, amply illustrates this point. For the message conveyed by those statistics is that Australian farmers and mining companies have to sell three times as much produce overseas today as they did in 1953 to buy the same volume of imported goods, machinery etc. That is a luxury which the country cannot go on supporting for ever, no more than it can support present levels of overseas debt indefinitely.

Significantly, there has been no improvement in the balance of payments situation world-wide since the introduction of flexible exchange rates in the early 1970s. Indeed, the evidence clearly indicates a worsening of the trade imbalance situation, thus giving the lie to the

---

[203]   Galbraith, John Kenneth, *The Great Crash*, Penguin, London (1961).

theory, so beloved of today's monetarist economists, that the prices of goods and services and the value of currencies will move to equilibrate the volume of goods and services imported into and exported from any given country. The significant trade surpluses which a nation such as Japan has accumulated and the corresponding fears of economic domination which their enormous economic power has engendered throughout the world, provide abundant evidence of the disutility of equilibrium theory.

Economists are beginning to realise that, on account of the price inelasticity of demand for most, though not all internationally traded products, the J-curve only works when the nations engaging in trade have similar products to sell. The theory of comparative advantage, like its faithful ally and compatriot, *"laissez-faire"*, ignores real world situations. Indeed, it is apt *"to sell at a big discount during periods of major macroeconomic dislocation"*, as Paul Samuleson correctly observes.[204]

" Joan Robinson summarised the argument very well in 1966 when she wrote: *"The economist's case for free trade is deployed by means of a model from which all relevant considerations are eliminated by the assumptions. Each country enjoys full employment. There is no migration of labour, no international investment, however great the differences in the level of profits in different countries may be. At the same time there is perfect mobility and adaptability of factors of production within each country. Perfect competition prevails. Fixed exchange rates are taken for granted. Equality between the values of imports and exports of each large country is quickly established, in the face even of large disturbances, by movements of relative prices brought about through the international monetary mechanism."*[205]

It is well recognised in economic circles that protection comes with a price tag attached to it. It is all too often forgotten, however, that the price which a nation pays is the price of apprenticeship, the price of acquiring those skills which other nations have but which one's own nation does not possess. Every industrialised nation has had to pay that price at some time or other; without paying that price, however, none of the industrial nations would have risen to the heights which they have done. The Third World, Australia included, would do well to remember that.

---

[204] Samuelson, Paul, *Economics*, 13th ed., McGraw Hill, New York (1989).
[205] Robinson, Joan, *The New Mercantilism, Collected Economic Papers*, Vol.4., Basil Blackwell, Oxford (1973), p.1.

The protagonists of Classical Economics, however, fail to recognise that Free Trade, no less than protectionism, comes with a price tag attached to it. The history of the two nations which David Ricardo took as the basis for his original model to demonstrate the theory of comparative advantage, namely Portugal and Britain, illustrates this point very well.[206] Portugal signed a series of free trade treaties with Britain between 1654 and 1702, whereby British goods could enter Portugal duty free, in return for which Portugal received the protection of the British navy, a one-sided arrangement if ever there was one. Modern nations contemplating following the theory of comparative advantage would do well to heed the words of Pombal, Portugal's chief minister who, in 1768, remarked that: *"two thirds of our necessities are now supplied from England. Thus English producers sell and re-sell everything that is needed in our country. The ancient manufactures of Portugal have been destroyed."*[207] They would also do well to ponder the loss of national independence which would almost certainly have been the lot of both the Portuguese and their neighbours, the Spaniards, forty years later if the British had not come to their rescue and evicted the French from their territory. They might also listen to the German economist, Frederick List who observed that *"The attempts which have been made by a single nation which is predominant in wealth and power, go to show us that in this way the prosperity of individual nations is sacrificed, without benefit to mankind in general, for the enrichment of the predominantly manufacturing and commercial nation."*[208] How right Pombal, the statesman, and List, the philosopher, were may be seen not only from the relative positions of Britain and Portugal today, but from those of the United States of America and Australia, exporters of raw materials and importers of manufactured goods, and Japan, an importer of raw materials and exporter of manufactured goods. Nations that allow their manufacturing industries to deteriorate are in grave danger not only of losing the capacity to defend themselves but of sacrificing the one attribute which they prize above all else, namely their own independence.

---

[206] Ricardo, David, *The Principles of Political Economy and Taxation*, Dent, London (1969).

[207] Cipolla, Carlo M., *Before the Industrial Revolution. European Society and Economy 1000-1700*, 2nd. ed., Methuen (1976), p.63.

[208] List, Friedrich, *The National System of Political Economy*, Longmans Green & Co., London (1885).

Economists would do well to remember that Ricardo formulated his theories in the aftermath of the Napoleonic Wars, in the safety and security of the British Isles in the full knowledge that the country which his family had made their home provided perhaps the most secure haven on earth in which to engage in those pursuits which leisured gentlemen of the age were wont to engage, namely, making money on the Stock market, and writing dissertations on Political Economy. *"Under a system of perfectly free commerce,"* he once wrote, *"each country naturally devotes its capital and labour to such employments as are mutually beneficial to each."* In true Smithian fashion, he then went on to explain that *"This pursuit of individual advantage is admirably connected with the universal good of the whole."*[209]In a world devoid of nation states, it is possible to conceive of conditions of perfectly free commerce. In a world in which the number of nation states, each with its own national flag, national currency, national government, national laws and national defence forces, has escalated, with the demise of colonialism and the dismemberment of the old Soviet Union, from 22 before the First World War by a factor in excess of seven, it is difficult, if not impossible, to see conditions of perfectly free commerce emerging.

Empiricists are concerned to explain facts. Persistent trade imbalances, current account deficits and wide scale international indebtedness cannot be explained by means of the Ricardian theory of comparative advantage and its counterpart, David Hume's theory of the monetary regulator. The time, therefore, has come when economists must ask themselves whether the Ricardian theory of comparative cost advantage should not be given similar treatment to that which was meted out to the theory of the Iron Law of Wages. When economists were forced to confront the evidence of steadily increasing real wages, as the nineteenth century progressed steadily into the twentieth century, they quietly allowed the theory to lapse. Economics, after all, claims to be an empirical science, and one of the hallmarks of genuine science is that theories which do not explain facts are discarded.

KARL MARX

Ricardo's greatest critic was Karl Marx. Indeed to understand the intricacies of Marx's thought, one needs to read Ricardo first. Marx

---

[209]   Ricardo, David, Quoted in Samuelson, P., *Economics*, 3rd Australian edition, McGraw Hill, Sydney (1992), p. 531.

was essentially a philosopher, a fact which is born out by the influence which the German philosophical school of Hegel and Fichte exerted on his mind in the form of the concept of dialectical materialism, a concept which lies at the root of all his ideas, economic, as well as philosophical. Marx, however, is remembered today principally for his famous critique of the capitalist system, *"Das Capital"*. It is this work that has moulded the thinking of millions of people around the world, has inspired class hatred, political revolution and the establishment of the one party totalitarian state.

In addition to being a philosopher, economist, lawyer and student of literature, Marx also had a grasp of history, an understanding which enabled him to develop his own unique convictions about the manner in which history would develop. For Marx believed that capitalism and the capitalist society was but a short phase in the history of mankind which had developed as a result of the breakdown of the old feudal system and would in due course be superseded by an entirely different order, namely the socialist system.[210] The downfall of the capitalist system would, argued Marx, only come about as a result of a political revolution, for the bourgeoisie who controlled political power in capitalist society would have to be ejected by violent means. Marx was adamant on this point; he held the complementary view that socialists who believed in the reformist rather than the revolutionary approach were not true social scientists. Although Marx was very deterministic in his thinking, and determinism underlay his whole approach to history, yet he believed passionately in the need for the workers in the industrial state to unite in preparation for the downfall of capitalism. Accordingly, he strongly supported the creation of cells of workers within each factory who, when the time was ripe, would rise up and overthrown the bourgeois government and substitute a proletarian government in its place. The revolution, Marx claimed, would take place in the industrial states first. Thereafter, it would spread throughout the world. Socialism would then be established, but, in course of time, it would give way to a purely communist society. The end result would be a society in which men worked, not for personal gain, pecuniary profit or social advancement, but for the good of the community at large, a society devoid of class antagonisms, in which men and women were rewarded, not according to effort, social standing or economic power, but according to their needs. In short, a materialistic Utopia. Indeed, it is

---

[210]   Freedman, Robert, *Marx on Economics*, Penguin Books (1961).

not unfair to describe Marx's work as but one in a long series of attempts by Europeans to establish paradise on earth.

Revolutionary socialism came to power, not as Marx predicted, in the highly industrialised, literate nations of western Europe, but in the predominantly peasant society of Russia where the scope for political and economic reform by constitutional means had been very largely frustrated by the autocratic government of the Romanovs. The Great War, into which, with extraordinary ineptitude, the last of the Romanovs had plunged the country, made far greater demands on backward Russia's ill-equipped defence forces, her inadequate railway network, and generally low-level of industrialisation than it had on the industrially more prosperous belligerents of western and central Europe. Recognising that the government of Kerensky, which had assumed office in March 1917 on the abdication of the Tsar had failed because its leaders had not taken Russia out of the war, the leader of the Bolsheviks, Lenin, decided immediately after seizing power to cease hostilities. The decision he had to make was indeed a very tough one, for it involved the handing over by the revolutionary government of all the agriculturally productive lands of the Ukraine to the Germans. Lenin, however, recognised that continued fighting was useless, particularly as the peasants were voting with their feet and leaving the army in droves to take up the lands which they now believed would, under the new government, be theirs.

Opposition to Lenin's policy was strong both within and without Russia. In 1918, the position worsened when Civil War broke out and the security of the revolution was jeopardised by the White Russians, who with the help of the Allies, wanted to restore a government in Russia which would further Allied War aims. The situation required strong measures both political and economic. A wholesale nationalisation program, known as war communism and dictated more by military necessity than economic need, was forced through. All industrial undertakings of any size and most agricultural land was brought under State control. The ensuing breakdown of the economy was catastrophic. By 1921, agricultural output had dropped to a half of what it had been in 1913, cattle stock was reduced to a third of what it had been, and other livestock were similarly effected. A drought in the lower Volga region in 1920 exacerbated the problem and resulted in the loss of five million lives. Industrial output was even more seriously effected. Steel production was a mere 5% of pre-war figures, coal was little better at 10% and manufactured consumer goods only one seventh of what they had been. The railway network was so severely damaged as to be almost unusable. The Great War, Civil War and famine cost Russia one sixth of her total population.

A crisis of this order called for resolute action; Lenin supplied it. Conceding that war communism had failed, he developed an alternative strategy based on the concept of State Capitalism and known to history as the New Economic Policy. In a country such as Russia, where the peasantry constituted over three quarters of the population, and where bourgeois capital had never developed on the scale on which it had in the west, there could be no direct transition to socialism. Compromise between the ruling proletariat and the peasantry was essential for the survival of the revolution. Accordingly, Lenin decreed the abolition of the practice of requisitioning grain and the re-establishment of a market economy for agricultural produce. Russia's first experiment with socialism had failed!. Although he was defeated on the agricultural front, Lenin, nevertheless, did manage to retain control of the large industrial enterprises. Indeed, only 5% of the output of the industrial sector remained in private hands. The remainder was subject to State control and direction, including the all important areas of banking and finance, transport and foreign trade. Under the new policy, a steady improvement in the indices of economic output became apparent until, by 1927, five years after Lenin's death, the economy had returned to pre-war production levels.

In the course of the next fifty years, the Russian economy grew at a very rapid rate from a very low level of productive output. In 1928, Russia could still be regarded as one of the backward countries of the world. Her industrial output was negligible in comparison with such countries as America, Britain, Germany or France. The standard of living of her peoples was still miserably low when compared to that enjoyed by most other Europeans, particularly the British, the Germans and even the French. Whilst agriculturally, she had recovered from the worst effects of the war and the drought, her methods of production were still very primitive when compared to more advanced societies. Industrially, her output was minimal. Yet, within twenty years, she was able, almost single-handedly to inflict defeat on Nazi Germany and thereafter to go on to establish herself as one of the two leading military and industrial powers in the world.

The Russian experiment is of considerable interest to the student of comparative economics as it was the first attempt by any nation in modern times to adopt the *"planned"* approach to the task of economic development. Stalin's First Five Year Plan arose out of the need to safeguard the country from external aggression, as he put it, "make socialism safe in one country". The Russians, however, have adopted the imperative planning technique ever since. In a country with a long tradition of political centralisation and autocratic government, imperative planning has its advantages, particularly in the circumstances of the 1930s when Russia needed to be placed on a war footing. Heavy criticism has been levelled at the Soviet system of imperative planning by western economists. Merchandise, it is said, is of poor quality, specifications for raw materials and intermediate parts are inadequate, stock-holdings are too large, managements frequently overstate their requirements for labour and materials, prices are too inelastic, since they are based on the Marxian theory of surplus value rather than on scarcity factors, performance measures are inadequate, because they only pay attention to gross output, the absence of profit as an economic yardstick poses problems for the measurement of the effective use of resources; alterations to plan are apt to create chaos in the administrative system. Ministries are always anxious to start projects, knowing that funds will always be made available for their completion. The list is almost endless. Yet, there is nothing in it which would be new to the managing director of a large multi-national western based company, other than the observation about the absence of profit as an economic performance indicator. The capitalist economy is just as capable of turning out poor quality merchandise, specifications for material are frequently inadequate, managers are guilty of over-ordering and over-stocking and prices can be just as inelastic under a market economy as in a planned economy.

The greatest problem with the planned economy is the high degree of centralisation inherent in the planning process. With the passing of time, the Russians have realised the need for decentralisation and they have accordingly divested the ministerial head offices in Moscow of some functions and left them to the provincial governments and other regional bodies to handle. Nevertheless, the sheer problems of size, of attempting to plan gross output for around 20,000 commodity groups, and the informational uncertainties entailed, are a much greater and a much more serious problem when a *nation* is trying to plan its future requirements than it is for a multi-national company. The scale of operations is such that a three-tier bureaucratic planning system is required; even then breakdowns in production and delivery schedules frequently occur, causing chaos.

For all its short-comings, however, the Russian technique of imperative planning has served the nation well, as the record of industrialisation and the production of producer goods has demonstrated all too clearly. The state has played a critical role in the economic development of modern Russia from the time of Peter the Great to the present day. Stalin's monumental achievements in the 1930s, a time when the western capitalist nations were attempting to recover from the vicissitudes of the great Depression are a poignant testimony to the thesis that economic development is most effective when governments determine the objectives to which the nation should orientate its energies, and then delineate strategies in accordance with those objectives. The Russian achievement of the middle decades of the twentieth century, the scale of the industrial effort in the 1930s, the military achievements of the Great Patriotic War, as the Russians have described the Second World War, and the continued industrialisation of the country since the war can best be understood in these terms. The Russian state's great failing, a fact which has become all too apparent in the 1980s with *"perestroika"* and *"glasnost"*, is its inability to satisfy demand for consumer goods. What the Russian experiment has demonstrated all too clearly is that, while the state has a very positive role to play in the promotion of economic development, both managerial and regulatory, as will be seen later, it cannot usurp the function of the market. The ordinary day to day transactions of life necessitate the operation of a market system.

Marx dreamed of a society in which there would be only one class, the proletariat, which he envisaged would eliminate the feudal aristocracy and the bourgeoisie and take over the reins of government. The classless society which would emerge from the revolution would know nothing of the advantages of privilege, rank, heredity, wealth or social position. The fruits of productive enterprise would be available to all according to their need, and not according to their social position or economic status. The Soviet Union, as it used to be called, knew nothing of the classless society; rather, it was a society in which the privileged, the members of the Communist Party, the only political organisation, enjoy not only the perquisites of political power, but the not inconsiderable economic advantages that go along with those positions, cars, country houses, seaside villas and luxury flats in cities. The elite in the modern Communist State are those who enjoy political power or whose contribution to the state is of such a high order that they warrant inclusion amongst the top social and economic strata. The route to wealth and power is through the ranks of the party hierarchy. Not surprisingly, there is evidence that corruption is even more rampant in Russia today than it is in our highly decadent western society.

Marx dreamed of a society in which the principle of *"from each according to his ability, to each according to his need"* would be the operative factor. The State, he claimed, would ultimately wither away and the need for money be entirely superseded. Neither in Russia nor China nor any other Marxist state has there been any tendency for the State to wither away. On the contrary, the State is as much in evidence today as it has ever been. The perfectibility of man, that hoary old dogma of the more Utopian socialists is no basis for the erection of a political theory, yet alone a nation state. Men are neither perfect nor perfectible. Nor is avarice, as Marx was inclined to suppose, the perquisite of the bourgeois class. Greed and the passion for material possessions are attributes of all classes of humanity, as Marx would have known had he listened to the Founder of Christianity. The principle that men should be rewarded for their efforts is the basis on which pecuniary emoluments are made in both the Communist as well as the capitalist world. Unionists in capitalist states and workers in socialist states are every bit as ready to preserve the principle of the wage differential for more arduous work or work with greater responsibility.

Marx has been criticised as the man all of whose predictions have proved false. Whether that is true or not is irrelevant. For the all-important prediction which he made concerning the occurrence of the revolution in Britain proved totally erroneous. It is important that we ask ourselves why the great philosopher was so far wrong in this, one of his most important beliefs. Marxists have long been divided about their mentor's teaching on the conditions of the working classes. Some have argued that Marx believed that they would steadily worsen, i.e. that there would be a decline in the absolute share of the workers in the national cake. Others have argued that what Marx meant was that the workers' share of an increasing national income would decrease. Whichever way we interpret Marx, he was wrong, and disastrously so! For nineteenth century England witnessed a steady, though not uninterrupted improvement in the standards of living of the English people. Twentieth century economists, particularly those of the Classical School, are apt to attribute this phenomenon to the untrammelled operations of the free market system. Technological innovation, contrary to the expectations of the nineteenth century

Classical Economists, outstripped population growth in the long run, with the result that standards of living rose, albeit slowly. For those who have a naive faith in the operations of the market system, such an explanation may well be acceptable. They fail, however, to take account of the very real role played by governments, through the social legislation which they enacted, in improving the lot of the ordinary people. *"Laissez-faire"* was not a policy which British governments in the nineteenth century paid much attention to. The English Social Historian of the period, G.M. Trevelyan,[211] has emphasised the vitally important role of the reform movement in English society in the nineteenth century, a movement which drew its inspiration, not from Adam Smith and his disciples who taught that the pursuit of self-interest would result in conditions of social optimality, but from the Christian reformers who, recognising that market systems do not necessarily work to the mutual benefit of everybody in society, particularly the poor, the weak, the powerless and the unfortunate, intervened both to limit the exploitation of man by his fellowman and to provide those minimal conditions of life which were considered every person's birthright. The role of the Evangelicals in the reform movement in the nineteenth century has been well recognised. In her book, *"The Bible and the Sword"*, Barbara Tuchman sums up the historiographical situation very appositely. *"It hurts the economic historians, the Marxians and Fabians, to admit that the ten hours bill, the basic piece of nineteenth century labour legislation, came down from the top, out of a private nobleman's private feelings about the gospel, or that the abolition of the Slave Trade was achieved, not through the operation of some law of profit and loss, but purely as the result of the new humanitarianism of the Evangelicals. But take an historian who is not riding the economic hobbyhorse and you will find him concluding, like Halevy, that it is impossible to overestimate the influence of the Evangelicals on their time."*[212] It was Christian action on behalf of the workers and their social conditions that rendered the tenets of Marxism false!

The failure of the Marxist system in Eastern Europe has demonstrated all too clearly one of the cardinal tenets of this book, namely that while the state performs a critical role in the economic development process, as we have indeed seen in the case of Russia, the role of the market cannot be ignored. The failure of the Soviet

---

[211] Trevelyan, G.M. *English Social History,* Longman Green & Co. (1942).
[212] Tuchman, Barbara, *The Bible and the Sword*, Ballantine Books.

government to provide an adequate supply of consumer goods is ample testimony to the all-important and essential role which the market fulfils. However, the concept of consumer sovereignty has quite justly been strongly attacked in the economic literature of the western world and with good reason. Developments in economic thinking this century have made us increasingly aware of how inadequately the market system often functions. The thesis of imperfect competition which Chamberlin and Robinson gave us in the 1930s has done much to provide a more realistic model of the operation of the microeconomic world than the neo-classical school had done. The recognition that oligopoly is a pervasive reality of the modern industrial and commercial world, particularly of those areas of heavy industry, such as steel chemicals, electrical goods, electric power generation, aviation, automobiles and energy, gives the lie to the multi-producer, multi-consumer competitive model which the classical school of economists were so fond of. Those familiar with business history know only too well the tendency for amalgamation and mergers of business firms to result in concentrations of economic power which are inimical to the smooth functioning of the competitive market economy of Adam Smith and his disciples. Governmental intervention to prevent price collusion, output restrictions and similar efforts to prevent market forces working effectively, speak volumes about the imperfections of the actual functioning of the market system.

The failure of the market system to deal effectively with the problem of the depletion of common property resources, such as forests, waterways, lakes and oceans has led this century to a volume of legislation at national level, and to hundreds of conferences at international level designed to preserve what we can of nature's heritage before it suffers extinction. Other environmental problems, such as pollution, likewise testify to the inadequacies of the economic arrangements according to which nineteenth century societies were content to conduct their affairs. The record of planned economies in this sphere, however, is no better than that of the market economies, if anything significantly worse, as the condition of Silesia, Lake Baikal and the Aral Sea, to name some of the serious disaster areas, testify.

While markets perform with considerably less satisfaction than the Classical Economists would like us to believe they do, their capacity to produce goods and services to satisfy consumer needs and desires know only the limits of current technology. The vast proliferation of material wealth which has been the lot of man in the more advanced societies of the twentieth century testifies to the effectiveness of the capitalist system's capacity to meet needs. The ability of the price system to co-ordinate the requirements of thousands of firms and millions of households throughout the economy is indeed, as Dennis Hay has remarked, *"an amazing achievement"*.[213] Nobody was more aware of capitalism's mighty achievements than Marx himself.

"The Bourgeoisie," he wrote, *"during its rule of scarce a hundred years, had created more massive and more productive forces than have all preceding generations together. Subjection of nature's forces to man, machinery, application of chemistry to industry and agriculture, steam navigation, railways, electric telegraphs, clearing of whole continents for cultivation, canalisation of rivers, whole populations conjured out of the ground - what earlier century had even a presentiment that such productive forces slumbered in the lap of social labour?"*[214]

At the same time, Marx was only too well aware of Capitalism's very significant deficiencies, above all, its inability to distribute the wealth that it had produced with any degree of equity. It was Marx's solution to the problem which has caused such untold heartache and suffering for millions of people. Violence begets violence as the Marxist experiment, both in Russia, China, Cuba and Eastern Europe has shown. To the millions of war dead that Russia has suffered this century must be added the twenty to thirty million people who, because they refused to adhere to the tenets of the rulers, were denied freedom and in many cases, life. We who have lived to see the price which has been paid in blood and treasure to establish Marxist Utopias around the world - the Civil War in Russia (1918-21), the ruthless collectivisation of agriculture undertaken by Stalin in the 1930s, the pathological slaughter of the Red Army leadership in 1937, the waves of refugees from Eastern Europe to the West following World War II and the establishment of satellite states in that part of the world, the Gulag Archipelago, the Maoist Revolution in China, the Great Agricultural Crisis of 1958, the Cultural Revolution which followed a decade later, the slaughter of students in Tiamen Square, and the final collapse of the socialist system in country after country in Eastern Europe, are only too well aware of the inadequacies of philosophies and ideologies which are not founded on a realistic view of human nature.

---

[213]   Hay, Dennis, *Capitalism*, Grove Booklets, UK.
[214]   Quoted in Freedman, Robert, *Marx on Economics*, Penguin Books (1961).

Men have yet to come to live with the reality of themselves, and they will not do so until they realise the truth which is enshrined in the words of the Nazarene, namely that it is *"from within, from men's hearts and minds, that evil thoughts arise, lust, theft, murder, adultery, greed, wickedness, deceit, sensuality, envy, slander, arrogance and folly."*[215] Only when man is changed can society be changed. It is only when his conscience is enlightened, as was that of the Christian reformers in the early nineteenth century that society can be to any degree improved. That can only be done at all effectively through peaceful change, not by revolution.

MILTON FRIEDMAN

The perfectibilist market system has enjoyed a strong renaissance in the last twenty years due to the crusading enthusiasm of Milton Friedman. Friedman's thesis is based on two fundamental convictions:

i) belief in the free-wheeling market economy, in the perfectibilist market theory developed by Smith in the eighteenth century;

ii) the conviction that, as bullion is no longer the basis of the monetary system, that governments therefore must intervene to control the money supply.

Friedman provides empirical evidence for his theories. His argument for the market economy is based upon the performance of the British Economy in the second part of the nineteenth century (1850-1915) - the so-called Liberal Era - and also upon the performance of the economy of Hong Kong after World War II. Like Marx, Friedman is most impressed with the achievements of capitalism. Friedman's reaction, however, is entirely different from that of the German philosopher. For no contemporary advocate of economic liberalism preaches on behalf of his cause with as much zeal as Milton Friedman. In his two books, *"Capitalism and Freedom"*[216] and *"Free to Choose"*[217], Friedman makes his case with all the fervour of an evangelist. Taking up Smith's observation about natural liberty as the basis of his thinking, Friedman argues that it is only when men and women are free to choose that they

---

[215]   Mark 7:20.

[216]   Friedman, Milton, *Capitalism and Freedom*, Phonex Books, Chicago (1963).

[217]   Friedman, Milton, and Rose D., *Free to Choose*, Harcourt, Brace and Jovanovich, New York (1980).

can consider themselves to be free at all. This freedom of choice, he claims, extends not only to the economic sphere where such institutions as the free market and free trade epitomise his theory, but to the political arena as well. True to his American heritage, he has profound reverence for the Constitution and the Bill of Rights as the ultimate safeguard of political freedom. America's remarkable progress since Independence he ascribes to the fact that men and women have migrated there to enjoy not only the political benefits which life in a democratic society under the rule of law confers, but also the material blessings which a society committed to the economic doctrines of *"laissez-faire"* capitalism provides. In Friedman's thinking, political liberty and economic freedom are inseparable. Any breakdown of the one is likely to result in a corresponding breakdown of the other. The great period of American Capitalism was, in Friedman's view, the nineteenth century, for that was a period when republican governments, governments committed to the *laissez-faire* economic philosophy, prevailed. America's greatest President was Abraham Lincoln, on account of his role in granting freedom to the Negro slaves. Twentieth century history, Friedman sees as dominated by Democrat governments which he considers have interfered with the natural process of economic development with such programs as the New Deal and the Great Society. In consequence, claims Friedman, economic growth has not been as spectacular as it should have been.

It is less with America's economic achievements that Friedman is so enthusiastic, however, as with Great Britain's economic ascendancy in the nineteenth century. To Friedman, Britain's success was due to the policies of free enterprise, competitive marketing, free trade and *"laissez-faire"* government which Adam Smith and the Classical Economists advocated. It was through the pursuit of policies based on these ideas, claims Friedman, that Britain was able to establish her world-wide dominion and the British people were able to enjoy a higher standard of material welfare than ever before in history. The free market system, continues Friedman, whenever and wherever it is allowed to operate, facilitates the growth of trade and the expansion of the economy by unleashing those pent-up forces within man that enable him to use his initiative, his native wit and the technical skills at his command, to provide a better way of life for himself and his dependants, at the same time providing a service to the community at large. In any society only a small proportion of men have the initiative, courage, vigour and stamina to achieve great things. It is essential, therefore, that no impediments should be placed in their way by governments or any other authority. Britain progressed as rapidly as she did, continues Friedman, in the nineteenth century because the economic conditions for growth were favourable; liberal governments followed *laissez-faire* policies, trade with other countries was subject to little or no restriction, and the domestic market was expanding. In Friedman's view, growth has been less spectacular in the twentieth century because British governments, like their counterparts in America, have interfered in the economic operations of the country by protecting obsolete industries, maintaining uneconomic businesses and by funding expensive health, welfare and education programs.

It is these activities by paternalistically minded governments that Milton Friedman so strongly condemns, for they interfere, he argues, with the beneficent operations of the market system, a system of economic organisation which is always and everywhere superior to the collectivist approach. State aided health schemes, minimum wage legislation, subsidised housing and rental accommodation, and state funded education have all at one time or another come under heavy fire. State aided health, welfare and education schemes undermine the quality of services available to the public, engender waste and discourage young people from becoming doctors and teachers. Minimum wage legislation ensures that more people receive unemployment relief than would be the case if the market fixed the price of labour. Subsidised housing has resulted, so Friedman tells us, in a decline in both the quantity and quality of units available to the poorer sections of the community. The collectivist approach, asserts Friedman, with little regard to the evidence, will not work. It has undermined the British economy, because it has undermined those very qualities of character, self-reliance, individual initiative and enterprise which made the nation the world leader in the nineteenth century.

The bicentennial celebrations in America in 1976 provided Friedman with a unique opportunity to proclaim yet again his profound faith in economic liberalism.[218] The conjuncture of circumstances that saw the publication of *"The Wealth of Nations"*, Adam Smith's great treatise extolling the virtues of economic liberalism, in the same year as the American colonists penned their memorable *"Declaration of Independence"* in defiance of the mother country's efforts to enforce mercantilist legislation, was too great an opportunity to miss! Smith's

---

[218]   Published in the International Institute for Economic Research Paper 5, December (1976).

work, continues Friedman, was published at a time when the burden of regulation weighed heavily on the British people. The next one hundred years in British history saw the gradual de-regulation of the economy and the steady introduction of economically liberal trading arrangements. This pattern, argues, Friedman, was reversed at the end of the century when the collectivist school of thought began to make its presence felt and its views heard. The result, contends Friedman, has been a marked growth in the role of government, particularly since the Keynesian Revolution of the 1930s. All is not lost, however, declares Friedman. There are strong indications that the end of the collectivist era is in sight. People are becoming more and more disenchanted with *"Big Government"*, and its inability to deliver the goods and services expected of it. Perhaps, after all, they say, the market system had its advantages. With a note of triumph, Friedman concludes that the next one hundred years might see the revival of economic liberalism.

Friedman frequently contrasts the nineteenth and twentieth centuries always to the advantage of the former and to the detriment of the latter. *"The combination of economic and political freedom produced a golden age in both Britain and the United States of America in the nineteenth century. The United States of America prospered even more than Great Britain. It started with a clean slate, free from the vestiges of class and status, fewer governmental restraints, a more fertile field for energy, drive and innovation, and an empty Continent to conquer."*[219] Friedman even goes so far as to assert that the long period of peace in nineteenth century European politics was due to the liberal trading arrangements adopted by Britain and the Pax Britannica. *"The century from Waterloo to World War I offers a striking example of the beneficial efforts of Free Trade on relations among nations."*[220] Insofar as the twentieth century is concerned, restraints on trade, both at the domestic and the international level, have, Friedman assures us, inhibited economic growth. Economic liberalism has, however, survived in East Asia, observes Friedman.[221] Hong Kong is a choice example of what can be achieved when liberal trading policies are pursued. Singapore and Taiwan are also deemed eligible for consideration.

---

[219] Friedman, Milton, and Rose D., *Free to Choose*, Harcourt, Brace and Jovanovich, New York (1980).

[220] Ibid.

[221] Ibid.

A detailed critique of Friedman's claims is beyond the scope of this book. Enough, however, has already been said on the subject of Free Trade to render Friedman's views on that score nugatory. The weakness of his argument about the Pax Britannica is dealt with in Appendix 1 of this work. Since the nub of his argument concerns the performance of the British economy in the latter half of the nineteenth century and the behaviour of the economy of Hong Kong in the aftermath of World War II, it is with these two periods of history which we shall concern ourselves with in this work.

Regrettably for Friedman, the Great Liberal Era in British History does not validate his thesis that economies progress most rapidly when economic liberal doctrines are followed. For it was during that period that both the United States of America and Imperial Germany, neither of whom, as we have already seen, pursued economically liberal doctrines during their era of industrialisation, closed the gap which the British had established by being first in the technological race in the eighteenth century. Germany's economic growth rate between 1870 and 1914 was 21% per decade as opposed to Britain's 12% per decade.[222] By 1914, Germany had almost closed the gap between herself and Britain; in terms of per capita income, Britain was still marginally ahead. In certain technical areas, e.g. the electrical and chemical industries, Germany was ahead.

The period between the American Civil War and the Great War was also the era during which the United States of America closed the gap on her rival, Britain.[223] American coal production, always a good indice of the economic performance of a country in the nineteenth century, first outstripped Britain's in 1890. At the same time, America, thanks to Edison and Du Pont, had acquired a significant advantage over Britain in the electrical and chemical industries respectively.

The reasons for Britain's comparatively poor performance in the latter part of the nineteenth century have long been debated. Some observers will be inclined to agree with Friedman and assert that America had considerable advantages insofar as economic opportunity was concerned on account of its relative freedom from the vestiges of the past, her boundless natural resources and the fact that she had an empty continent to fill. It is an argument, however, which is difficult to

---

[222]   Henderson, W.O., *The Rise of German Industrial Power (1934-1934)*, Temple Smith, London (1975).

[223]   Bagwell, P.S., Mingay, G.E., *Britain and America - A Study of Economic Change (1850-1939)*, Routledge & Kegan Paul, London (1970).

substantiate in the light of developments which have taken place in the second part of the twentieth century, in particular the comparative performance of the American and Japanese economies. Japan is endowed with far fewer natural resources than either Britain or America, and yet she has outperformed both of her rivals. There were plenty of opportunities for Britain to continue expanding economically in the nineteenth century; the British simply refused to take advantage of them.

Nor does Freidman's collectivist argument have any substance in it. As Friedman well knows, Germany was the first country in Europe to adopt socialist legislation in the 1880s, when she enacted legislation to provide for the worker's well-being in periods of sickness, when injured, or during old age. In this respect she was at least thirty years ahead of Britain. Nor is there any evidence that Britain was any more collectivist in her approach than the United States of America. Shaftesbury's Ten Hours Bill, enacted in 1847, had its precursor in Van Buren's Act of 1830. Moreover, the armoury of social legislation which the British Parliament passed to protect the interests of the unenfranchised and poorer elements of the population had its counterpart in the United States of America. To argue that these reform measures interfered with the smooth functioning of the market system and slowed economic growth as economic liberals are wont to argue, is to fly in the face of history. On the contrary, reform measures facilitated the operation of the market system by preventing that abuse of power which employers were only too ready to indulge in when it suited their interests, as indeed Adam Smith had observed when he wrote *"The Wealth of Nations"*.

The free market argument so beloved by Friedman receives a further blow when the conditions under which industrialisation took place are taken into account, for, as we've seen, both the United States of America and Imperial Germany industrialised behind high tariff barriers. In both countries, national governments significantly assisted the development and expansion of business in a variety of different ways. In America, impetus was given to the development of agriculture by the enactment of the Homesteads Bill in 1862 and the provision by the government of agricultural research stations. The development of rail transport was significantly assisted by the sale of land for railway construction at prices well below market values. At the same time, business was protected from the monopolistic power which railways frequently exercised by the Interstate Commerce Commission, whose function it was to ensure a fair deal for railway customers. The exploitation of labour was likewise impeded by the various pieces of social legislation which Congress enacted in the wake of the Civil Service Reform Bill of 1883.

In Germany, business was not only protected by the tariff, but was also permitted to develop on a cartel basis.[224] Indeed cartellisation of industry was very widespread during the Imperial era in Germany with the result that very little genuine competition occurred. Not only was price collusion a frequent occurrence, but so too were agreements relating to market share, either on a segmentation basis or on a regionalisation basis; in a few instances, firms even shared profits. The Germans, moreover, were not slow to imitate the British technique of economic advancement during the Mercantilist era. The German Historical School, whose writings belong to this period, were only too well aware of the advantages which Britain had scored as a result of being first in the field, and they were not averse to imitation.

The issue of tariff barriers caused not a little consternation in the Britain of the 1870s and 80s as cheap goods swept into British markets from America and Germany, neither of whom permitted British goods into their territories on similar terms. The British sent up the cry *"Fair Trade, not Free Trade"*. The advocates of liberalism, however, held the day and Britain remained a Free Trading nation until the outbreak of war. Free Trade came with a price tag, however; that price in Britain's case was the demise of agriculture.

The repeal of the Corn Laws in 1846 by the Conservative Government of Robert Peel, Friedman sees as inaugurating the great era of Liberalism in British History, and with good reason for it was his countrymen who benefited from that legislative repeal. The opening up of the North American prairies, following the completion of the Transcontinental railway in 1860, made it possible for American farmers to grow grain and ship it to Britain and sell it at lower prices than British farmers could produce it locally. British farmers, accordingly, switched their resources into the production of beef and dairy cattle, a victory for the theory of comparative advantage, as economic liberals would be quick to tell us. The British people and their government had cause to see the matter differently when in 1917 the country was within six weeks of surrendering to Germany due to the latter's highly effective submarine warfare. Adam Smith had been

---

[224]   Henderson, W.O., *The Rise of German Industrial Power (1934-1934)*, Temple Smith, London (1975).

180

realistic about the value of Cromwell's Navigation Acts for the safety and security of the country. He realised that a country must be able to defend itself in times of war, and that this necessitated the protection of English shipping and shipbuilding. Modern European governments, aware of the dangers of neglecting agriculture, have reversed the liberal process, much to the chagrin of the liberal economists who have not been slow to criticise the food surpluses that have resulted. In a world devoid of national conflict and tension, economic liberalism would work very well. Unfortunately, for the liberals such a world belongs to the realm of the idealistic, rather than the realistic. It is the recognition that politics, (national security and national self-esteem) is ultimately more important than economics that makes economic theory, liberalism in particular, unacceptable as practical policy.

Northcote Parkinson, in his book, *"Left Luggage"*, has argued that the relative decline of Britain began in the 1840s with the Anglican Church's embrace of the Tractarian Movement and the corresponding shift from Evangelical religion to Anglo-Catholicism.[225] He maintains that the British governed the empire less confidently thereafter, that, in short, that they were on the defensive. This is not the place for a full scale discussion of the relationship between Protestantism and the emergence of Britain on the forefront of the world's political and economic scene. Suffice it to say that Protestants have not been a whit less influenced by the Book than have the Jews. Nor is it entirely accidental that Britain has generally progressed more rapidly during periods when the Protestant faith has been most to the fore, e.g. the Elizabethan era, the Cromwellian period and the century or so which followed the Seven Years War (1756-63). Evangelicalism declined as a force in the 1860s with the publication of Darwin's *"Origin of Species"*, which the rationalist, T.H. Huxley used to refute the Creationist account of Scripture, and of J.S. Mill's *"Essay on Liberty"*, a critique of the influence of Evangelicals on society as a whole.

Economically speaking, Britain's downfall began in the very year, 1865, that Palmerston, her jingoistic foreign minister died. For it was in that year that the British Parliament enacted legislation which effectively inhibited the development of the motor industry in England. The Red Flag Act forbade the use of motor vehicles unless preceded by a man carrying a red flag. The nation that had led the world in the development of internal transport systems with canalisation in the

---

[225]   Parkinson, C. Northcote, *Left Luggage - From Marx & Wilson*, Pelican Books, London (1970).

eighteenth century and the railways in the nineteenth century now committed the monumental blunder of preventing the development of the horseless carriage. That very year, a Frenchman invented the petrol engine. Twenty years later, Benz incorporated that engine into the first motor car. In 1903, Henry Ford applied the technique of mass production to the automobile, thereby ushering in the age of mass transport.

Nor was it only in the field of vehicular transport that the British lost the initiative, but in chemicals, the electrical industry and aviation. For the pioneers in these fields, the successors of Boyle and Faraday, were either German or American. While Edison was laying the foundations of the electricity industry in America, and Siemens in Germany, the British continued to perfect the inventions for which they had been initially responsible, the steam engine, textile manufacturing machinery and shipbuilding. In consequence the development of the British chemical industry was left to the German businessman, Brunner, the Swiss chemist, Mond, the Swedish businessman, Nobel and to Americans such as Castner and Kellner. The British electrical industry, likewise, owes its foundation to the initiatives of American and German businessmen.[226]

Britain's decline followed, though there were few at the time who appreciated what was happening, such was the British intoxication with their remarkable achievements. A few perspicacious Englishmen realised that Germany posed a threat to Britain's leadership; they were ignored. The nation that had become the Workshop of the World was anxious to let the world know of its accomplishments, and so was organised the most illustrious exhibition yet seen in the history of mankind, the Crystal Palace Exhibition of 1851. Pre-eminence, however, is more difficult to maintain than to attain, as many a leader and many a nation has had cause to prove. The old adage that pride comes before a fall is all too often proven true, both for nations as well as for individuals. The lot that befell the Venetian Republic at the end of the fifteenth century and the Dutch Republic in the mid-seventeenth century, and has since befallen the United States of America, befell Britain in the 1860s.

The long steady relative decline of Britain in the world's economic league tables dates from the beginning of the Liberal Era in British political and economic life, a fact which does little to support

---

[226]   Jones, Robert, Marriott, Oliver, *Anatomy of a Merger. A History of GEC, AEI and English Electric*, Pan Books (1970).

Friedman's claim that this was a period of great economic progress in British history; rather it was a period during which the United States of America and Germany, in defiance of the tenets of economic liberalism, steadily closed the technological and economic gap which had opened between themselves and their rival, Great Britain, at the end of the eighteenth century. It was, as we have already seen, the Mercantilist period in British period (1650-1850) that witnessed Great Britain's rise to economic hegemony of the world.

Friedman and those who, like him, espouse the cause of economic liberalism, look to Hong Kong as an illustration of an economy that has developed a strong industrial base without the use of tariff barriers. There is some incongruity in the fact that a British colony, an outpost of empire as it once was, administered along traditional colonial lines by a British Governor appointed by the British Government, advised by a Legislative Council whose members owe their position to the Governor, should be regarded as a bastion of economic liberalism. For the government of Hong Kong was until recently, as illiberal a form of government as could be found anywhere. Nevertheless, it is true that the colony has been governed very well since World War II in the manner of a benevolent despotism and in the best tradition of British overseas administration.

The period of Hong Kong's history which most interests the economic liberals is the post-World War II boom era, in particular the twenty-five years following the establishment of the Chinese People's Republic. It was a period of dynamic expansion for the British Crown Colony, as indeed it was for many of Hong Kong's neighbours, mainland China, Taiwan, South Korea and Japan, not to mention Hong Kong's other trading partners, Britain and America. It was also a period during which Hong Kong experienced a considerable increase in population. Prior to the influx of Chinese refugees from the mainland in 1949 following Chiang Kai Shek's defeat and retreat to the island of Taiwan, Hong Kong had a population of two million. Within a year this had risen to two and a quarter million and by 1955 was standing at two and a half million. Further steady increases in the next fifteen years brought Hong Kong's population up to the four million mark. It was during this period that the colony was transformed from an entrepôt into a major manufacturing centre. The statistics on factory establishments speak for themselves. In 1940, Hong Kong had 800 manufacturing establishments; by 1950, this had almost doubled to become 1500. In the next decade, it rose to 5,100, and by 1972 was standing at 19,500.

Many of these establishments employed less than ten people. However, three quarters of the workforce were employed in large factories. The growth in the number of factories was matched by a corresponding increase in the size of the workforce which in 1960 stood at 229,000, and had by 1972 risen to the 600,000 mark.[227] Hong Kong's trade with the outside world, a life-line for a colony dependent on the import of food and raw materials for its survival, increased in proportions similar to the growth of the colony, with one important exception, the three year period which followed the end of the Korean War in the 1950s. The reason for this depression was the United States government's prohibition on the export of strategic materials to China. Since China was Hong Kong's principal trading partner this embargo, which was ratified by the United Nations Organisation and therefore supported by all America's allies in the Far East, including Japan, South Korea and Taiwan, seriously affected Hong Kong and resulted in a fall of 30% in her trade. The revival of industry and commerce in the mid-fifties which accompanied the government's industrialisation policy, continued unabated until the early 1970s.

The question that we have now to ask ourselves is what made this possible. If, as the Chicago School of Economists has argued, it was the result of the pursuit of economically liberal policies, we must ask ourselves why this policy was successful in the situation in which Hong Kong found itself. In this connection, three points need to be made. The first is that in 1949-50, Hong Kong received a large influx of people from the mainland, many of whom had been entrepreneurs in the days of the Nationalist Government of China. It was these people who provided the backbone, the skills and the business acumen that were needed to develop Hong Kong into an industrial state. The arrival of these people and their acceptance into the Hong Kong community contributed in no small way to the colony's very rapid industrialisation drive.

Secondly, the consistent improvement in Hong Kong's economic situation from 1955 onwards was very largely due to the policies of her major trading partners, who also were pursuing expansionist policies at the time. This was particularly true of Japan, whose manufacturing concerns viewed Hong Kong as a very suitable emporium for the products of their rapidly recovering economy. It was also true for America, with whom Hong Kong increased her trade sixfold during the

[227] Rabushi, Alvin, *Hong Kong - A Study in Economic Freedom*, Graduate School of Business, University of Chicago (1979).

1960s. It was also true for Britain with whom Hong Kong increased her trade threefold during the same period. The Republic of China also saw a substantial increase in economic output during this period, although while China's exports through Hong Kong increased fourfold between 1950 and 1971, imports, reflecting China's increasing self-sufficiency, declined to a mere $HK60 million. The increasing prosperity of all the nations in the Far East, as well as America and Britain, goes a long way to explaining why Hong Kong's adoption of economically liberal policies was so successful. A nation can trade very successfully with other nations provided that it has goods which are in demand and provided that no restrictions are placed on their import. Thanks to the expansionary policies being pursued by the governments of Britain and America during this period, by Japan in its attempt to establish itself as one of the leading industrial powers, by Taiwan and South Korea, both of whose governments were, for various reasons, anxious to strengthen their countries, militarily as well as economically, and by mainland China who was herself on the road to industrialisation, Hong Kong's prosperity was guaranteed. If, therefore, we see Hong Kong's highly successful and very rapid industrialisation against this backdrop, we shall see that Hong Kong's adoption of economic liberalism was a very sensible move in a world of expanding international trade and rapid economic development. It is worth observing that with the downturn in world trade in the 1970s and the increasing tendency among developing and developed nations to erect tariff barriers, Hong Kong is not faring so well. Economic liberalism is a very fine theory, but it is very questionable whether it has applicability outside the level playing field, and in the real world, level playing fields do not exist. It worked well for the British in the nineteenth century because they were the technological leaders of the world. It worked to Hong Kong's advantage during the post-World War II boom, because of contemporary trading conditions. It would work well in a world devoid of mistrust, suspicion, greed, the abuse of power, lust and fear. Such a world is well removed from reality.

A third factor in Hong Kong's very successful economic expansion is the enlightened policies pursued by colonial governments. A significant portion of government revenues, sometimes as much as 60%, and generally never less than 25% in the 1960s, was spent on public works' projects. Land reclamation, a top priority in a territory which attempts to accommodate four million people on 400 square miles of land, has been given a significant portion of the funds, as has the building of resettlement estates and the construction of low-cost housing for the workers employed in the new factories. (Needless to say, the free market system failed to provide housing of sufficient quality for the worker in Hong Kong as elsewhere in the world.) Road and reservoir construction have also received a fair proportion of the funds. Government spending on education and health, while small in relation to the population as a whole, nevertheless represents a worthwhile contribution to the benefit of society. The role of government in providing the infrastructure for the development of the colony, ensuring a basic standard of decency where the market system failed to provide it, and in providing the colony with the rudiments of an educational system can not be ignored in any fair assessment of the colonial economy's performance.

Friedman has used history to justify his belief, not only in economic liberalism, but also in his doctrine of monetarism. The key propositions of monetarism, according to Friedman, are that *"there is a consistent though not precise relationship between the rate of growth of the quantity of money and the rate of growth of nominal income, that, in the short run, monetary changes affect primarily output, but that over decades the rate of monetary growth affects prices. Inflation is always and everywhere a monetary phenomcnon. A change in the growth of the money stock lowers interest rates initially but, as spending increases, it stimulates price inflation and produces an increase in demand for loans which will tend to increase interest rates."*[228] The bases for Friedman's conclusions are the monumental work which he produced, in conjunction with Anna Jacobson Schwartz, on the monetary history of the United States of America from 1867 to 1960, which he followed up with a similar study of Britain's monetary history.[229] Friedman's belief that the money stock is the principal determinant of economic activity in the short run leads to his all-important policy conclusion, namely that modern governments should manage the money supply and leave all else to the gyrations of the market place.

When, in 1929, disaster struck the citadel of capitalism in terrifying proportions, Milton Friedman was one of the few economists

---

[228]   Friedman, Milton, *The Counter-revolution in Monetary Theory*, First Wincott Memorial Lecture. Pt.IV. "The Propositions of Monetarism", Institute of Economic Affairs (1970).

[229]   Friedman, M, Schwartz, A.J., *A Monetary History of the United States of America, 1867-1960*, Princeton University Press (1963).

who retained their faith in the institutions of the free market unsullied. When many economists adopted the Keynesian view that the depression was the outcome of a failure of private investment and could therefore be corrected by liberal doses of government spending, Friedman stuck to his convictions. Government intervention to cure economic ills would constitute a major breach of the liberal economic creed. Convinced that the Depression was the result of a tragic mismanagement of the money supply by the Federal Reserve Bank of New York, an agency constituted by government in 1907 to avert banking crises, Friedman, in conjunction with Schwarz, set about the formidable task of collecting, analysing, sifting and collating a mass of statistical data to prove the theory. The work, which was presented to the public in the 1960s, traced the history of monetary movements in the American economy over a ninety three year period (1867-1960). The thesis was clear! Business cycles, during the period under review, could, in every case, be associated with movements in the money stock, albeit with time lags. There was, argued Friedman, an automatic and invariable relationship between the money supply and national income. Most significant of all, continued Friedman, was the contractionary policy of the Federal Reserve Bank in 1929 when it reduced the base money supply by 2½%, thereby effecting a reduction of one-third in the total stock of money in circulation. The Great Depression, urged Friedman, should be regarded as the consequence of the Great Contraction of the Money Supply.

The conclusion, contended Friedman the empiricist, was that governments universally would have to accept responsibility for the management of their country's money supply. With what reluctance Friedman accepted this breach in the walls of the economic liberal fortress, we shall probably never know. A return to the Gold Standard is not practical, contends Friedman. The New Deal economic policies of F.D. Roosevelt, which did so much to facilitate America's economic recovery in the 1930s, Friedman has little use for. He does, however, commend the President warmly for his FDIC legislation, whereby the banking fraternity has been authorised to deposit some of its holdings with the Federal Reserve Bank in the event of a major debtor or debtors defaulting on their loans, arguing that it has averted another financial disaster on the scale of 1929. The capitalist system can survive, he claims, as long as governments control the money supply.

Monetary management, sound, effective and responsible, Friedman sees as the key to economic stability and growth. Mismanagement of the money supply was, in his opinion, a contributory factor in the rise to power of Adolf Hitler in Germany in 1933. During the Great German inflation of 1923, many thousands of middle-class Germans lost their life savings; their disgust with the governments of the Weimar Republic, modern Germany's first experiment with democracy, for failing to address the much more serious problems confronting Germany in the wake of the Great Depression, when the nation found itself with six million workers idle, made them support the man who promised to restore the country's economy. Inability to manage the money supply lies behind the persistent inflation which nations around the world have experienced since World War II. Full employment policies, argues Friedman, are not compatible with price stability. There is, he contends, a natural rate of unemployment which may well vary from country to country and from time to time. Price stability cannot be maintained if governments pursue policies which ignore that factor. Weak governments, moreover, will be strongly inclined to accommodate price increases by increasing the money stock. There is a strong tendency for this situation to become self-perpetuating, warns Friedman, and the only way to counteract it, he claims, is to maintain strict control over monetary aggregates.

Friedman's thesis, that the cure for inflation is strict control of the money supply, has come in for heavy criticism at the hands of economists, with justification. Six years after Friedman opened the war on inflation with his address to the American Economics Association in 1967, the OPEC countries proved the weakness of his thesis by increasing the price of a barrel of oil at the well head by a factor of four, thus forcing governments around the world either to increase the money supply to meet the demands of the domestic economy for more funds, or to suffer significant increases in the level of unemployment. OPEC's actions demonstrated the extraordinary ineptitude of the monetarist solution. It highlighted the undeniable weakness of governments to combat inflation with monetary weapons, particularly when the source of that inflation was external. Money, as many economists had already realised, was no different from other commodities; the supply of it was determined by demand, and demand, it soon became apparent, was determined by the controllers of prices. If prices rose, governments had no option but to increase the money supply. Other policies based on *"fight flation first"* principles only led to unacceptably high levels of unemployment, and declining economic growth rates.

It is the controllers of the prices of the factors of production who determine the level of inflation in any society, and, since, to a very large extent today, we live in a society in which big business controls the prices of the goods which we buy, the unions the price of labour, and the professions the price of the services which they provide, it is these three institutions which have, in some measure, the responsibility for determining the level of inflation. Gone are the days of the free market, if indeed they ever existed. Our modern world is dominated by oligopolies and oligopsonies, in which the key actors are big business and unionised labour. The only significant contribution that modern governments can make concerns the price of money, for the long term association between the interest rate and the inflation rate is now realised by most economists. whatever their explanation for that phenomenon may be, as the comparison between the level of interest rates and the inflation rate during the twenty-five year period which followed World War II and the twenty year period of the 1970s and 80s, demonstrated Governments that do not want to see inflation can contribute towards controlling it by keeping interest rates low.

Few economists would deny that monetary stability is desirable. Monetary stability is only obtainable in modern society, however, when the nation is agreed on how wealth is to be distributed by the various income earners in modern society, and then it is only possible if there are no external shocks to the monetary system such as were administered by OPEC during the 1970s. Nations which enjoy relative freedom from inflation, namely Switzerland, Western Germany and Japan, are those whose people accept the current distribution of wealth in their countries. Countries such as Argentina, Brazil *et al* which experience high rates of inflation do so because there is no agreement on how wealth is to be distributed in their societies. Actual wealth distribution, it should be noted, has no bearing on the inflation rate. It is society's views on that wealth distribution and the behaviour which its members adopt to change it which determines the level of inflation in any one society. Inflation cannot be controlled by governments as Friedman avers, as the history of the last twenty years has demonstrated. Inflation is a national disease which only the nation can control if it has the collective will to do so.

Monetarism was abandoned by governments in the 1980s and with good reason. The task of determining the money supply at any one point in time has proved to be a far more incalculable exercise than Friedman had led the world to believe it would be when he first expounded his theories in the 1960s. The monetarist experiment, however, like all experiments, came with a price tag attached to it, as the Anglo-Saxon countries, in which Friedman's influence has been greatest, can testify. America, which was unquestionably the economic and military leader of the world in the 1960s, now lies in second place to Japan in terms of per capita industrial production. America's exports to Japan comprise agricultural goods and industrial raw materials; the only high technology goods which America has sold Japan in recent years have been aircraft, and soon Japan will be self-sufficient in this field. Britain, once the leading industrial nation in the world, now lies at the bottom of the industrial nation's league table in terms of Gross National Output, having been overtaken since World War II by Western Germany, Japan, France and Italy, a dismal record for a once great nation and one which the Thatcher government's mediocre performance has done little to allay and much to assist. Australia, once top of the per capita league tables, has slipped well down the ladder. In the 1960s, Australia saw herself, with good reason, as the super-state of the twenty-first century. She was fortunate enough to possess an abundance of material resources and a development potential, with her small population, which would be difficult for any other country, besides Canada, to surpass. So rapidly did the nation's self-confidence evaporate that, in the 1980s, two Australian authors gained considerable prestige by claiming that Australia was travelling fast down the Argentinian track.[230]

The question must be asked, however, whether monetarism was necessary in the first place. It is, when all is said and done, economic growth that nations most want today, and economic growth, as Friedman has conceded, may take place with or without inflation.[231] Likewise, inflation may occur with or without economic growth. All four scenarios, he tells us, are possible. The last twenty years have witnessed economic growth throughout the world, but the rate of growth has been significantly slower in many countries compared to what it was during the Keynesian era (1945-70). It is also pertinent to observe that statistics for the United States of America show a strong growth correlation when Democrat governments are in office. Poulson, who is a firm believer in Classical Economics, has conceded that two of the great growth periods in twentieth century American history occurred when Democrat governments were in office, namely 1937-53

---

[230]   Duncan, T., Fogarty, J. *Australia and Argentina on Parallel Paths*, Melbourne University Press (1984).

[231]   Friedman, M., *Money and Economic Development*, Horowitz Lectures of 1972, Praeger, (1973) p.41.

& 1960-67.[232] On both these occasions America enjoyed the advantage of having governments which knew what they wanted to achieve and also how to achieve it. Roosevelt was committed firstly to getting America out of the Depression and thence to victory in war. Truman was concerned to ensure, as were many of his political colleagues on the other side of the Atlantic, that the conditions of the Depression did not return after the cessation of hostilities in 1945. Kennedy, on arrival in office, committed himself to America's greatest ever endeavour, the lunar landing, which was finally achieved as he purposed in 1969.

Monetarism's infatuation with price stability, moreover, finds little support in history. Price instability, rather than price stability, has been the lot of mankind throughout history as Braudel's compendious work has shown. Deflation as well as inflation has been the experience of mankind throughout the era of the bullion based currency. It is unreasonable to suppose that mankind will overcome the problem of constantly changing monetary values simply because it has abandoned metallic standards in favour of nominal monetary systems.

Friedman must certainly be given credit for the warnings which he has issued to the world about the dangers of Big Government. Lord Acton's dictum - *"Power tends to corrupt, and absolute power corrupts absolutely,"*[233] - should never be forgotten. Too much power in the hands of governments is always dangerous, and can all too easily lead to the denigration of freedom, as America's recent history has shown. The modern state, however, has a responsibility to manage the economy effectively, and, as this book has attempted to show, that cannot be done simply by managing the money supply and leaving all else to the vicissitudes of the market place, as Friedman would like us to believe. Governments have a responsibility in the modern technocratic age to determine the projects which are going to yield the greatest return to the community at large, and to see that they are carried out. It is only when governments perform their managerial task effectively that the nation moves ahead satisfactorily on its chosen growth path. Only then can the resources of the nation be effectively utilised and the scourge of unemployment be avoided.

Governments, however, not only have a managerial role to perform; they also have a regulatory responsibility. It is this aspect of

---

[232]   Poulson, Barry, *The Economic History of the United States of America*, MacMillan, New York (1981).

[233]   Acton, Lord, originally cited in letter dated 24th May 1882 addressed to Bishop Creighton.

governmental activity which has occasioned so much criticism in the past. Adam Smith's diatribes against the obsolete legislation on the English Statute Book in the eighteenth century are well-known. It is all too often forgotten, however, that, while it was undoubtedly necessary to remove all the antiquated legislation which dated from the pre-industrial era from the Statute Book if Britain was to have an effective market economy, the industrial era created situations which called for state intervention to redress the wrongs which the emergence of new forms of power and their inevitable abuse created. The spate of legislation which the British Parliament enacted in the nineteenth century to protect the interests of the under-privileged, the poor and those who were unable to defend themselves, is clear evidence, not only of the inability of the market system to operate with the efficiency and effectiveness which Friedman would like, but of the need for society to correct those manifest evils which are the consequence of the abuse of power. Regulation can stifle progress, if legislation is left on the Statute Book after the need for it has ceased to exist. There would be few today who would argue in favour of the removal of all factory legislation from the Statute Book. Minimum standards of safety, health and hygiene are an essential part of the operation of our society. De-regulation in this sphere would not be acceptable either to union leaders or to society at large.

Nor is Friedman's solution to the problem of unemployment in any way acceptable. Negative Income Taxes are a reprehensible form of remuneration. People are entitled to work, as the Declaration of Human Rights affirmed in 1948: *"Everybody has the right to work."* The world has had one warning this century of what can happen when human rights in this respect are ignored. The Nazi menace arose in a Germany in which there were six million people unemployed. Nazism was the immediate outcome, not of the Great German Inflation of 1923, but of the Great Depression of 1929-33.

Friedman is right to warn the world of the dangers of Big Government. The voucher system for education is not the way to tackle the problem, however. The responsibility for health, education and welfare rests with the family, and 80% of families in the western world could, given a full employment economy, fulfil those responsibilities themselves. For those who are too poor to provide for themselves, a wealth tax to transfer funds from the rich to the poor is necessary and justified, in view of the inability of market systems to operate effectively.

Friedman is to be commended for his espousal of the flexible exchange rate system. The fortunes which were made by speculators under the fixed exchange rate system provided a sufficiently strong case for dismantling it. It is not possible to determine the value of one nation's currency in relation to that of another on a permanent basis. However, too much reliance should not be placed on the ability of flexible exchange rates either in the short term or the long term to correct the trade imbalances which currently afflict nations that are exporters of raw materials, other than oil, and importers of manufactured goods. History demonstrates the validity of the tariff as the sole means by which this can be done effectively, Joan Robinson's zero sum argument notwithstanding.

Perfectibilist market systems were a product of the eighteenth century, an age which divorced freedom from responsibility, an age which witnessed, in consequence, one of the bloodiest revolutions in modern history. The Declaration of the Rights of Man ignored the all important corollary, namely the duties of man. A society which concentrates on rights and ignores duties is in real danger of a military dictatorship. It is all very well to talk of people's right of choice. The critical question is whether they accept that the responsibilities inherent in that freedom. If those responsibilities are denied, if we do not accept that we are our brother's keeper, that we have some responsibility for our neighbour's welfare, then trouble lies ahead. If we persist in believing, as the economic liberals do, that social optimality will be achieved through the pursuit of self-interest, we shall err grievously. Britain and America were spared the catastrophes which befell France at the end of the eighteenth century because Protestant Christianity was the dominant influence in those countries at that time. In France, the salt had lost its savour; Catholicism was identified with privilege and power. France, in consequence, became a deeply divided nation, a nation whose form of government changed no less than five times in fifteen years (1789-1804) and seven times in the next sixty years (1804-70). The rift between the clericals and the anti-clericals was to dominate French politics throughout the nineteenth century and well into the twentieth century. The reform measures for which Britain and America are justly praised did not in many cases take place in France until very much later and impeded the course of economic development in that country. France became a divided nation, and *"a kingdom divided against itself cannot stand"*, [234]as the events of 1940 showed.

The exponents of Classical Economics, Friedman et al, would do well to remind themselves of the truth of Keynes' dictum; *"Classical Economics is the world as we would like it to be, not the world as it really is."*[235]

PAUL SAMUELSON

To single out Paul Samuelson as one of the most influential economists of our time requires little justification. Samuelson is the author of one of the most popular textbooks on Economics which is now in its thirteenth edition. A whole generation of American students have been brought up on Samuelson as he himself attests. *"The book has served as the standard bearer for the teaching of elementary economics since the 1948 edition."*[236] The significance of Samuelson's work, however, is that it is not only a student textbook, but the basis on which most other textbook writers on Economics have based their work whether they agree with him on details or not.

Samuelson's approach, however, highlights the difficulties which economics textbook writers have when writing on the topic of Economic Principles, namely the obsession, shared by almost all economists, with the concept of equilibrium. A perusal of any modern economics textbook, be it Samuelson's or any one else's, will confirm the extent to which economic thinking is dominated by this concept. Markets are said to be in equilibrium when the prevailing price for the good is just sufficient to clear production without either increasing or decreasing inventories, in other words, when aggregate demand equals aggregate supply. Firms are said to be in a state of equilibrium when production levels are consistent with either the marginalist principle (MC=MR) or the averaging principle (AC=AR). Much debate currently surrounds the question what constitutes a full employment equilibrium; the notion that the economy can operate at some level of real output without experiencing either significant inflation or a high level of unemployment still continues to dominate contemporary economic

---

[234] Mark 3:24.

[235] Keynes, J M, *The General Theory of Employment, Interest and Money*, Macmillan, London (1935).

[236] Samuelson, Paul, *Economics*, 13th edition, McGraw Hill, New York (1989).

thought. What, it must be asked, then, is meant by the expression equilibrium?

Equilibrium, Samuelson defines as *"the state in which an economic entity is at rest or in which the forces operating on the entity are in balance so that there is no tendency for change."*[237] Within the context of the macroeconomy, equilibrium is therefore the point at which aggregate demand and aggregate supply are in balance. When that occurs, indeed, whether it ever occurs, is a moot point. For, it can well be argued that the equilibrium situation, in which all goods and services supplied within an economy are demanded at that price level, is a purely hypothetical one. If we take the first of Samuelson's definitions, namely that an equilibrium is a state of rest, we have a problem because the modern economy can never meaningfully be described as being in a state of inertia. The modern economy is characterised by constant change, as every economic historian appreciates. Equilibria, whether defined as a state of rest or as a state of balance between opposing forces, in this case, aggregate demand and aggregate supply, do not exist in the real world. Markets do not repose themselves into states of inertia, or even states of balance. The forces of change are constantly at work with the result that prices, output, income and employment levels are likewise constantly changing. This is particularly true of those markets in which the competitive principle enjoys unrestricted sway, e.g. international markets where prices of commodities vary hour by hour, and domestic markets for fresh produce where prices vary daily. But it is also true for markets for manufactured goods whose prices tend, in the jargon of economists, to be *"sticky"*, i.e. resistant to change. Even here, the gyrations of the so-called business cycle ensure that output levels do not remain constant for any length of time. Indeed, the very concept of the business cycle is an admission that the modern economy is constantly in a state of flux. Those economists who argue that the economy is always in a state of disequilibria have history on their side.

The obsession with the concept of equilibrium has important consequences both for contemporary economic theory and for contemporary economic policy, for contemporary macroeconomic objectives are stated in terms of equilibrium theory. Indeed, Samuelson believes, (and here he has the support of most modern economists,) that a modern economy should aim for high economic growth, high

---

[237]   Tobin, James, Quoted in Samuelson, P. *Economics*, 13th edition. McGraw Hill, New York (1989).

employment levels, stable prices, (or, if these are unattainable, then a low rate of inflation), a stable exchange rate and a reasonable balance on merchandise trade. Some economists would even add a further factor, namely a more equitable distribution of wealth. The virtual impossibility of finding an economy in the modern world that corresponds to this idealistic situation is a sure measure of the impracticability of the task which our omnipotent economists, in their wisdom, demand of modern governments. And it is precisely because modern governments have been given a task which is well and truly beyond their capability that economic policy has performed such amazing gyrations in the last twenty to twenty-five years. For no government, however clever, can hope to achieve all those objectives simultaneously, as the Hawke government's performance in Australia over the last ten years has shown.

All might be well if modern governments concentrated on the one area in which they can make a significant difference, namely that of economic growth. This they have not done. Had they listened to James Tobin, economic performance would have been much better than it has been. Sadly, Tobin's advice, contained in the following words - *"The whole purpose of the economy is the production of goods or services for consumption now or in the future. I think that the burden of proof should always be on those who would produce less rather than more, on those who would leave idle men or machines or land that could be used. It is amazing how many reasons can be found to justify such waste: fear of inflation, balance of payments deficits, unbalanced budgets, excessive national debt, loss of confidence in the dollar."*[238] - was ignored.

Tobin was ignored because modern governments have given a relatively low priority to economic growth, and one reason, though not the only one, why economic growth has been given a low priority, is because it receives a low priority in modern economic thinking. A glance at any of the modern textbooks on Economics will indicate the truth of that assertion, for economic theory is no longer concerned to demonstrate how the economic growth process has taken place, which was Adam Smith's purpose in writing *"The Wealth of Nations"*. Economic growth is generally treated as a subject of minor importance and relegated to the closing chapters of the book. Not until economic growth and development come back centre stage in our economic

---

238   Samuelson, Paul, *Economics*, 13th edition, McGraw Hill, New York (1989).

thinking will modern governments extricate their stricken economies from the recession into which they have thrown them.

If economic growth and development are to be restored to their rightful place, economic history will have to be given a much more important role in the economics curriculum than it enjoys at the present time. Currently, economic history is all too often treated as the Cinderella of Economics Departments in Universities. Economic history, however, should be the king pin of an Economics Degree course, since it is economic history, the growth and development process, which economic theory should explain. Economics students should therefore receive a thorough grounding in economic and business history in their first year at University before they attempt to come to grips with economic theory. The value of history is twofold: firstly it provides students with an understanding of the economic growth and development process; secondly, it enables them to understand why the economic theorists wrote in the way in which they did at the time when they did. For theory can only be properly understood against the background of the times in which it was written.

Students need to understand that in a world of intense commercial and political rivalry, the pre-occupation with external stability which marked the economic writers of the seventeenth and early eighteenth centuries was thoroughly comprehensible. Theirs was a world of nation states each competing with one another for economic and political hegemony. Wealth was the basis of power, and national security a primary consideration. Mercantilism, with its emphasis on developing domestic industries, was the answer. They should be forgiven for thinking that the world of the twentieth century with its economic blocs and its power blocs is any different. Indeed, they would be right to ask themselves whether countries such as Australia which insist on adopting liberal policies at a time when the rest of the world is moving in the opposite direction, should not pay more attention to the lot which befell Portugal as a result of her adoption of liberal trading arrangements in the seventeenth century.

Economic liberalism, on the other hand, should be seen for what it undoubtedly was, namely a luxury which the Classical Economists, living in Britain in the latter part of the eighteenth century and the first half of the nineteenth century, could safely espouse because Britain was the leading industrial nation at that time in history. Economic liberalism is a creed that only rich and powerful nations can afford to emulate. Nobody understood that better than the economists of the German

Historical School, whose very strong appreciation of the relevance of history to economic development enabled them to see the weaknesses of the classical position.

Marxist economics was a product of the acute social divisions which a century of industrial change had created. Few people understood this better than Karl Marx who, realising that the wealth of the nation was concentrated in the hands of the aristocracy and the middle classes, made income distribution the central theme of his work. So strong was the Marxists' dislike for capitalism that they rejected the market system altogether with consequences that the nations of the newly constituted Commonwealth of Independent States are currently coming to terms with.

Keynesian economics was a product of the Great Depression, of the era when classical economics had failed; the focus accordingly was on raising the level of aggregate demand through fiscal policy in order to reduce the unprecedentedly high levels of unemployment which the industrial world in the early 1930s experienced. The Keynesian/Welfare State policies of the post-war era occasioned an increase in the level of governmental control of the economy which triggered a strong reaction in the late 60s and 70s from the monetarists. Monetarism condemned collectivism as inimical to the smooth operations of the market system. At the same time, it exploited the growing concern with inflation which half a century's experiment with nominal monetary values had occasioned. Monetarism's demise in the 80s has left a vacuum which will only be adequately filled when governments pursue policies based upon the principles of managerial macro-economics. Economic thought is, par excellence, a product of the era in which it is written. In consequence, it is often found wanting by a later group of analysts.

The Mercantilists were not mistaken in teaching the world the importance of external stability. In every age, national self-esteem and national security require that nations pay attention to their economic relationships with other nations. Continuous surpluses or deficits in the balance of trade, or, for that matter the current account are undesirable, as indeed is chronic indebtedness, for indebtedness only leads to economic dependence, which in time leads to either political or cultural dependence or both.

The Classical Economists were not wrong in teaching the world the importance of the market. At a time when transport systems were being rapidly developed and national markets were coming into existence, Britain needed to be told that regulation on the scale to which it had been accustomed was no longer necessary. They were mistaken in assuming that the state no longer had either a managerial or a regulatory role to perform, as the German Historical School correctly perceived.

Marx was right to draw attention to the disparities of wealth which the capitalist system had created. He was wrong in assuming that they could be abolished by creating a new society.

Keynes showed the world how governments could return economies in a state of recession to prosperity. His solutions worked well in the 1930s when every nation adopted fiscal expansionary policies behind high tariff barriers, and again in the 1950s and 60s when the industrial nations were all pursuing the same objectives. They failed in the 1970s and '80s because they were all too often implemented against the background of the open economy, with the result that governments intending to give their national economies a boost, all too often found themselves with current account deficit problems.

The monetarists were not wrong in drawing attention to the importance of sound management of the money supply in view of the debacles which had afflicted the twentieth century economy. They were mistaken in assuming that all that was required was correct monetary targeting. The solutions are never that simple.

Economic growth and development is a long term process, for the simple reason that nations survive in the long term. The economic policies, therefore, that a country must adopt to achieve its goals are determined by the circumstances in which it finds itself at any point in time.

For the record, however, we need to remember that history demonstrates that:

- issues of equity are more important than issues of efficiency and that if equity issues are ignored for too long, the security of the state may well be jeopardised;
- the state has a major role to play in the economic development process, both in a regulatory sense and in a managerial sense;
- nations that set long term goals and stick to them are most likely to achieve their ends;
- external stability is a priority concern for any nation concerned for its own security or self-esteem;
- full employment is possible without galloping inflation;

- price instability, not price stability, has been the experience of mankind.

Economics courses that do not incorporate those ideas into their curriculum are not fulfilling the role which they should in our society.

EQUITY

It is one of the paradoxes of history that the Father of Classical Economics should himself have occupied the Chair in the University of Glasgow, not of Economics, which in the eighteenth century had not been elevated to the distinction of a separate field of study in its own right, but of Moral Philosophy. Our forefathers were wiser than we sometimes give them credit for. They realised that Political Economy, as it was then called, dealing as it did with man's use of the natural resources of the world to satisfy his material needs and desires, was essentially a moral science. They recognised, therefore, that all economic issues were essentially moral issues in essence, that economics was inextricably linked to ethics because man was a moral being. This realisation should have led them to the conclusion that equity is of greater importance than efficiency, that moral issues take precedence over the purely material. Unhappily that has not happened. Contemporary economic thinking tends to assume that equity and efficiency can be traded off against one another, a dangerous hypothesis which leads to the conclusion that morality is negotiable.

One of the themes of this book is that moral considerations take precedence over the material, in other words, equity is more important than efficiency. To argue that history supports that view may well be considered tendentious in the extreme. After all, the European nations, those in which the Christian influence was strongest, established their supremacy over the rest of the world between the fifteenth and the nineteenth centuries at the point of the gun. Even more reprehensible from the moral point of view was their enslavement of significant numbers of the Negro peoples and their exploitation at the hands of the cotton and sugar growers of the Caribbean and the United States of America. The shipment of many thousands of Indians from their home country by the British Raj during the nineteenth century to other parts of the world to work as indentured labourers has likewise raised questions about the morality of colonial governments. Perhaps, the ultimate cruelty ever inflicted on one nation by another was committed by the

British, just nine years after they had abolished slavery in their Empire and were intent on getting the rest of the world to follow their example, when they forced the Chinese at gun point to open up their country to the opium trade.

A less tendentious view than that stated above recognises that, however detrimental some of the European influences may have been, much of positive value to Afro-Asian societies has eventuated. The description of Africa by enlightened nineteenth century Europeans as the Dark Continent was no euphemism. For a continent enslaved in fetishism, voodoo, black magic and witchcraft was in no position to engage in economic development. Likewise, India's comparative backwardness is, in no small measure, due to the fearful inhibitions of the Hindu caste system which so weakened Indian society that the country fell victim first to the Mughals and later to the British.

There was little improvement in the conditions of the people during the era of the slave-owning empires of the Ancient World, Egypt, Assyria, Babylon, Persia, Greece and Rome. With the steady manumission of slaves from the third century onwards in the Roman Empire, the way was slowly opened up for the introduction of labour saving techniques. The pace of progress was inhibited by the advent of serfdom in Western Europe in the ninth century, but its abolition during the later Middle Ages paved the way for another spate of inventions. C.M. Cipolla has shown that it was in those European countries which took steps to rid themselves of beggary that economic advancement was greatest.[239] Putting the nation's manpower to work was one of the secrets of economic growth, a secret which our politicians do not yet appear to have learned.

Modern economists have, to a large extent, evaded the issue of equity. They have retreated from the loftier planes of ethics and even politics in the name of positive economics and have perforce concentrated their attention increasingly on the issue of efficiency. Efficiency, as the title of this book implies, is undeniably important, but it should never be made the first consideration in human affairs. Issues of equity and justice should always take pride of place in economic theory and policy. Normative issues, in other words, should always take priority over positive issues, a fact which economists, with their penchant for efficiency, try to ignore.

---

[239] Cipolla, C M, *Before the Industrial Revolution. European Society and Economy. (1000-1700).* Methuen (1976).

One of the reasons why economists have tended to ignore moral issues is that it is a field which is thwart with difficulties for the unwary. It is much easier therefore to concentrate on those areas in which general agreement can be obtained. This, of course, constitutes an evasion of the real issues, which are admittedly complex, but not beyond the capacity of men of goodwill to grapple with. Currently there are five issues in modern economic life, employment, remuneration, taxation, foreign trade and inflation, which deserve examination from a moral standpoint. Indeed, if we delineate the moral principles underlying the policies which we adopt, our economic growth rate would improve immeasurably.

Employment is probably the most contentious moral and economic issue of our time. Providing work for everyone who is able and willing to work has never been an easy task. The assumption, so beloved by the Classical Economists, that there is always work available at some price finds no support whatever from history. The evidence, indeed, suggests very strongly that there has often been insufficient work available to satisfy the requirements of the available workforce, with the consequence that unemployment and, in previous centuries, beggary, has been the lot of many thousands of people. We have seen how Elizabethan England dealt with the problem. Industrial societies in the twentieth century have tackled it firstly by providing transfer payments to those temporarily unemployed, secondly through the provision of retraining schemes for those whose skills are no longer appropriate, and thirdly through the Keynesian technique of managing aggregate demand. The latter has occasioned a voluminous economic literature in the course of the last thirty years, none of which has effectively demonstrated why unemployment, other than the purely frictional, should continue to be tolerated. It is well known, and has been for thirty years now, that the solution to structural unemployment, is retraining. Cyclical unemployment is generally, if not always, due to mismanagement of the economy by governments and can therefore be overcome given the political will. The employment issue, unhappily, has become clouded by the spurious argument that it is in some way related to inflation. The evidence, however, suggests that they are in no way related.

It is generally recognised in our society that a man should work for his living. (The idle rich - and not all rich people are idle - may be regarded with envy in some quarters, or as parasites on the community in others; either way, they constitute what many decent minded people would consider an undesirable exception to the norm. The bludger, likewise, calls forth our scorn.) Our society, however, also accepts the principle that rates of remuneration should take account of the level of skill, and therefore education, required to do a job. Ipso facto, it accepts the fact that wealth distribution will therefore not be even, that some people will have more than others. Significantly enough both capitalist and communist societies recognise this principle, and pay their workers accordingly. It would be fatuous to argue, however, that remuneration for all jobs undertaken in our society is based on the equity principle. The power factor plays much too important a role in real life. Wealth distribution, consequently, becomes very uneven.

Governments in modern times have recognised this injustice and have introduced progressive direct taxation as a means of countering it. Progressive direct taxation, however, works not on the principle of taxing the rich to subsidise the poor, but on the principle of taxing the income recipient to pay those who do not receive incomes, a highly dubious practice indeed! Moreover, it raises the question why there are some people in our society who do not receive any income. If, indeed, wealth is unfairly distributed due to inequities in the distribution arrangements, then it is wealth and not income which should be made the basis of the taxation system. That, and that alone, should be the basis on which transfer payments should be made.

The taxation issue, however, raises some very critical questions which modern governments are loathe to tackle, the first of which concerns the appropriate spheres of governmental authority. Abraham Lincoln once remarked that *the state should do for people what needs to be done, but which they cannot by individual effort do at all, or do as well for themselves.*" If this rule were followed, the domain of modern governments would be considerably diminished, taxation would be significantly reduced and the family's sphere of responsibility restored.

The state clearly has a responsibility for providing those public goods, e.g. national defence and the maintenance of law and order, which only it has the resources to provide. The state, moreover, should be responsible for common property resources, whether these be fishing grounds, forests, public parks or recreation grounds. The state is justified in retaining control over land utilisation, since the use to which private property owners may wish to put land may not be in the interests of society. The state also has a responsibility for ensuring that standards of housing and sanitation suffice to prevent the spread of infectious disease through the community, and that conditions in the workplace conform to acceptable standards. The enforcement of standard weights and measures throughout the land is another state responsibility. So too is the provision of an adequate transport and communications infrastructure. The education of the young, the health and welfare of the family and the care of the elderly, however, are all responsibilities which the family should shoulder, wherever possible.

Given this division of responsibilities between the state and the family or the individual, the question of who should pay and how they should pay arises. Since everybody benefits from the services provided by the State, the principle that everybody should pay would appear to be a fair one. That, however, does not justify resorting to poll taxes, which are both difficult and expensive to collect. Taxes should, as Smith asserted, be relatively inexpensive to collect - the efficiency principle applies. The method used by governments throughout history, namely that of indirect taxation, should be adhered to in this case. Resource taxes are preferred, not only because they are the easiest to collect and therefore the least expensive, but also because the taxpayer contributes in proportion to his level of consumption. Poll taxes are to be avoided, not only because they are extremely expensive to administer, but because they raise the vexed question of how much tax each citizen should pay. Taxes on income, whether individual, family or company, should be abolished.

The fourth area in which issues of equity arise is that of international trade, the current trade imbalances reflecting the differing levels of wealth prevailing amongst the world's nations at any point in time. Japan, being technological leader of the world, has a massive trade surplus. The erstwhile leader, the United States of America, currently runs a current account deficit, very largely on account of its imbalance of trade with Japan. Oil rich nations, such as Saudi Arabia, the Gulf States and Brunei, likewise enjoy fabulous surpluses. South American countries in general live in a chronic state of indebtedness, often because of the desires of their wealthier elements to live on the same material plane as they would if they lived in the United States of America.

Economists are divided over the effect which indebtedness will have on the international situation. The liberals, with their amazing penchant for ideology, argue, in complete defiance of history, that the market system is self-correcting, when experience shows that it clearly is not. Even over a decade, as the recent history of Australia has shown, trade imbalances will not necessarily correct themselves. Other economists express the well-grounded fear that, if not dealt with soon, the world's monetary system will collapse.

Free trade is often defended on the ground that tariffs force consumers to pay more for goods than they would otherwise do. There is a more important moral issue at stake here, however, and that is whether or not a nation should be permitted to live beyond its means. If the answer to that question is negative, then tariffs and quotas and all the other paraphernalia of import controls are justified, for they provide the means by which countries can not only concentrate on the goal of balanced development, but live within their means. Moreover, it behoves the West to remember that indebtedness leads not only to economic dependency, but to cultural dependency. Hence the Deuteronomic prohibition.

Inflation has been given pride of place in the pantheon of macroeconomic objectives for much of the last twenty years, thanks very largely to monetarism. Yet, the monetarist solution reveals a complete lack of understanding of the essential nature of the problem, for inflation is not a problem which governments can cure, as we have already seen. Inflation is a social evil which only society can hope to control, if society has the corporate will to cure it. Societies which are driven by greed, as indeed capitalist societies are, will, however, always encounter great difficulty in dealing effectively with inflation. The reason for this is that the root of social evils is not to be found, as Jean-Jacques Rousseau and the philosophers of the so-called Enlightenment would have us believe, in society, but in ourselves. Shakespeare's immortal words, put into the mouth of Julius Caesar - *"The fault, dear Brutus, lies not in our stars, but in ourselves"* - reflect the true nature of the problem. And a problem it is, for if Shakespeare is right, then all our brave attempts to establish a world based on fair play, justice and integrity will founder, unless man can be changed.

Moreover, prudent men know that the problem cannot be circumvented in the manner in which economic liberals, Smith and Friedman in particular, would like to circumvent it, namely by arguing that the pursuit of self-interest is in the public interest. Nor can it be overcome in the manner of Marx by arguing that greed is the perquisite of the bourgeoisie. Moreover, we deceive ourselves if we fall into the trap which so many philosophers from Plato to Marx have done and imagine that we can construct our own model society. For man lost his real freedom when he usurped the place of his Maker and made himself the centre of the universe, and his freedom will only be restored when he reverses that initial decision and accepts his need for regeneration.

The contribution which the Jews have made to the economic development of modern Europe and the modern world has been out of all proportion to their numbers, such is the influence which they have wielded. Jews who deny their faith, however, and give their allegiance to one another of the rationalistic philosophies which have competed for the mind of man in the last two to three hundred years, not only betray the remarkable heritage which is their birthright, but seriously mislead the world into paths which are detrimental to its well-being. it ill-behoves the philosophers to ignore the words of the great Hebrew prophet, Jeremiah: *"The heart of man is deceitful above all things."*[240]

---

[240]   Jeremiah 17:9.

9 Policy Implications

Twenty-five years ago, Australia saw itself as the super-state of the twenty-first century. The euphoria which the minerals boom of the late 60s had engendered in the nation had been dissipated as the phenomenon of stagflation, marking the end of the long boom of the post-war period, began to make its presence felt. There was, nevertheless, still a high degree of confidence in the country's ability to perform well economically, as the nation's resource endowment and its potential for development, so clearly indicated.

Then came the Whitlam years and policies which had stood the country in good stead for decades were either abandoned, reversed or revised. The Club of Rome published its negative scenario on the prospects for economic growth world-wide, and the cause was taken up in Australia by the advocates of Zero Population Growth. Immigration, the traditional source of new supplies of labour and the principal factor behind Australia's economic expansion, was reduced. Tariff protection, behind which Australia had built up a small, but quite successful manufacturing industry, was abandoned. Unemployment continued to rise, as the Second Slump, as Ernest Mandel described it, occasioned by the OPEC price increases, took effect.[241] Simultaneously, inflation, in defiance of the Phillips curve, approached double-digits. The economic doctors diagnosed a severe bout of stagflation, an infectious disease now enveloping the world-wide body politic and economic. The remedy, the then increasingly popular doctrine of monetarism, was applied by the new Liberal leadership, under the slogan "fight 'flation first". The record of the Fraser years speaks for itself. Economic growth averaged 1.8% per annum; unemployment remained stubbornly above

---

[241]   Mandel, Ernest, *The Second Slump. A Marxist Analysis of Recession in the 1970s*, NLB. London (1978).

5% and inflation above 8%.[242] Worse still, Australia's refusal to follow the rest of the world in the early seventies and float its exchange rate led to one revaluation or devaluation after another. The incompetence of the Fraser government was manifested when in 1982 the economy registered a negative economic growth rate for the first time since World War II with both unemployment and inflation running into double-digits.

The performance of the Australian government under Hawke's leadership is an example of what happens when governments attempt to target the impossible. Confronted with an economic recession more serious than anything Australia had experienced since the grim days of the Great Depression, Hawke adopted - with complete disregard for the experience of such countries as Britain, under Heath, and France, under Mitterand, both of whom had adopted similar policies against the background of an open economy - a typical Keynesian style fiscal expansionary policy. In terms of reducing unemployment, and for that matter inflation too, the policy enjoyed some success, but Hawke had ignored external factors at a critical time in Australia's history. On few occasions have the terms of trade moved so strongly against the nation as they did in the first half of the 1980s, with the consequence that the government was forced to revise its priorities in 1985 and concentrate on external stability. Fear of an inflation/devaluation spiral led to the abandonment of the initial wages agreement negotiated with the Trades Unions in 1983 whereby worker's incomes were fully indexed to the Consumer Price Index. The consequence was that Australian workers experienced, under a government led by a former President of the Australian Council of Trades Unions, a fall in real wages of 6% in two years. Such a state of affairs could not continue, and so a further change of policy followed in 1987, when Accord III, a more equitable level of income distribution being the goal this time, was entered into with the unions. Meanwhile, pump priming of the economy by governments world-wide in the wake of the October 1986 Stock Market Crash (fears of a repercussion of October 1929 being the instigating factor) led to a situation euphemistically described as 'overheating' of the economy. A further reversal of policy followed with price stability the catch cry this time. Ignoring the universal experience of the twentieth century, contractionary monetary policy was applied and Australia slid into its third recession in twenty years.

---

[242]   Dyster & Meredith, *Australia in the International Economy*, C.U.P. (1990), p.271.

The experience of the Hawke government is by no means exceptional. It merely demonstrates the inanity of attempting to pursue a multitude of economic objectives successfully. All might have been well, in this instance, if the government had dealt with the problem of the current account deficit by reversing the policy of the Whitlam years and reintroduced tariffs. The Hawke government was not game to do that, however, with the result that it was forced to change the direction of policy every two years or thereabouts. In other words, policy began to be dictated by the needs of the moment, a series of knee jerk reactions to changing situations. Understandably the nation failed to perform at its best.

Can Australia break out of the recurrent cycle of recessions with which she seems to be afflicted? The answer is that she can, provided that she is prepared to take responsibility for her own future, and not allow the rest of the world to dictate it to her. The lessons of history are clear. Expansionism must be the order of the day. Australia must increase her immigrant intake, build new cities, develop new forms of city transport, thus reducing passenger travel time and goods distribution costs, re-build her battered manufacturing sector, become more self-reliant and less dependent on other countries for finance capital and capital goods, and develop her own space shuttle construction industry so that her people can commute to Europe without having to traverse other nations' airspace. She must also undertake desert reclamation and afforestation schemes so that she can meet her own increasing demands for timber.

Few countries in the world today enjoy a greater potential for development than Australia. Endowed with a small population of seventeen million people scattered across a Continent covering three million square miles, the country enjoys one of the lowest densities of population in the world. At the same time, it is blessed with a significant acreage of good grazing lands, in consequence of which, until the middle of the twentieth century, much of Australia's wealth lay on the backs of its sheep; in 1980, the country had an ovine population in excess of 200 million, though this has been drastically reduced due to the fall in the price of wool. Despite being climatically very dry with extensive areas of desert, the continent possesses significant areas of good cultivable land. Most of this is located in the south east, in the area described by Geoffrey Blainey as the boomerang coast.[243]. A rich

---

[243]   Blainey, Geoffrey, *The Tyranny of Distance*, Sun Books, Melbourne (1966).

supply of mineral deposits, gold, silver, lead, zinc, bauxite, iron ore, uranium and coal are to be found in various parts of the continent. The nation's greatest resource, however, is its people, and this is no less true for Australia than it is for any other country in the world. The Australian population is predominantly European in character; the British predominance, however, is much less marked today than it was in the nineteenth century as increasing numbers of Continental Europeans and Asians have been given residency rights. The Judaeo-Christian tradition and value systems still enjoy a high measure of acceptance. A relatively stable government, an incorrupt judiciary, and an independent press testify to the virtues of that tradition.

Blessed with advantages such as these, it is hard to understand why Australian governments have not pressed ahead with a vigorous expansion policy in the same way as the United States of America did in the nineteenth century. The Australian Continent can comfortably accommodate 100 million people without any strain on existing resources given existing technologies; with changes in technology, even greater population levels could be sustained. The nation's wealth of agricultural and mineral products suffices to ensure the enjoyment of relatively high living standards for a much larger population than Australia currently possesses. Critics of expansion argue that Australian cities are already too heavily populated and that over-population will result if more pressure is placed on them. Others tend to see the aridity of the Continent, in particular the western half, as a serious obstacle to expansion. A vigorous policy of city building on the one hand and desert reclamation on the other could, however, overcome these problems. Desert reclamation schemes could lead to significant changes in rainfall patterns in the drier part of the continent and to a welcome increase in the acreage of afforested land elsewhere. Similarly, a program for the construction of cities throughout the Continent is not only highly desirable but essential if economic development is to go ahead as it should.

The case for expansion enjoys the very considerable support of history. For Australia has enjoyed two long booms, one in the nineteenth century (1860-90), the second in the twentieth century (1945-70). In both periods, rapid population growth was accompanied by rapid economic expansion. During the first period (1860-90), population, which had taken seventy years to reach one million, increased threefold to three million in the next thirty years. During the second period, the population which had taken fifty-five years (1890-

1945) to increase from three million to seven million, almost doubled again in the next twenty-five years to reach thirteen million by 1971. Real per capita economic growth in the period during the first long boom averaged 1.3% per annum, whereas *"only a slight increase is recorded in per capita GDP over the half century between 1890 and 1940."*[244] By contrast, the twentieth century post-World War II boom was to witness a very rapid increase in real per capita GDP of 2.5% per annum. Both population growth and economic growth have slowed since the early 70s.

Critics of the development hypothesis, of the go it alone approach, have observed that Australia's economic expansion has been determined by events external to Australia. Australia, they argue, is a small open economy which has to take the world as it comes. If the rest of the world performs poorly economically, so too will Australia. If the rest of the world fares well, so too will Australia. Countries which export raw materials and import manufactured goods are at the mercy of world market conditions. The performance of other national economies, Britain in the nineteenth century and America and Japan in the twentieth, have determined how well the Australian economy has performed. The hypothesis is an attractive one, the more so because evidence can always be adduced in support of such views. It can always be argued that Australia's economic recessions (1843, 1893, 1929, 1982 and 1992) have coincided with economic recessions elsewhere in the world. Similarly, it can also be argued that Australia's two long booms, have coincided with periods of expansion elsewhere in the world, though this claim is open to some objections. Deterministic interpretations of economic history are always popular with politicians, their great virtue being that they exonerate the political leadership, partially if not wholly, from responsibility for what has happened. They are particularly popular whenever the country is in recession or the economy is either faring relatively poorly or is perceived by its critics to be seen to be in that position. The thesis, however, is open to objection on two accounts. Firstly, it ignores the lessons of European history which, as we have already seen, support the view that economic development is the product of conscious policy making and implementation by governments. Secondly, it ignores the realities of Australian history.

---

[244]   Maddock, Rodney and McLean, Ian (Editors), *The Australian Economy in the Long Run*, C.U.P. (1987).

National economic performance is the result of the collective efforts of the people whether expressed through individual enterprise or through the co-operative powers of government. Australia is no exception in this respect. Individual enterprise has played a key role in Australia's history as the development of Australia's agricultural and manufacturing sectors testifies. The role of government in Australia's economic development has, however, not been given the importance which it merits. Yet government has played a significant role in Australia's economic development from the very beginning. The settlement of Australia in 1788 was a British government initiative. A complex set of factors, with which we do not need to be concerned here, lay behind that decision. The subsequent growth of the colony was slow, due largely to the fact that the British government was engaged in the French Revolutionary and Napoleonic Wars. From 1815 onwards, however, colonial governments played a significant role in the economic expansion of their states by encouraging and supporting the migration of free settlers, and by building roads. After 1860, state involvement in the economic growth process intensified as governments took responsibility for the construction of railways and telegraphs, for the development of irrigation schemes aimed at increasing the acreage of land under cultivation, and for the establishment of agricultural research stations and agricultural colleges. In Victoria and Western Australia, state governments provided tariff protection for industry. The period 1860-90 saw gross domestic capital formation increase fivefold. Public investment accounted for half of this.

In the twentieth century, the Commonwealth Government has continued the process of involvement in the economic development of the nation by establishing the Commonwealth Scientific and Industrial Research Organisation, by constructing a national network of railways, roads and telecommunications, by developing hydro-electric schemes, by providing grants to higher education and by providing funds for the development of harbours and ports. The long boom of the post-World War II era, undoubtedly owed much to the Commonwealth Government's expansionist policy. The decision to populate or perish which the nation accepted as its objective in 1945 and which entailed raising the population to thirty million, a figure as yet not reached, was the principal factor behind the excellent economic performance record experienced during that period.

Moreover, the fact that similar policies were being followed in many other countries of the world at that time reflected the influence of

Keynes on the one hand and the conviction shared by the political leaders of the world of that period that, under no circumstances should there be a return to the appalling conditions of economic depression which had been the scourge of the advanced nations of the world during the 1930s and which had presented Adolf Hitler with his opportunity. The relatively poorer performance of the world economy since 1970 must in the main be attributed to monetarism and the corresponding resurgence of economic liberalism which has placed this country's weaker manufacturing sectors at the mercy of competitors who enjoy the immense advantage of bigger markets.

One of the messages of this book is that the state is the critical factor in the economic development process, that it is economic policy which determines what a nation can achieve. It is not denied that events outside Australia will effect the way in which the Australian economy behaves. Indeed, a strong argument can be made out to substantiate the view that much of Australia's serious inflation since World War II has been imported. The wool boom generated by the Korean War (1950-52) resulted in Australia's worst ever post-World War II inflation when prices rose 19% in one year. The OPEC price rises (1973 & 79) increased the price of imported goods in the mid-seventies and the early eighties giving rise to the serious inflations of those years. Australia's comparatively poorer performance in the eighties with regard to inflation, however, is due to government policy, in particular with reference to interest rates, which for several years were kept at a high level in order to attract foreign capital into the country to offset the current account deficit. To argue, however, that Australia's economic performance is always determined by external events is unhistorical and unacceptable. Australia's future lies, not in the hands of the rest of the world, but in the hands of her people, and more importantly, in the hands of the leadership. It is the poor quality of that leadership that has led to the relatively poor performance of the country over the last twenty years.

Small nations do not have to wait for the rest of the world to expand before they do, as the history of the maritime nations of western Europe demonstrates all too clearly. The leaders of Portugal in the fifteenth century, of the Dutch Republic in the seventeenth century, of Great Britain in the seventeenth and eighteenth centuries saw the opportunities which lay open to them and took advantage of them. It is small nations that have changed the world's history. The Portuguese only numbered one and a half million people when the nation set out on its transoceanic voyages of discovery at the end of the fifteenth century. The Dutch, similarly, only numbered approximately the same figure when they created their East India Company in 1605 and began their century of expansion. Britain, likewise, only had four or five million people when she launched out on her career of overseas empire building in the seventeenth century, and still only ten million when confronted by the might of France with thirty million under Napoleon. America only numbered two and a half million people when she fought the War of Independence.

Australia has the capacity to become a world leader in the twenty-first century; this she will only do if she produces a leadership capable of realising that potential. Australia needs men of vision as leaders, men who appreciate the enormous potential which the continent possesses and who can turn that vision into reality. A change of economic policy is essential if this is to happen. The model is there. Britain was, after all, in the mediaeval era a wool producer and exporter just as Australia became in the nineteenth century. The model, however, does not have to be slavishly followed. Australia does not require Navigation Acts; indeed, shipping is a function which she would be well advised to leave to other nations to handle. There are other more important transport facilities for Australia to concentrate on producing, e.g. electronic cab track systems, of which more later, and inter-Continental spacecraft. A pre-requisite to success, however, is a willingness to manage the economy effectively, and this can only be done when external events are not allowed to dictate policy as has happened for the last ten years(1985-95). Australia does not have to rely on imported capital goods; she is quite capable of manufacturing this equipment herself. She has the raw materials, she has the technology, what she lacks is a sufficiently large enough market to enable her to compete with other producers; consequently, her prices are higher than those of her competitors. Nor, for that matter, does she have to depend on foreign capital for economic expansion to take place. Australia has generated by far the bulk of her total capital requirements herself; there is no reason therefore why she should not imitate the Japanese example and provide all her capital requirements from within her own financial resources. Capital dependency leads to economic dependency and economic dependency leads, in turn, to political dependency. Neither are desirable. Australia must learn to become much more self-sufficient.

Australia's heavy reliance on the export of primary products for her income is quite unsatisfactory, for it places her at the mercy of the rest of the world to a degree which is both unnecessary and undesirable. All of Australia's economic recessions, 1843, 1893, 1926-34, 1982 and 1992, have been caused by over-investment in the export sector of our very vulnerable primary industries based economy. These recessions can be attributed to the indubitable propensity of Australians to over-invest in marginal lands, in dubious mining ventures, in urban land speculation and in unprofitable railway construction. Governments must inevitably bear some responsibility for their part in this process. The tendency, still very much with us today, to rely on the export of primary products as the country's main source of income, has all too frequently led to an over-expansion of supply. The present situation is but one more example of what will continue to befall this country as long as its major source of export income is derived from primary products. The solution to this problem necessitates the abandonment of the doctrine of comparative advantage, according to which current economic policy is being conducted, and its replacement by a policy of balanced development

Australia needs to reverse the trading policies so prematurely adopted in the early 1970s. Her leadership needs to recognise that only those nations which are economic leaders can afford the price which liberalism exacts from those who obey its teachings. Australia is as yet not in the position where she can pay that price without dire consequences. The lessons of history, as we have seen, are clear on that point.

Australia must recognise the supreme importance of the need for a balanced development of her economy. It is to the credit of Australia's early rulers that they, like the Mercantilists before them, saw the wisdom of a policy which encouraged the development of indigenous manufacturing. For they realised that countries that added value to the materials which they produced were in a far stronger position insofar as international trade was concerned than those that did not. The tragic reversal of trade policy over the last twenty years has undermined Australia's none too strong manufacturing industry, and forced her to rely more heavily on primary production. Hence her current weak international payments position is one which she should not have fallen into given the abundance of resources which she possesses. It has been the lot of the Judaeo-Christian nations, more specifically, the Anglo-Saxon nations, to have provided the economic and political leadership of the world in the nineteenth and twentieth centuries. It ill behoves those nations now to let that leadership slip from their grasp. Tragically, that is exactly what they have done! The time has come to reverse that situation, and no country is better placed to do just that at the present time than Australia!

Australia's first goal must be a larger population. The negative scenarios associated with the Club of Rome's gloomy Malthusian predictions and enshrined in the doctrine of Zero Population Growth should be banished, along with Malthus, into the shades of history. Australia must grow; she must expand, for only as she expands can she fulfil her destiny and become the prosperous, dynamic, teleologically orientated, technologically innovative country that she has the potential to become. There are, mercifully, some signs that this is happening. Recent studies conducted into the impact which immigration has had and is likely to have on the development of the Australian economy have concluded that net immigration should continue at the rate of 125,000 persons per annum.[245] In this way, it is believed, Australia's population will reach 26 million by 2030, a 50% increase in 40 years. While this will allow for a more rapid rate of economic expansion than would have been possible had the country abandoned immigration altogether, it is not fast enough if the Continent is to achieve its potential as a world leader in the twenty-first century. A more appropriate target for Australia's future population would be 100 million by 2050; that would involve a doubling of the present rate of immigration bringing the figure up to 250,000 persons per annum. If, however, Australia is to develop its resources on a continent wide basis, instead of remaining hemmed into the south east corner of the Continent, she will require a much larger population than she currently possesses. If Australia is to undertake the development schemes which modern science and technology render possible, schemes such as desert reclamation, afforestation and fisheries development, she will require greater labour resources than are currently available. More significantly, only when Australia has a much larger population will she be able to overcome her inferiority complex and take a more responsible attitude towards herself and the rest of the world. Only when she has a larger population will she be able to play a role in world affairs commensurate with her position as the occupant of one of the largest continents on earth. Only when she has a population of 100 million will she be able to compete on

---

[245]   Dyster and Meredith, *Australia in the International Economy*, C.U.P. (1990), p.271.

anything like equal terms with the technologically advanced nations of the world, Japan, America and the European Economic Community, or with those who, like her, have the capacity to develop.

Australia's immigration policy in the past has been motivated by a mixture of fear, compassion and economic necessity, all three factors playing a simultaneous role at times. Fear dictated the White Australia policy which emerged in the latter part of the nineteenth century and was a response to the influx of Chinese on the Eastern States' gold fields. Fear of invasion, together with the recognition that a population of seven million was insufficient to protect Australia's long coastline, was one factor, though by no means the only one, in Australia's determination to expand after World War II. Less emphasis is placed on the defence factor today, greater reliance being placed on Australia's superior weaponry, a dubious policy, to say the least, in view of Australia's alignment with Israel, very appropriate as that may be, and the attitude of the Oriental nations, Australia's northern neighbours, towards that state.

Compassion has also been a factor in Australia's immigration program since the 1920s & 30s when the refugee problem first began to rear its ugly head, and some 15,000 European Jews were admitted to Australia. In the post-war years, many thousands of refugees have migrated to Australia from Eastern Europe. A similarly compassionate policy has led to the admission of Asian minority groups in larger numbers in the last thirty years.

Economic necessity, however, has been the principal factor in Australia's immigration policy both in the nineteenth and twentieth centuries. The recognition that Australia offered enormous scope for settlement and development has motivated both colonial and commonwealth governments to encourage immigration. The realisation that if the potential of the Continent was to be achieved, it would have to be peopled first, has led successive governments to undertake expansionist programs. As we have observed, there has been a lack of consistency over the long term in these programs, the level of success or failure which they have experienced being an influencing factor on the way in which policy was changed for the ensuing period. Economic factors certainly predominated in the findings of the Fitzgerald Report of 1988 which recommended that youth, skill and business entrepreneurial capability together with a ready facility in the English language are prime considerations in selecting suitable immigrants.[246] Certainly, a knowledge of the English language is one facility which should be part of every immigrant's stock-in-trade. Australia should not have to teach its newcomers the English language now that English is the world's international language.

Australia has always been a highly urbanised society. Along with high levels of urbanisation there has gone a relatively high standard of living. Urban society, as Adam Smith observed two centuries ago, tends to promote specialisation of labour, and with specialisation there occurs greater proficiency in the performance of tasks, higher levels of skill and correspondingly higher levels of pecuniary reward. Smith's observations have been more than justified in the light of Australian history, for at the end of the nineteenth century Australia was not only deemed to have been the most highly urbanised society on earth, but also to have enjoyed the highest standards of living on earth. Australia is now a society with a very large component in the tertiary sector, 75% of her population find work, not in the primary production area or even the manufacturing sector, but in the services' sector. Australia, consequently, has a service economy, and service economies only flourish in urbanised societies. Australia's future population will therefore live in cities to an even greater extent than their forefathers did. Since further expansion of Australia's already burgeoning cities is unrealistic and undesirable, especially for Sydney and Melbourne, new cities must be built.

The city is traditionally a meeting place for people to exchange goods and services, to enter into contractual arrangements, to engage in trade and commerce. Whenever people meet together, however, it is not only the economic life of the nation which benefits, but the cultural, aesthetic, religious and educational life of the people as well. So it is that cities become not only centres of economic life and seats of government, local, provincial or national, but centres of learning, culture, education, entertainment and worship. A city, if it is to fulfil its function effectively must meet as many of these needs as it reasonably can.

Cities in Europe and Asia have traditionally grown up in river valleys, the river being the only means of inland transport prior to the coming of the railway in the nineteenth century. The city acted as the entrepôt for the region in which it was situated, the villages in the

---

[246]   Ibid. p.306.

hinterland supplying the food and raw materials required by the city's inhabitants, the city supplying the specialist services for its own inhabitants and any who cared to make the journey either from the villages or from other cities. To some extent this pattern was adopted by the British when they came to Australia. The sites which they chose as their future cities all had a river traversing them. Their coastal orientation was determined by their need to trade with the outside world. The key difference, however, between European and Asian cities on the one hand and Australian cities on the other is that, whereas the former had grown up in river valleys because that was the natural thing for them to do, Australian cities were government sponsored creations.

In his highly enlightening study of Australia's early history, Geoffrey Blainey tells us that it cost the British government in excess of £1 million to get the new Botany Bay colony established in the 1790s, a huge sum of money for a country to commit itself to spending at a time when it was fighting with its back to the wall against a much more populous nation.[247] Yet the British government committed the necessary resources. Nor was Sydney alone in being a state sponsored creation. The Moreton Bay colony, established in 1824, likewise owed much to the initiative of Thomas Brisbane. The Swan River colony, established five years later, was an attempt by the British Government to forestall French designs on the western half of the Continent. Only Adelaide was a private enterprise initiative, and even that owed its ultimate success to the government. In the twentieth century Australia has made only one successful attempt to build a city, namely Canberra, which was, like its American counterpart, Washington, a government creation.

The construction of cities in Australia then owes much to state initiative, and there is no reason to believe that the pattern of the past will be any different in the future. If Australia is to have more centres of population, more cities, it will only happen if the Commonwealth Government takes the initiative in their construction, since it is only the Commonwealth that has the capacity to raise the necessary funds to embark on such expensive projects. It is frequently argued that cities can only be viable if industries are established which make them so. The industry first, city next thesis is based on the sequence of events in Europe during the Industrial Revolution when cities grew up around the new manufacturing centres. Certainly, cities do need some form of

---

[247]   Blainey, Geoffrey, *The Tyranny of Distance*, Sun Books, Melbourne (1966).

industry, though industry, whilst essential for the well being of a modern nation, does not play the part which it once did in the life of the nation. The principle of industry first, city next, has been very largely reversed in the history of Australia, a fact which Australia's politicians will need to bear in mind when they plan the construction of more new cities.

Australia's major cities are all located around the country's perimeter. The harsh, comparatively barren nature of much of the continent has had much to do with this. Lack of effective inter-state land communications until comparatively recent times together with Australia's overseas orientation have been among other factors contributing to this state of affairs. Moreover, Australia has had comparatively little success with inland centres as yet, there being only about half a dozen inland cities with populations in excess of 50,000 people. History dictates therefore that settlement should continue to be in the coastal zone. It is the western side of the continent that requires development, and the potential for the construction of new cities in such places as Geraldton, Albany and Esperance is great. Other possibilities exist in such places as Ceduna in South Australia, and the coastal towns of Central Queensland.

One of the themes of this book is that improvements in transport systems lower costs of travel and goods distribution and simultaneously increase the size of markets and the quantity and quality of goods and services available to the community. The galley, the dhow and the junk were adequate for moving people and cargo around the Mediterranean, across the Arabian Sea or up and down the China Sea for several millennia of human history. They were totally inadequate for the task of moving goods and people across oceans, from one continent to another. That only became possible with the invention of the three masted sailing ship, the vehicle which, as we have seen, was the means by which Europe established its control over the oceans of the world and thereby its commerce, and effected significant reductions in the cost of transporting goods over long distances.

Canal construction, undertaken on a large scale in seventh century China and later in eighteenth century Britain, likewise had similar results in terms of reducing internal transport costs and facilitating the creation of national markets. In the nineteenth century, the railway revolutionised the whole process of land transport, opening up whole Continents, facilitating a much more direct movement of goods and people than had been possible before that time. Railways crossed mountain ranges, opened up prairies, swept through jungle and bush, desert and scrub. They linked city to city and town to town. Wherever the railway went, travel and transport opportunities multiplied, and markets burgeoned as distribution costs fell. Railways became, par excellence, the symbol of economic development. Wherever the railway went, the life of the inhabitants improved. Countries with the highest density of rail facilities usually enjoyed the highest standards of living.

The railway, however, was superseded in the twentieth century by the petrol engined motor vehicle. As governments opened up highway networks, gravel and bitumen superseded steel and ballast as the new form of permanent way and the automobile, the omnibus, the van, the truck, and the heavy lorry took the place of the railway. The latter survives in the advanced countries of the world, mainly with the help of government subsidies. As a means of moving large numbers of people to and from their workplaces in city centres, the rail system has definite advantages, even though it is not an economic proposition. Inter-city expresses continue to provide an alternative mode of transport to the airline in most European countries. Only as a means of hauling bulk goods, iron ore, bauxite, coal, uranium, wheat, or even wool, is the railway ever an economic proposition. Elsewhere it is fast being superseded by road transport; yet, as a means of transport, it has much to offer, not only in terms of safety, but in terms of speed, comfort and convenience.

Why did the motor vehicle win? It was cheaper, faster, more flexible and cleaner than the railway. Moreover, the motor vehicle could go to places which were inaccessible to railways. It was in the city where the motor vehicle first came into its own, for the delivery vehicle provided a safer and more economic mode of goods distribution than the horse and cart. It was cleaner and more reliable and less subject to breakdown. Speed, reliability and comfort ensured that the taxi replaced the hansom cab as the principal means of conveyance for the wealthy in cities. Simultaneously, the motor bus replaced the horse drawn omnibus as the means of transport for the poorer sections of the community. In time, the motor coach provided a competitive form of transport for those wishing to travel long distances, and the motor lorry challenged the goods monopoly which the railways had established in the latter part of the nineteenth century. The ubiquitous automobile not only provided a much faster - traffic conditions permitting - and more flexible means of conveyance than any other previous invention, but it also came to determine the layout of cities and suburbs. In time, in Europe and America, such were the demands placed on conventional highway networks that new rapid transit motorways had to be built to facilitate the movement of goods and people over long distances.

Just as every technological innovation in transport has brought advantages to mankind, so every invention has had its drawbacks. Those who undertook the arduous journeys of transoceanic exploration in the sixteenth, seventeenth and eighteenth centuries not infrequently risked not only their health but their lives. Ocean going travel had none of the certainties which it does for us today. The risk of contracting scurvy was very high due to the lack of fresh fruit and vegetables. Disease was a very real problem, and it was not unknown for half of a ship's crew to be lost at sea, with the result that the remainder would be transferred to another ship and the vessel abandoned. Ships were always at the mercy of the wind; too little of it, and they were becalmed; too much of it, and they were in danger of being driven onto rocks or into icebergs. For centuries, the art of navigation was an art rather than a science as it is today with modern instrumentation. Add to these difficulties the prospect of piracy on the high seas, and the realities of transoceanic navigation take on a degree of risk not experienced in modern times.

Railways, likewise, spawned a spate of problems which were inherent in their construction. The task of constructing railroads over land that was uneven, rocky or marshy, provided plenty of challenge to the then infant civil engineering profession; bridging and tunnelling, whilst not new undertakings, had nevertheless not been undertaken on such a scale before. Signalling presented its own problems with the ever recurring possibility of a disastrous accident if for some reason the system malfunctioned. Timetabling, in particular, became a nightmare as more and more trains had to be accommodated on the same tracks in order to cope with demand during peak hours. One delay on a main line could wreck the scheduling system for a whole day.

The motor vehicle, like its predecessors, has spawned its own set of problems of which the most serious are traffic accidents, traffic congestion and pollution. The statistics on loss of life and limb are not such that we can be complacent about the safety aspects of motoring. Vehicles have been made safer and many of the more dangerous sections of roads have been eliminated; and some steps have been taken to deal with the problem of bad driving. Traffic congestion, however, remains the single biggest problem that motorists have to contend with due to the inadequacy of the highway network to cope with peak hour demands. Congestion, like accidents, cannot be eliminated given the existing transport system on account of the freedom which the individual owner has to take his privately owned vehicle on to the public highway at any time to suit his own convenience, thereby occasioning some measure of inconvenience to all other road users.

Pollution is the third biggest headache associated with the motor vehicle. To some extent progress has been made in reducing Carbon Dioxide levels in the atmosphere now that emission control devices have been fitted to vehicles. There is still a long way to go, however, before environmental pollution comes down to acceptable levels particularly in the cities of the Third World, which have older vehicles in general and more lax methods of control.

Every improvement in transport technology has necessitated high capital costs, but has resulted in lower operating costs and lower costs per passenger or per unit of material moved. Simultaneously, level of service, convenience, efficiency and reliability have all improved, with the result that travel has now become a part of the daily lives of millions of people. The market for goods and services has simultaneously widened thus facilitating higher standards of material welfare. There is, however, room for further improvement as the problems currently encountered indicate. Moreover, the technology is now available to facilitate that improvement, the use of electronic centrally controlled vehicle systems providing the flexibility, speed, safety, reliability and convenience required by the modern user.

The cab track system will therefore combine the speed, reliability and convenience of the motor vehicle with the safety and efficiency of the railway, and thus provide the twenty-first century urban dweller with what he needs, namely a transport facility which will enable him to move freely from any urban location to another without unnecessary delay, and therefore more rapidly than is possible at present given conventional traffic systems. The latter are no longer able to perform this task efficiently as the capacity limitations of highway networks becomes increasingly evident. Nor will the problem of traffic congestion be adequately overcome by constructing more roads, even supposing that sufficient land is available for the purpose, an assumption which, in countries such as the Netherlands, Britain, Japan or Singapore is unjustified in view of the high density of population. Twentieth century urban planners have had to recognise that uncontrolled increases in the number of vehicles using public highways at any one time only leads to congestion and is therefore self-defeating from the point of view of the user. The congestion problem can be overcome with the cab track system because the number of vehicles in the system at any one time will be determined by the central control system. The system, in other words, will be designed to ensure that no vehicle enters the network unless the capacity exists for it to reach its destination without impediment. Any journey, therefore, undertaken for whatever purpose, will be completed on time unless the system fails.

This objective, however, can only be achieved if the principle that public highways are for the use of the public, and therefore are only available for use by publicly owned vehicles, is observed. Current congestion problems arise because this principle is not observed. Possession of a motor vehicle currently guarantees the owner unrestricted use of the highway regardless of the congestion and chaos that results from the use of that vehicle during peak periods. The principle that public transport networks are for the use of the public in publicly owned and operated vehicles is one that mankind is going to have to learn if progress is going to be made in the field of transport.

The reduction in the number of vehicles using the network at any one time, especially during peak periods, will be very considerable. Conventional vehicular transport occasions a very significant waste of resources insofar as the use of both roads and vehicles is concerned. Motor vehicles demand more space on conventional highways than electronically controlled cabs operating on rail or some form of tracking device for the simple reason that rail eliminates the need for manoeuvrability. Consequently, larger highway networks have to be built to accommodate motor vehicles than would be necessary if the electronic cab track system was adopted. Moreover, such is the design of conventional highway network that all lanes into the Central Business District are choked with traffic in the morning rush hours and all lanes out of the area are similarly clogged in the evenings. Very few cities have had the foresight to do as Manchester has, namely to have four lanes of traffic on a six lane highway open in the morning to ingoing traffic, and four lanes open in the evening to homeward bound traffic.

Conventional vehicular systems are also very wasteful insofar as the use of vehicle space is concerned. Casual observation of the motor vehicles on our highways shows that on average vehicle utilisation is of the order of 1.3 persons. In other words, three vehicles in every four carry only one person, the fourth carries two. Conventional transport systems, therefore, utilise only one quarter of the available vehicular space. The waste of resources inherent in this system is therefore phenomenal.

The elimination of the driver is another advantage which the cab track system provides. Not only will this measure enhance the safety of urban transport, but it will also eliminate the necessity for licensing both of vehicles and of persons. A considerable volume of policing time therefore will be saved. The number of accidents with all the heartache and sorrow which they entail, not to mention the financial burden to the community, will also be reduced. Families will also benefit because mothers will no longer be required to run taxi services for their children, as the latter will be able to operate the system themselves.

A further advantage of the cab track system is that its implementation entails the complete separation of vehicular and pedestrian traffic, a goal to which urban planners have been slowly groping ever since the motor vehicle appeared on the scene. The safety of the pedestrian is too important to be left to the vicissitudes of the driver. The elimination of the driver will necessitate the complete separation of pedestrian and vehicular traffic. A transformation in the design and layout of our cities will follow as separate access ways are built for pedestrian use on the one hand and vehicular use on the other. The principle which has been incorporated into the design of shopping centres will now be observed in the design and layout of cities and their suburbs. A much more efficient use of land will result.

The fundamental principle on which the electronic cab track system operates is that only a limited number of vehicles will be permitted to use the system at any one time. Network control will be achieved by means of a regional control unit; all cabs operating within the orbit of that control unit will come under its control while in that region. Regional control units will control the number of cabs entering the region at any one time and the speed with which they travel. They will have built into them a map showing all the tracks in the region. They will also know the exact location, at any point in time, of all cabs operating in the region, including those parked in public cab parks awaiting use.

Cabs will be activated by means of messages transmitted from the potential user or users via the regional control unit to the individual vehicle. These messages will be transmitted from the home based computer through the telephone wiring network to the regional control unit. Messages will specify the user's address, the location to which the user wishes to travel, and the time at which he wishes to travel. If he has an appointment to meet, the system will calculate the duration of the trip, taking into account known traffic conditions, and will inform him when his cab will arrive to collect him from his property. If the trip is one which he makes regularly, e.g. to school or work, the message will be recorded accordingly in the regional control unit and relayed to the cab at the appropriate time. Clearly the more notice the regional control unit is given, the greater the chance that the user will be able to reach his destination on time, particularly if his journey involves peak period travel. Under normal conditions, however, vehicles will be available for use at a moment's notice, and no delays should therefore occur.

When the regional control unit receives a message from a potential user, it first of all ascertains whether the tracks over which the user wishes to travel are sufficiently clear to permit the use of one more cab on the network. If so, a cab is then instructed by the regional control unit to proceed to the user's address. If the service is demanded during peak periods, the regional control unit will compare messages received from users to ascertain which users can be accommodated in the same vehicle. Users, for example, who travel daily to the same destination from one suburb or neighbouring suburbs will be expected to make the journey in one cab. In this case, the cab will be instructed to proceed to the locations of all vehicle users in succession before proceeding to the desired destination or destinations. Considerable economy in both time, energy and finance is thus envisaged: time, because delays due to traffic congestion will be eliminated; energy, because driving is eliminated, thus giving the user an additional relaxation period during which to read or sleep; finance, because the system will be cheaper to operate than conventional transport systems.

Responsibility for routing of cabs between journey termini will rest with the regional control units. It is envisaged initially that at least one thousand cabs will be controlled by one regional control unit. A city, however, will require several regional control units depending on its size, density of population, user travel requirements and geography. The major network arteries in any metropolitan area will be controlled by arterial control units. Traffic on these major arteries will therefore be under the control of one control unit; this will facilitate rapid transit through metropolitan areas. Moreover, the system will be devised in such a way that cabs travelling on the arterial network will be linked together to form trains when they are all proceeding to one destination, e.g. a Central Business District. If, at any time, one particular artery or section of the network is congested, the regional control units will devise an alternative route for the users. Similarly, if the network itself is congested, users will not be able to make their journeys. The saving in user time by this facility alone will be considerable.

A further great advantage of the electronic cab track system, however, is that it facilitates the movement of goods far more efficiently than conventional vehicles, by virtue of the fact that the driver is eliminated. Indeed, cab track systems will accomplish a virtual revolution in goods distribution. Shopping, in particular, for food items and similar articles of general consumption, will become superfluous. For the housewife of the future will be able to do her shopping without even visiting the supermarket. Shopping in the twenty first century will be conducted by means of the television set. At the press of a button, the housewife will have access to the warehouses of the various food distributors in the city, to their range of goods and prices, and from these she will make her selection. Her food parcel will then be collated by the warehouse robots and despatched by means of the cab track system to her residence at such time as she designates. Security on freight vehicles will be such that goods will not need to be accompanied en route. Freight vehicles will be fitted out with lockable compartments, the combination number of which will be known only to the despatcher and the recipient. They will be available in an number of different forms, as at present, on account of the wide variety of goods which require transport at one time or another, from pianos on the one hand to small parcels of food on the other.

Not only will the delivery of goods become a much easier task than it is at present, so too will the whole waste disposal system. Garbage collection systems will be fully automated as robotised vehicles pick up household refuse each week and take it to the waste disposal area. Additional services will be available to a householder on request.

The electronic cab track system is ideally suited to implementation initially in the Central Business Districts of large metropolitan areas, where the unrestricted use of the motor vehicle creates severe traffic congestion problems. Once implemented in these areas, the network can quite readily be extended to cover the whole metropolitan area. Implementation will be a time consuming and costly exercise, and will inevitably extend over many years in the case of larger cities. The benefits, however, to urban dwellers will be immense. The day is envisaged, moreover, when the electronic cab track system becomes the sole means of land transport, when indeed it will be possible to move goods across continents by cab track rather than by conventional rail and road systems. Integration of the cab track system into conventional rail systems will not be difficult in view of the similarities between the two.

Transport innovations have always been a very costly exercise. The great argument against Portugal undertaking the voyage to India at the end of the fifteenth century was that such a project was beyond the resources of a small nation. Indeed, the majority of the royal council advised against the undertaking. Fortunately for Portugal and the rest of the world, King Manuel II was not so easily deterred. Both canalisation and railway construction had to overcome formidable obstacles in their early days, not the least of which was the availability of funds on the scale required.

The very considerable capital requirements of railways were even greater in the case of Britain than they were for America, on account of the high cost of land in the former; indeed, the construction of American railways was significantly facilitated by the very low price at which the state made land available to railway operators. High capitalisation has been a feature of most, if not all, transport systems. The ultimate success of any new transport system arises out of its superior performance over its predecessors. The electronic cab track system will have no difficulty in establishing its credentials in this respect. Moreover, the first nation to develop the system successfully will do as Great Britain did in the nineteenth century when she built the railways of the world, for it will be that nation's privilege to provide a more efficient method of transport for the rapidly increasing number of city dwellers which twenty-first century living will entail for many millions of people throughout the world.

The user pays principle should be the basis on which payment for the use of the cab track system should be made. The price charged should be sufficient to provide a normal profit. Prices, however, should be geared to reflect demand, the highest rates applying to those periods when the system is most in demand, i.e. during the morning and evening peak periods, the lowest to those periods when demand is lowest, (i.e. midnight to 6 am in most cities). Peak period travel will therefore be the highest; the sharing principle, however, will significantly reduce the actual cost to the user. The preferred method of charging is that which is currently used by the suppliers of such public services as electricity distribution and telephonic communication, with the proviso that accounts are rendered and settled monthly. All users will be required to pay a bond three monthly in advance, in much the same way as they currently pay their telephone rental. The inconveniences of cash handling will thereby be eliminated.

The development of the electronic cab track system is well within Australia's capabilities. She has the technology to implement the system, she has the natural resources with which to manufacture both the vehicles and the network on which the vehicles will run. Above all, she needs a better city transport system, especially in view of the very high proportion of people living in her large cities. The question is whether she has the political will. Is our much vaunted commitment to improvements in efficiency a reality or is merely something which we trumpet to the rest of the world? Will Australia put her purse where her mouth is? We can be sure that if she does, she will not only provide her own cities with the most efficient transport system the world has ever seen, but she will find a ready export market for her inventions in many other countries throughout the world. Just as Britain built the railways of the world in the nineteenth century, so Australia will be able to build the cab track systems of the world in the twenty-first century. The clever country can do it!

Appendix

Free Trade & the Pax Britannica in Nineteenth Century Europe (1815-1914)

Milton Friedman has argued in his work, "Capitalism and Freedom" that the long peace which Europe enjoyed between 1815 and 1914 was due to the Pax Britannica and to the adoption by Britain of Free Trade Policies. Friedman's view deserves comment.

The period of European history between 1815 and 1914 may be divided into three eras:

a)   the era of peace, 1815-1848;

b)   the era of political instability and change 1848-71;

c)   the era of Germany's ascendancy, 1871- 1914.

The first period, the era of peace, was marked by the absence of any major European conflict. It was the time when the European powers were very anxious not to permit any further outbreaks of war on the European Continent; indeed, every effort was made by the former Allied Powers, Britain, Prussia, Russia, and Austria, under the leadership of the Austrian Chancellor, Metternich, to ensure that France did not erupt into revolutionary fervour again as she had in 1789 and envelop Europe once again in war. The diplomacy of the earlier years was directed towards the holding of regular conferences between the powers to deal with any manifestations of liberalism or nationalism within their borders. 1830, however, saw a change of government in France as the Bourbon monarchy was replaced by the Orleanist royal house. It was also the year of Belgian independence, Palmerstonian gunboat diplomacy being the means by which the Belgians secured their liberty. Politically, the years between 1815 and 1848 were years in which European governments were more concerned about the enemy within than the enemy without. Economically, it was a period of protection, though Britain, increasingly aware of the enormous technological advantages which she enjoyed, moved steadily in the direction of trade liberalisation from 1820 onwards. The Germans, recognising the threat to their nascent industries posed by British predominance, moved steadily in the opposite direction, from 1818 onwards, culminating in the formation of a national customs union, the Zollverein, in 1834.

The era of peace ended in the year of Revolutions, 1848. The repressive measures which Metternich and the Prussian king, Frederick William IV, had taken, brought their own retribution. In Eastern Europe, however, autocracy remained in control. In France, a short-lived republic was replaced by a second imperial era, and Europe was once again resorted to war as a means of settling differences. None of these conflicts was of any great duration, though the Crimean War, fought to resist Russian encroachments on the Turkish Empire, lasted for three years(1853-56). A succession of conflicts followed in the 1860s, the object of which was the unification of the two nation states, Germany and Italy, both of which had remained since mediaeval times, a patchwork of principalities, ecclesiastical as well as secular.

Economically, this era, (1848-1871), goes down in the textbooks as an era of economic liberalism. There is, however, little evidence to support this view. Britain, certainly did adopt a Free Trade stance, but she was the only country to do so with any degree of consistency. France did sign the Cobden treaty with Britain in 1860 whereby duties on a range of goods being traded between the two countries were reduced. The three Eastern Empires, however, while engaging in some superficial tariff reductions, remained basically protectionist.

Period three, the era between the Franco-Prussian war of 1870/1 and the Great War (1914-8), was the age of German ascendancy. It was, throughout, a period of considerable international tensions, and, although in the main, the Great Powers managed to contain themselves by directing their expansionist tendencies into colonial adventures, a general European conflagration was only narrowly avoided on several occasions. Tension mounted after the retirement of Bismarck in 1890. In 1893, the French, growing increasingly alarmed about the increasing power of a united Germany, signed a mutual defence pact with Russia. The German Army responded two years later by drawing up the plans for a war on two fronts, while the Naval High Command expanded its forces in anticipation of a general European conflict. From 1878 onwards, when a conflict was only just averted, all the European nations concentrated on building up their armaments. Tension became acute with every new crisis - Agadir, Morocco and finally Sarayevo, which triggered the conflict which everyone had been expecting for the last decade or more.

Period three was, likewise, a period of strong protectionist sentiment as each power built up its armaments' industry behind high tariff barriers. Russia increased tariffs on imported goods in 1877 after a brief period of liberalisation; duties were imposed to pay for the war with Turkey. Germany followed suit in 1879, France in 1881, and Italy in 1883. Only Britain remained committed to Free Trade, though even in that country there were those who wished to abandon unilateral free trade in favour of imperial free trade.

It is chimerical, therefore, to speak of Europe enjoying a century of peace between 1815 and 1914. More pertinently, it is completely false to argue that the relative tranquillity that Europe enjoyed was in any way influenced by the Pax Britannica. The British Navy acted as the world's policeman in the nineteenth century, in much the same way as the American navy has done since 1945. The British, being a trading nation, had a vested interest in keeping the sea lanes of the world open, not only to their own commerce, but to the commerce of other nations. Since they had the largest mercantile fleet afloat, it was they who benefited most from the charting of the oceans, the eradication of piracy, and even the abolition of the slave trade.

Moreover, it must not be forgotten that Britain was engaged in conflict after conflict in the colonial territories throughout the nineteenth century, that a price was paid in blood and treasure for the laurels of empire, which cannot be ignored in any reckoning of the cost of empire. Nor was Britain alone, for, from 1880 onwards, the hunger for overseas possessions embraced all the Great Powers of Europe, the Russians who expanded into Central Asia, the Germans who acquired colonies in East and West Africa and New Guinea, the French who acquired much of North Africa and the Italians who conquered Libya.

If, however, we wish to get a clearer view of the reasons why Europe enjoyed a long period of comparative peace in the nineteenth century, we shall need to look more closely at the change in the international balance of power. Whereas during the Napoleonic Wars, it took the combined forces of Britain, Prussia, Austria and Russia to defeat the French, in the Great War of 1914-18, it required the combined forces of the British Commonwealth, France, Italy, Russia, and, for the last eighteen months, America to defeat the forces of the Central Powers. France, in other words, had ceased to be the dominant power in Europe, and her position had been taken by Germany.

Fundamentally, this change in the respective positions of the two nations can be explained as the product of demographic factors. France's population, which numbered about thirty million in 1800, did not grow at a rate remotely comparable to that of Britain or Germany in the nineteenth century. Consequently, it is probably true to say that French hegemony came to an end with the Battle of Waterloo in 1815. German hegemony of the Continent of Europe was probably well established when Prussia defeated France at the Battle of Sedan in 1871. Thereafter, international peace depended on what Germany did and said. When, in 1914, the Germans gave the Austrians a *'carte blanche'* for their attack on Serbia, in spite of the latter's acceptance of all the important conditions of the ultimatum, a general European conflagration was unavoidable.

The title of A.J.P. Taylor's work, *"The Struggle for the Mastery of Europe (1848-1914)"*, makes it clear that it was European hegemony that the Great European Powers were pursuing. Economic factors had little do with it, except insofar as political power had military and, therefore, economic connotations. Politics, once again, whether we like it or not, took pride of place over economics.

Bibliography

General

Butterfield, Herbert, *The Origins of History*, Basic Books, New York (1981).

Chisholm, Michael, *Modern World Development,* Hutchinson, London (1982).

Drucker, Peter, *The Practice of Management*, Pan Books (1968).

Hooykaas, R., *Religion and the Rise of Modern Science*, Scottish Academic Press, Edinburgh (1972), pp 76,78.

Keller, W., *Diaspora: The Post-Biblical History of the Jews*, Pitman (1971).

McCandlish Phillip, *The Bible, the Supernatural and the Jews*, Bethany Press, Chicago (1984).

Merton, R.K., *Science, Technology and Society in Seventeenth Century England*, Fertig, New York (1970).

Parkes, James, *A History of the Jewish People*, Penguin Books (1964).

Roth, Cecil, *A Short History of the Jewish People*, East & West Library, London (1969).

Sombart, Werner, *The Jews and Modern Capitalism*, Transaction Books, London & New Brunswick (1982).

Tawney, R.H., *Religion and the Rise of Capitalism*, Penguin Books (1938).

Trevelyan, G.M. *English Social History,* Longman Green & Co. (1942).

Tuchman, Barbara, *The Bible and the Sword*, Ballantine Books.

Weber, Max, *The Protestant Ethic and the Spirit of Capitalism*, Unwin Uni Books, London (1930).

Economic History

Abu Lughod, Janet, *Before European Hegemony. The World System, 1250-1350,* New York, O.U.P. (1989).

Bagwell, P.S., Mingay, G.E., *Britain and America - A Study of Economic Change (1850-1939)*, Routledge & Kegan Paul, London (1970).

Braudel, Fernand, *Civilization and Capitalism: The Fifteenth to the Eighteenth Centuries*, Vol.3. The Perspective of the World. Fontana Press, London (1985).

Cipolla, Carlo, M., *Guns, Sails and Empires. Technological Innovation and the early phase of European Expansion, 1400-1700.*, Sunflower University Press, Kansas (1965).

Cipolla, Carlo M., *Before the Industrial Revolution. European Society and Economy 1000-1700*, 2nd. ed., Methuen (1976).

Gerschenkron, Alexander, *Economic Backwardness in Historical Perspective*, The Belknap Press, Harvard University Press (1966).

Hecksher, Eli, *Mercantilism*, Garland, New York & London (1983).

Higgins, Benjamin & J.H., *Economic Development of a Small Planet*, W.W. Norton & Co., New York.

Jones, Robert, Marriott, Oliver, *Anatomy of a Merger. A History of GEC, AEI and English Electric*, Pan Books (1970).

Knowles, L.C.A., *Economic Development in Nineteenth Century France, Germany, Russia and the United States*, Augustus M. Kelly, New York (1968).

Mandel, Ernest, *The Second Slump. A Marxist Analysis of Recession in the 1970s*, NLB. London (1978).

Meier, Gerald M., *Leading Issues in Economic Development*, 5th edition, O.U.P. (1989).

Moulder, F.V., *Japan, China and the Modern World Economy. Towards a Re-interpretation of East Asian Development*, C.U.P. (1977).

Rostow, W.W., *The Process of Economic Growth*, W.W. Norton, New York (1952).

Rostow, W.W., *The World Economy - History and Prospect*, Macmillan (1978).

Schmoller, Gustav. *The Mercantile System and its Historical Significance*, by Augustus M. Kelly New York, London (1967).

Van Duijn, *The Long Wave in Economic Life*, Allen & Unwin (1983).

Economic Theory

Avineri, Schlomo, *The Social and Political Thought of Karl Marx*, C.U.O. (1968).

Butler, Eamonn. Milton Friedman, *A Guide to his Economic Thought*. Gower, Aldershot, England (1985).

Donaldson, Peter, *Economics of the Real World*, Penguin Books (1973).

Freedman, Robert, *Marx on Economics*, Penguin Books (1961).

Friedman, Milton & Rose, *Free to Choose*, Harcourt, Brace & Jovanovich, New York (1980).

Friedman, Milton, *Capitalism and Freedom*, Phoenix Books, Chicago (1963).

Galbraith, John Kenneth, *A History of Economics. The Past as the Present*, Hamish Hamilton (1987).

Hayek, F.A., *The Road to Serfdom*, Dymock Books, Sydney (1944).

Keynes, J M, *The General Theory of Employment, Interest and Money*, Macmillan, London (1935).

Kuznets, Simon, *Towards a Theory of Economic Growth*, W.W. Norton & Co, New York (1968).

List, Friedrich, *The National System of Political Economy*, Longmans Green & Co., London (1885).

Parkinson, Northcote, *Left Luggage. From Marx to Wilson*, Pelican Books, London (1970).

Ricardo, David, *The Principles of Political Economy and Taxation*, Dent, London (1969).

Robinson, Joan, *The New Mercantilism, Collected Economic Papers*, Vol.4., Basil Blackwell, Oxford (1973).

Smith, Adam *The Wealth of Nations*, Edited by Edwin Cannan. Norman Berg, Georgia (1976).

Money and Inflation

Cumes, J.W.C., *Inflation - A Study in Stability*, Pergamon Press, Australia.

Friedman, Irving S., *A World-wide Disaster*, Houghton Mifflin, Boston.

Friedman, Milton, *The Counter-revolution in Monetary Theory*, First Wincott memorial Lecture. Pt.IV. "The Propositions of Monetarism", Institute of Economic Affairs (1970).

Friedman, M., *Money and Economic Development*, Horowitz Lectures of 1972, Praeger (1973).

Tew, Brian, *The Evaluation of the International Monetary System (1945-81).*, 2nd ed., Hutchinson, London (1977).

Vila, Pierre, *A History of Gold and Money (1450-1920)*, NLB, London (1976).

Africa

Harris, Richard, *The Political Economy of Africa*, Schenkman, Cambridge, Mass. (1975).

Hopkins, Anthony, *An Economic History of West Africa*, Longmans (1973).

Australia

Barnard, Marjorie, *A History of Australia*, Angus & Robertson (1962).

Blainey, Geoffrey, *The Tyranny of Distance*, Sun Books, Melbourne (1966).

Butlin, Barnard and Pincus, *Government and Capitalism*, Allen & Unwin (1982).

Chapman, Bruce (editor), *Australian Economic Growth*, Macmillan (1989).

Crough and Wellwright, *Australia - A Client State*, Penguin Books (1982).

Duncan, T., Fogarty, J. *Australia and Argentina on Parallel Paths*, Melbourne University Press (1984).

Dyster and Meredith, *Australia in the International Economy*, C.U.P. (1990).

Fitzpatrick, Brian, *British Imperialism and Australia (1783-1833). An Economic History of Australia*, Allen & Unwin (1939).

Fitxpatrick, Brian, *The British Empire in Australia (1834-1939)*. Melbourne University Press (1941).

Maddock, Rodney and McLean, Ian (Editors), *The Australian Economy in the Long Run*, C.U.P. (1987), p.14,17.

Shann, Edward, *An Economic History of Australia*, C.U.P. (1930).

Shaw, A.G.L., *The Economic Development of Australia*, 7th ed., Longman Cheshire (1980).

Sinclair, W.A., *The Process of Economic Development in Australia*, Longman Cheshire (1976).

Britain

Ashley, Maurice, *Financial and Commercial Policy under the Cromwellian Protectorate*, Frank Cass (1934).

Ashton, T.S., *The Industrial Revolution 1760-1830.*. O.U.P. (1968).

Bindoff, S.T., *Tudor England*, Penguin Books (1950).

Clapham, J.H., *An Economic History of Modern Britain*. C.U.P.

Cunningham, W., *The Growth of English Industry and Commerce*, Kelley, New York (1968).

Davis, Ralph, *English Overseas Trade 1500-1700*, Macmillan, London (1973).

Davis, R., *The Rise of the English Shipping Industry in the Seventeenth and Eighteenth Centuries*, David & Charles (1962)..

Deane, Phyllis, *The First Industrial Revolution*. C.U.P. (1979).

Hartwell, R.M., *The Industrial Revolution and Economic Growth*, Methuen & Co. (1971).

Hill, Christopher, *Reformation to Industrial Revolution*, p.30. "Pelican Economic History of Britain". Vol.2. (1969).

Hobsbawm, E.J., *Industry and Empire*, Wiedenfeld & Nicholson, (1968).

Jones, J.R., *Britain and the World 1649-1815*, Fontana Press (1980).

Lee, C.H., *The British Economy since 1700, A Macroeconomic Perspective*, C.U.P. (1986).

Mathias, Peter, *The First Industrial Nation: An Economic History of Britain. (1700-1914)*, Methuen & Co., London (1968).

Minchinton, W.E., *The Growth of English Overseas Trade*, Methuen (1969).

Morgan, Kenneth (Ed)., *Oxford Illustrated History of Britain*, O.U.P. (1984).

Morris, James, *Pax Britannica*, Penguin Books.

Mun, Thomas, *England's Treasure by Foreign Trade*, Blackwell (1967).

Nef. J.U., *The Rise of the British Coal Industry*, Vol.1. Frank Cass & Co..

Plumb, J.H., *England in the Eighteenth Century*, Penguin Books (1950).

Pollard, Sidney, *The Development of the British Economy (1914-80)*, 3rd edition, Edward Arnold, London.

Thomson, David, *England in the Nineteenth Century*, Penguin Books (1950).

Toynbee, Arnold, *Lectures on the Industrial Revolution in England*. Augustus M. Kelly (1962).

Unwin, George, *Studies in Economic History. The Collected Papers of George Unwin*. ed. by R.H. Tawney., Frank Cass, London (1958).

Wilson, Charles, *England's Apprenticeship, 1603-1763*, Longman, London (1965).

Wright, J.F., *Britain in the Age of Economic Management. An Economic History since 1939*, Oxford University Press (1979).

China

Cottrell, L., *The tiger of Ch'in*, Evans Bros. London (1962).

Dawson, Raymond, *The Chinese Experience*, Chas. Scribner's Sons, New York (1978).

Eckstein, Alexander, *China's Economic Revolution*.

Elvin, Mark, *The Pattern of the Chinese Past*, Stanford University Press (1973).

Fairbank & Reischauer, *China: Tradition and Transformation*, George Allen & Unwin, Sydney (1979).

Feuerwerker, Albert, *China's Early Industrialization*, Harvard University Press (1958).

Haegar, J.W., *Crisis and Prosperity in Sung China*, University of Arizona Press (1975).

Ho, Ping-Ti, *Economic and Institutional Factors in the Decline of the Chinese Empire*.

Hsu, Immanuel Chung-Yueh, *The Rise of Modern China*, Oxford University Press, New York (1970).

Latourette, K.S., *A History of Modern China*, Penguin books (1954).

Li, Dun J., *The Ageless Chinese*, J.M. Dent and Sons, London (1965).

Shiba Yoshinori, Yamane, Yuko, *Markets in China during the Sung, Ming and Ch'ing Periods*, Honolulu East-West Centre (1967).

Swanson, Brian, *A History of China's Quest for Seapower*, Naval Institute Press, Annanpolis (1982).

Wright, A., *The Sui Dynasty (AD 581-617)*, Knopf, New York (1978).

France

Caron, F., *The Economic History of Modern France*, Methuen (1979).

Dutôt, Political *Reflections on the Finances and Commerce of France*, Augustus M. Kelly (1974).

Henderson, W.W., *The Industrial Revolution on the Continent. Germany, France, Russia, (1800-1914)*, Cass, London (1961).

Germany

Balfour, Michael, *West Germany. A Contemporary History*, Croom Helm (1982).

Henderson, W.O., *The Rise of German Industrial Power (1934-1934)*, Temple Smith, London (1975).

India

Bettleheim, Charles, *India Independent*, MacGibbon & Kee, London (1968).

Frankel, F.R., *India's Political Economy (1947-77)*, Princeton University Press (1978).

Griffiths, Percival, *Modern India*, 4th edition, Benn, London.

Iran

Katouzian, Homa, *The Political Economy of Modern Iran (1926-79), Despotism and Pseudo-Modernism*, MacMillan (1981).

Italy

Chambers, D.S., *The Imperial Age of Venice (1380-1580)*, Thames and Hudson, London (1970).

Cronin, *The Flowering of the Renaissance*, Collins, London (1969).

Longworth, Philip, *The Rise and Fall of Venice*, Constable, London (1974).

Norwich, Julian Lord, *Venice, The Rise to Empire*, Allen Lane, London (1977).

Symonds, J.A., *The Age of the Despots*, 2nd edition, Smith, Elder, London (1880).

Japan

Allen, G.C., *A Short Economic History of Modern Japan (1867-1937)*, Allen & Unwin.

Bergamini, David, *Japan's Imperial Conspiracy*, Granada, London (1976).

Bieda, K., *Structure and Operation of the Japanese Economy*, Wiley, New York (1970).

Halliday, Jon, *A Political History of Japanese Capitalism*, Pantheon, New York (1975).

Halliday, Jon & McCormack, *Japanese Imperialism Today. Co-Prosperity in Greater East Asia*, Monthly Review Press, New York (1973).

Lockwood, W. *The Economic Development of Japan, (1868-1938)*, Princeton University Press (1954).

Smith, Thomas C., *Political Change and Industrial Development in Japan: Government Enterprise (1868-80)*, Stanford University Press (1955).

Takahashi, Kamachichi, *The Rise and Development of Japan's Modern Economy - the Basis for Miraculous Growth*, Jiji Press, Tokyo (1969).

Yoshihara, Kunio, *Japanese Economic Development. A Short Introduction*, Oxford University Press, London (1979).

The Netherlands

Boxer, C.R., *The Dutch Seaborne Empire (1600-1800)*, Hutchinson, London (1965).

Geyl, Pieter, *The Revolt of the Netherlands*, Vol.1., (1555-1609), Vol.2., (1609-48), Benn, London.

Portugal

Boxer, C.R., *The Portuguese Seaborne Empire 1415-1825*, Hutchinson, London (1969).

Diffie, Bailey W., & Winius, George D., *Foundations of the Portuguese Empire 1415-1580.* University of Minesota Press (1977).

Diffie, Bailey W., *Prelude to Empire. Portugal Overseas before Henry the Navigator*, University of Nebraska Press (1980).

Newitt, Malynn, *The First Portuguese Empire*, University of Exeter (1986).

Oliveira De Marques, A.H., *History of Portugal*, Vol.1 "From Lusitania to Empire". Columbia University Press (1972).

Russia
Dyker, David, *Soviet Economy*, Crosby, Lockwood, Staples, London (1976).

Spain
Elliott, J.H., *Imperial Spain 1469-1716*, Penguin Books, London (1970).

Lieberman, Sima, *The Contemporary Spanish Economy. An Historical Perspective*, Allen & Unwin, London (1982).

Ortiz, Antonio, *The Golden Age of Spain 1516-1659*, Basic Books, New York (1971).

Sri Lanka
Ponnambalam, Satchi, *Dependent Capitalism in Crisis. The Sri Lankan Economy (1948-80)*, Zed, London (1981).

Sweden
Hecksher, Eli, *An Economic History of Sweden*, Harvard University Press (1954).

Turkey
Hale, William, *The Political and Economic Development of Modern Turkey*, Croom Helm (1986).

United States of America
Caroll, P.N. & Noble, D.W., *The Free and the Unfree. A New History of the United States*, Penguin Books (1977).

Coates, A.W., & Robertson, Ross M., *Essays in American Economic History*, Edward Arnold (1969).

Faulkner, H.U., *American Economic History*, 7th.ed., Harper (1954).

Friedman, Milton & Schwarz, Anna J., *A Monetary History of the United States of America (1867-1960)*. Princeton University Press (1963).

Galbraith, John Kenneth, *The Great Crash*, Penguin, London (1961).

Heilbronner, *The Economic Transformation of America. A Short Introduction in collaboration with Aaron Singer*, OUP.

Poulson, Barry W., *The Economic History of the United States of America*, MacMillan, New York (1981).

Vatter, H.G., *The Drive to Industrial Maturity. The U.S. Economy (1860-1914)*, Greenwood (1975).

Index